THE NEGRO PRESS IN
THE UNITED STATES

THE UNIVERSITY OF CHICAGO PRESS
CHICAGO, ILLINOIS

THE BAKER & TAYLOR COMPANY
NEW YORK

THE CAMBRIDGE UNIVERSITY PRESS
LONDON

THE MARUZEN-KABUSHIKI-KAISHA
TOKYO, OSAKA, KYOTO, FUKUOKA, SENDAI

THE MISSION BOOK COMPANY
SHANGHAI

THE NEGRO PRESS IN
THE UNITED STATES

By

FREDERICK G. DETWEILER

THE UNIVERSITY OF CHICAGO PRESS
CHICAGO, ILLINOIS

Composed and Printed By
The University of Chicago Press
Chicago, Illinois, U.S.A.

TO
MY WIFE

PREFACE

When Colonel Robert T. Kerlin's book, *The Voice of the Negro*, appeared, it startled a great many people into serious thought about the Negro press. Professor Robert E. Park's *The Immigrant Press and Its Control* was then almost ready for the public, and the idea of making that public better acquainted with another of its great minority groups had for me a strong appeal. Colonel Kerlin, too—who has been consistently helpful—held that his study of Negro newspapers as they appeared during a certain four-month period should call out an extended inquiry into the actual numbers, circulation, history, economic connections, and social implications of such papers.

It is impossible to name here all those who have helped in the production of the present book. Negro editors have responded courteously to many letters of inquiry. The newspaper men in Chicago, where the study was carried on during the greater part of two years, have especially deserved mention. The gentlemen of the Associated Negro Press have been very generous in offering the use of their exchanges and in countless other favors.

To Professor Park a debt of gratitude is due which these rather formal phrases cannot be expected to discharge. His wide knowledge of the field of Negro life, his kindly interest in this undertaking, and his unique way of offering criticism and suggestion have been indispensable.

In presenting the results that follow, the author has probably failed of that degree of objectivity he desired to attain. The purpose has been to describe rather than interpret, to set forth facts in as straightforward a way as possible, and to let the Negro press speak for itself. If there is any contribution here which might help the races to understand each other better, well and good. It may be, however, that these pages will be to many readers what they have become in the author's thought—an offering of materials for the further study of human nature.

DENISON UNIVERSITY
GRANVILLE, OHIO
August, 1922

TABLE OF CONTENTS

CHAPTER I

VOLUME AND INFLUENCE OF THE NEGRO PRESS

Somerville, Tenn., Feb. 7—White people of this city have issued an order that no "colored newspapers" must be circulated in this town, but that every "darkey," the petition reads, must read the *Falcon*, a local white paper edited by a Confederate veteran. The whites stated this step was being done in order to keep the "nigger from getting besides himself, and to keep him in his place." Since the invasion made in this city by newspapers of our race, people have been leaving by the wholesale, seeking better opportunity and development in northern cities. The edict was issued against the newspaper when white men were forced, because of the lack of help, to plow the fields.

Somerville is the county seat of Fayette county. There are 20,000 of our people residing in this section and only 7,000 white. Our people furnished five soldiers to one white soldier from this district to the National Army in the fight for democracy.

Items like the above, which appeared early in 1919, lead the inquiring reader to ask what is meant by the "colored newspaper." This particular piece of news could be traced to the weekly edited in a northern city by a black man from the South. Within a stone's throw of his desk other similar papers have offices, which contain exchanges from cities and towns all over the country. What are the facts about the entire situation?

There are nearly 500 periodicals published by Negroes in the United States. While accuracy in the statistics is not possible, it is true that there is evidence for the existence, in the summer of 1921, of 492 papers.

Only ten states in the Union are not represented by these publications, and these are the three northernmost in New England and seven in the sparsely settled West. The state of New York has twenty-one titles; Alabama, thirty-five; Arizona, two; Michigan, six; and Virginia, twenty-six. Naturally the greater number belongs to the South, but of the 149 north of Mason and Dixon's line many have a large circulation and wide reach of influence. Of the twelve great urban areas in the United States containing over half a million of people each, only Baltimore and St. Louis could be called southern; and all of these are centers of Negro journalism, producing a total of seventy-six papers. In the 310 that are published in cities with population ranging down to 10,000, the South is better represented. It may be said that smaller towns and rural villages publish altogether only 106 papers that have come to general notice.[1]

Until recently the existence of such a press has been virtually unknown to the white group. To Ray Stannard Baker, writing in the *World's Work*, this fact is alarming. "Few white people realize that there are

[1] These statistics result from an extensive correspondence with publishers on the basis of the list in the *Negro Year Book for 1918-19*, Tuskegee Institute, Alabama, Monroe N. Work, Editor, pp. 460 ff., and Ayer and Son's *American Newspaper Annual and Directory for 1921*, Philadelphia, 1921, pp. 17 f. and 1271 f. The Tuskegee Institute Department of Records and Research, the National Negro Press Association, Nashville, and the Associated Negro Press, Chicago, have also been consulted.

The *Year Book* gives a total of 450 periodicals, but, if one counts the titles listed, the sum amounts to only 391 (for the United States). The larger total assumed is justified by the extreme difficulty in securing complete returns. The results embodied in the text are to be thought of as holding good for midsummer, 1921. During the two years in which this study has been in progress many periodicals have begun and many ended their careers, not to speak of consolidations and changes of title.

more than four hundred and fifty newspapers and other publications in America devoted exclusively to the interests of colored people, nearly all edited by Negroes. . . . . The utter ignorance of the great mass of white Americans as to what is really going on among the colored people of the country is appalling—and dangerous."[1] Warren G. Harding, however, when still a member of the Senate, was typical of an awakening interest. He wrote in 1920:

It would be a very sorry contradiction to the policy of the developing of democracy if the Colored people of the country should not find marked advancement in this fluid state of world civilization, and it is very pleasing to note the growth of Colored publicity service, which means that educational advancement and intelligent enlightenment which always speaks of the progress of any people.

Publicity is going to be the greatest weapon of all in furthering the cause of the Colored people of the United States.[2]

There is still a great deal of the "ignorance" Baker refers to. Out of fifteen individuals interviewed for the Chicago Commission on Race Relations as representing the more intelligent members of the white community, several had no knowledge of the Negro press even in Chicago. On the other hand there is a growing desire to learn the facts about the Negro. The editor of the Des Moines *Bystander*, a colored weekly, told of a speaker of his group who was asked to address a white audience on the condition of Negro people. He took with him to

---

[1] Quoted by the *Crisis*, August, 1916, p. 183. With reference to the Washington riot of 1919, Robert T. Kerlin says (*The Voice of the Negro, 1919*, New York, 1920, p. 76): "But how the Negro viewed that riot, what to him the causes of it were, who the instigators and real rioters were, doubtless it never occurred to one white person in a hunded thousand to consult a Negro newspaper to discover."

[2] Letter to the Associated Negro Press, Chicago.

the meeting a large assortment of Negro newspapers; and, as he later described it, nothing evoked so much curiosity as that exhibit. The papers were eagerly passed from hand to hand and thumbed carefully as though to make sure they were real. Stephen Graham, an Englishman who went on foot throughout the South and followed the trail of Sherman's march to the sea, writes, in *The Soul of John Brown*, of a "passion for journalism" outrunning racial capacities. Referring to Norfolk, Virginia, he says: "I visited the publishing office of the *Journal and Guide*, where the Negroes not only edit a paper but manufacture their own type and do everything themselves—one of a hundred Negro newspapers published in the United States."[1]

When we come to examine in more detail the character of these papers, we discover that they fall into classes somewhat as follows: eighty-three are religious, being official organs of some denomination or a means of edification resorted to by representative religious leaders; forty-five are accredited as journals of fraternal orders, labor organizations, or similar bodies; from colleges, institutes, and schools come eighty periodicals; thirty-one may be called magazines, these including a medical journal, four business periodicals, and five music magazines. Thus there are left 253 periodicals to be called newspapers. All these are first and foremost "race papers." In other words, they all keep race interests pre-eminent.

The avowed newspapers are all weeklies, with the exception of the *Washington Colored American* and the *Richmond Colored American,* which are printed as daily bul-

[1] New York, 1920, p. 58.

letins on one side of a large sheet. With the exception of a few monthlies and quarterlies, other Negro publications are weeklies. Why not dailies? The evident answer is that the Negroes in the United States belong to the same language group as the whites, share in American industry and politics, and are in general dependent on our entire machinery of social life. They dare not give up reading the great American dailies. In New York City Negroes have sometimes discussed the possibility of success for a daily paper there. The *Brooklyn and Long Island Informer*, April 23, 1921, wrote editorially, "as to a daily newspaper":

Recently the *National Review* . . . . carried an editorial in which mention was made of the fact that in a certain section of German East Africa, 3,000 white people were publishing three daily papers . . . . the writer drew a parallel of 180,000 Colored people in the most progressive city in the world, with only half a dozen weeklies to their credit, and badly written ones at that. The *New York Age* did not agree with the "impatience" of the *Review*, as it felt that the time is not ripe for a Negro daily in New York. . . . .

A Negro daily paper in New York is just as much a necessity as is a Negro bank. Fifty years ago we had to look to real estate men, undertakers, hairdressers, and even barbers, for economic leadership, but in these days of high specialization we must have bankers to organize banks, editors to edit papers, reporters to write news articles. To run a daily paper we must be able to vie with the great metropolitan dailies in point of capital, organization and literary efficiency. . . . .

It was said in a recent investigation "Negro newspapers are published weekly because they cannot compete with the daily papers in providing any part of the public with news from day to day."[1] It must be allowed, however,

---

[1] Unpublished notes, Chicago Commission on Race Relations.

that the two bulletins printed in Washington and Richmond seem to fill a special place. The large, one-page sheet can be posted on the wall, in a barber-shop for example, where individual reading may be followed by group discussion.

How far does the Negro press really represent the race? This depends upon the response the printed page receives and is first of all a matter of circulation. There are difficulties, as will easily appear, in reaching a very satisfactory knowledge of this subject. Circulation means different things to different editors. There is a feeling that the paper reaches many more people than its subscribers, and this makes one editor say, "Its circulation, based on 1,000 readers to every 100 copies of the paper, is a fraction over 50,000."[1] Only four papers in Ayer and Son's *Newspaper Directory*, out of a total of 217 listed for Negroes, make sworn statements of circulation. Foremost of these is the *Afro-American* of Baltimore with 18,916. Estimates generally furnished for advertising purposes suggest revision downward.[2] The two largest circulations are those of the *Crisis*, which represents the National Association for the Advancement of Colored People, and the *Chicago Defender*, a news weekly. The former averaged 62,417 copies monthly during 1920.[3] The latter has been said to have sold more than 150,000 copies an issue.[4] On the basis of all attainable information, one may say that the combined

[1] Personal letter.

[2] Two series of estimates of this sort have been consulted.

[3] *Eleventh Annual Report, N.A.A.C.P.*, January, 1921, New York.

[4] Both these periodicals sold more copies before the advance in paper and labor caused the price to be raised.

circulation of Negro periodicals in the United States is probably over a million.[1]

But the actual number of readers of the papers is no doubt far in excess of this figure. As long ago as 1905, L. M. Hershaw, writing in *Charities* said: "It is a difficult matter to find a Negro who can read, who does not read one or more of these race papers. He may not always be a subscriber, but failing in this he has an unfailing faculty of borrowing his neighbors' papers."[2] How the paper is passed from hand to hand, especially in the South, is emphasized by a communication received by the *Chicago Enterprise*. A copy of that journal, so thumbed and worn as to be scarcely recognizable even to its publishers, was returned as a sample for a new duplicate copy desired by the writer of the letter. A white man in a Virginia town, although wishing to get copies of Negro newspapers, does not attempt to find any among the local colored people, who are too busy borrowing and lending to have any papers to spare. If, as certain white people in Louisiana believe, the Negro wishes to keep the white man from reading his papers, whatever the ulterior motive, there is evidence of a very lively appreciation of their value on the part of the Negro himself. It is a common custom for a group to listen as someone reads the paper aloud. At about the time Hershaw wrote, an observer in the far South saw the *Freeman* of Indianapolis draw a circle of auditors in a small-town barber-shop soon after the paper arrived on

[1] There are various items on which to ground this estimate, some of them statements from individual publishers, some of them suggestions of persons who have seen presses in operation.

[2] Vol. XV, No. 1, p. 67, "The Negro Press in America."

the train.   An audience of this sort can still be quickly obtained in Georgia.

There are other indications of an interest in their press on the part of the rank and file of Negroes.   Some may be readers of the paper and yet be very slightly blessed with education.   Letters come into the newspaper offices so poorly spelled and written that they are hard to interpret, yet they show how greatly impressed the writers are with the possibilities of publicity.   The following is better written than many:

> I am this day writing you a few lines of business.   As I was looking over the *Chicago Whip*.   And Saw your warning to the Colored race to beware of March. beware of Ides.   Why yes I Say So my Self, because I have never seen any good that our race has every received from they White Brothers yet.   And I am 44 years of age.   if our race dont look for they own Selves.   and stays asking White mens to do this and the other for them.   Why we Will always be the White mens cows tail to keep the flies of him.   or I might say into another place.   We are his Bull dog.   he will keep our race tied down with a Slavery Chain. . . . . in close you will find 75c. for your *Chicago Whip* for three months. . . . .

The degree of literacy in letters which appear in print in the columns is, of course, not discernible.   But that all such represent different types of readers among the population is clear.   The next two are found in the *Hephzibah Herald* (Hearne, Texas, February 5, 1921) a paper that stresses the religious motive.   First a glowing personal tribute:

> Dear Editor and Saints and Readers of the *Hephzibah Herald*.   Greetings in Jesus' dear sweet name.   Love, joy and peace be multiplied unto you. . . . . I want to tell you all how I was healed.   I came home from church with a severe earache in both ears, and I suffered severely, and I took one of the *Hephzibah Herald* and placed it under my head and fell fast asleep.   I did not know when

the misery left. Children this is a great Savior, bless his dear name. . . . . I thank God for this paper and for the Editor a real man of God.

The second is from the agent-reporter:

Dear Editor. After reading and distributing a number of your wonderful papers I find it greatly appreciated and highly praised throughout our city. . . . .

Our readers and subscribers are growing daily. Enclosed please find remittance for papers sold. Please send me a good supply each week.

Here is the reaction of a West India girl to the *Negro World* of New York (September 11, 1920):

KEY WEST, FLA., Sept. 2.—When Mrs. Williams, a white woman of this city, imported Rebecca Hall, a 16-year-old Jamaica girl, from Panama, she had no idea that she was bringing to the Negroes of Key West such an able orator and splendid fighter for the right of self-determination among Negroes. But she learnt what she was up against last Friday when she ordered her domestic to throw away a copy of the *Negro World*, which she happened to be reading. "Throw away the darned paper, and never let me see you reading it again!" "Throw away this paper? You make me laugh, ma'am," replied the young lady from Jamaica. "This paper is worth more to me than all the jobs you can give me. If I am to go I shall go with this paper, and if I am to stay I'll stay with it."

More often, of course, the letters received are of a commonplace nature, but they all bespeak a peculiar interest and pride in the press. This is from Kentucky (*New York Age*, February 5, 1921):

Find enclosed postoffice money order for $2. Please enter my subscription for one year. I feel that this is the only source from which we can learn of what good Negroes are doing. The white press just will not publish anything good of us. All we can see from their papers is the bad side.

Another testimonial and one that seems to represent a different type of reader comes from Florida.

A lady whom I have known since childhood and lives at the Chicago Beach Hotel told me that she and her husband, who is a prominent man here, had a houseboat in Florida upon which they had a colored woman as cook—a woman who, as she said, had a wonderful fund of common sense. This woman had been a subscriber to the *Defender* almost since its beginning, and this white lady said she used to go out and talk to this woman and she found she too was a reader of the *Defender*. The white woman said, "To you what is the worst thing in your life?" And this woman answered, "To us the worst thing in our lives is that all hope for advancement seems cut out; that is, our general environment and atmosphere is such that there is no hope for advancement in the future." And this lady said to the cook, "What is the best thing that comes into your life?" The woman told her that the best thing that came into her life was the *Chicago Defender*.[1]

It is doubtless on general indications of this sort that the statement above is based, that every Negro who can read does read a race paper. It is a statement, indeed, that is made freely by leading Negroes. Charles S. Johnson,[2] who conducted investigations in Mississippi, Alabama, and Louisiana in connection with the Carnegie Endowment study of Negro migration during the war,[3] asserts most emphatically that this is true. Colored people of the South, when interviewed as individuals, say that the race papers are known in their communities, that local sheets sometimes have a very limited range,

[1] Unpublished notes, Chicago Commission on Race Relations.

[2] Now Director of Research and Investigation, National Urban League, New York.

[3] See Emmett J. Scott, *Negro Migration During the War*, Carnegie Endowment for International Peace, Division of Economics and History, New York, 1920.

but certain northern papers are very widely read. The quickest replies to inquiries come from those who know the cities. One man[1] instanced the advertisement of a labor organization inserted in a northern paper which brought a large number of replies from very small towns and villages in the South. True, many of the papers cover a small area, as is evidenced by the figures for circulation reported to the writer, which in some cases do not exceed 3,500 and are sometimes quoted as low as 1,000. There is even heard a note like this, the complaint of an editor whose paper has only a few hundred subscribers: "Some of my own race don't read any newspapers I am very sorry to say, and are not interested in any uplift." The *Houston Informer* also, May 28, 1921, says: "And yet we have some individuals within our race who boast that they do not read colored newspapers, but in the same breath tell you that they subscribe and pay for white newspapers. Let us hope that these racial impedimenta will stop fattening frogs for snakes!" It is probable that race members who do not read their own papers would not be so excoriated if their cases were not regarded as exceptional.

Curiously enough, it seems that the two assertions often made by colored newspaper men are consistent with each other: (1) that the entire literate portion of the race reads newspapers; and (2) that each paper sold has an average of five readers. The figures given out by the Census Bureau show that, in 1920, there were 6,211,062 Negroes over ten years of age who could read and write. At the rate of one copy to five readers a total circulation

---

[1] Robert L. Mays, president, Railway Men's International Benevolent Industrial Association.

of a million and a quarter would be enough for all. A speculation suggests itself as to how far the drop in the percentage of illiteracy from 30.4 in 1910 to 22.9 in 1920 is due to the spread of newspaper circulation.

The amount of response in the cities of the North—including Baltimore and Washington—can be estimated by the degree of competition existing among the papers that bid for the support of these populations.[1] Balti-more, with 106,390 Negroes, has the *Afro-American*, a paper with thirty years of history behind it and a sworn circulation approaching 20,000. There are six other publications in the city, including one weekly. The presence of papers from other large centers must of course be taken into consideration throughout the East. Washington, with 109,976 Negroes, has three weeklies and one daily. The keenness of the competition there is well set off by a bit of editorial writing, evidently from the pen of W. Calvin Chase, in the *Bee* (November 20, 1920).

The *Bee* does not have to write up minutes and desecrate the Sabbath by selling them in the churches. The *Bee* does not attempt to make statesmen out of scavengers, bankers out of crap-shooters, or editors out of fish-mongers.

The *Bee* has always stood on its merits and has braved storms and lightning. . . . . The *Bee* will deposit $50 in the hands of any reputable citizen, if any of its competitors can show a bona fide subscription list of 1,000—*Odd Fellows Journal* not included in this offer. That journal has a bona fide circulation. . . . .

This offer holds good for thirty days. The *Bee* wants a bona fide subscription list, and not a list of persons who are reading the paper without pay.

[1] Special bulletins and press announcements issued in 1920 and 1921 by the Census Bureau, Washington, are the basis for the statistics given here.

Philadelphia, with a Negro population of 134,000, supports fifteen periodicals, eight of these being weekly. New York, where there are now 153,088 colored people, has seventeen, among which are the well-known *New York Age*, the *Amsterdam News*, the *New York News*, Marcus Garvey's *Negro World*, the *Crisis*, the *Messenger*, and the *Crusader*. In Indianapolis five weeklies compete among 34,690 people. The *Bystander*, Des Moines, counts its local population as 10,000 and has 3,000 or more on its subscription list, according to the statement of its editor. Chicago, with almost 110,000 Negroes, buys from its news-stands such papers as come from New York and Indianapolis, besides the white dailies. The *Messenger*, of New York, is sold by local agent. In addition there are fifteen publications printed in Chicago itself, five of these being news weeklies. According to the best estimate the writer can make, the *Defender*, the *Whip*, and the *Enterprise* together sell more than 25,000 copies in the city each week.

Each of these thriving urban districts reflects its image week by week in its local press. The very existence of newspapers in such numbers is significant of what is going on in the whole social background. The development is rather uneven. Localities that in the past have had a strong nucleus of free Negroes are likely to be the strong centers of the press today. In the North and along the border, conditions have been most favorable. New Orleans, on the other hand, has over 100,000 of the race, and yet peculiar conditions there apparently do not allow the city to develop strong secular weeklies. But generally speaking the newspaper is an adjunct of city life, furnishing the requisite number of secondary social contacts. In the city one must be able to read constantly. And of late years the growth of Negro journalism has been only a normal element in the cityward migration of the people. Even in the efforts made by city papers to increase their circulation there is a rather significant reflection of Negro life. The *Louisville News*, offering $3,000 in prizes for subscriptions, included an automobile.[1] The *New York News*[2] and the *Chicago Enterprise* have had beautiful-girl contests. The *Progressive Citizen* of Texarkana[3] offered "a Tailor-Made Suit! a pair of Edwin Clapp Shoes! a J. B. Stetson Hat! a Liberal Purse of Money!" as inducements— these to be presented to the men chosen as the most "popular ministers. . . . . 5,000 subscribers in ninety days is our slogan."

Negro editors have noticed that the last decade has shown three tendencies: (1) a drift to the cities, accelerated, of course, by the industrial activity of war time; (2) the general tendency to go north, culminating in 1916 and 1917; and (3) some movement from the North and West to the South, whether this be dated earlier or later than 1916. The second of these movements is well known. Of the first the *Chicago Broad Ax* (February 5, 1921) says: "Figures so far available show a movement of the Negroes to the large industrial towns in every state and away from the smaller cities and agricultural districts." The *Washington Colored American* (December 19, 1921) reports, on the basis of a recent census bulletin, that 780,794 Negroes who were born in the South were found living in the North and West in 1920, and 47,223, born in the latter regions, were found living

---

[1] Issue of February 19, 1921.   Several others are using the plan.

[2] February, 10, 1921.   [3] February 19, 1921.

in the South in the same year. Surely the outstanding fact here is movement or migration, indicating less and less attachment to the soil, more economic freedom, more restlessness, more adventure. The spread of newspaper circulation is a part of this whole trend.

It is not surprising, then, to find that many an active northern paper has of late been making a stir in the South. The *New York Age*, the *Crisis*, and the *Chicago Defender* have gained largely there during this period, although some particularly outspoken southern papers have been noted also. The *Defender* sells over two-thirds of its issue outside of Chicago.[1] The *Chicago Whip*, a more recent arrival, has been competing for the southern reader. Its sworn statement to the local post-office counts 8,000 copies as going into the fifth "zone," most of these being destined for the far South. Referring to the former paper, R. H. Leavell writes:[2]

The northern Negro press has also had access through the mails or the express companies to the towns of Mississippi. Notably a weekly published in Chicago. . . . . This paper has a large southern circulation. Within a fortnight after some "booster" articles on northern conditions appearing in this sheet last spring, a Negro welfare agency received from its readers 940 letters from Negroes desiring to leave the South. Of these, 520 were analyzed and the distribution by states noted. The record follows:

Louisiana	85
Mississippi	87
Alabama	64
Georgia	102
Florida	79
Scattering	103
	520

[1] Statement made before Chicago Commission on Race Relations.

[2] *Negro Migration in 1916–17*, U.S. Department of Labor, Division of Negro Economics, 1919, Washington, pp. 29, 30.

Leavell also speaks of seeing, in Mississippi, Negro papers published in New York, Washington, and Indianapolis.

The geographical distance covered by a Negro periodical is often referred to with satisfaction by the publisher. Editor King, of the *Southwestern Christian Advocate*, New Orleans, says: "This paper serves the entire Negro constituency of the 350,000 members of the Methodist Episcopal Church." The *Crusader* writes:

> The Crusader serves . . . . the colored people of the world. It circulates in nearly every big town of the U.S., and in many rural communities. It has circulation in the West Indies and Panama, in South America, and in the coastal districts of West, East and South Africa, penetrating as far as Kano on the Nigerian railway, as far as Coquithatville on the Congo river, and in South Africa as far as Pretoria.

Indeed a reader in Sierra Leone writes to the *Negro World* (March 26, 1921): "We have been reading the *Negro World* for about two years. We have been reading other Negro papers, such as the *New York Age*, the *Washington Bee*, the *Crisis*, the *Colored American*, the *Liberian West Africa*, the *Liberian Register*." The *New York Age* (February 5, 1921) also prints a letter from a reader in Nicaragua. And the *Star of Zion* speaks of reaching Central and South America, Africa, and Europe.[1] Evidently this means a network of influences tending to bind together the Negroes of a much larger world than the United States alone.

The papers that remain within the country are largely distributed in the mails. What can easily be noted is the amount of space the newspaper gives to out-

[1] The writer has letters from this and other papers substantiating these statements.

of-town items. The presence of this news means readers in the places from which it comes. By simply counting the number of localities thus represented, in a few papers taken almost at random, the following number of out-of-town destinations may be noted:

Pike County (Ala.) News	5
Royal Messenger (Helena)	6
Savannah Tribune	8
Guardian (Boston)	12
Norfolk Journal and Guide	13
St. Louis Argus	13
Black Dispatch (Okla. City)	14
New York Age	15
Philadelphia Tribune	26
Baltimore Afro-American	27
Dallas Express	28
Chicago Defender	71

In order to extend out-of-town business, periodicals sometimes have traveling agents, or "field editors." The *Tulsa Star* (May 14, 1921) has this note:

Robert D. Durr, Secretary of the Des Moines Negro Business League and Traveling Editor and Advertising Manager of the *Bystander* will leave Des Moines, Iowa, May 6, for a speaking tour through eastern Iowa and Illinois, and then south into Mississippi, Tennessee and other southern cities.

Dublin's *Weekly Bulletin* of Memphis, a new journal, apparently still building its circulation, has a report (June 25, 1921) by its "field editor from points in Mississippi and Tennessee." Thus, many papers which depend first of all on some local clientèle attempt to push out farther and farther from home and cover as wide a field as possible.[1] It is impossible to measure the amount of

[1] The *Indianapolis Recorder* asserts (June 18, 1921) that it reaches more than 100 cities and towns in Indiana alone.

overlapping as each tries to serve the whole far-scattered group.

To the degree in which the facts above stated will seem typical and cogent, one can decide to follow Robert T. Kerlin in his assertion:

The colored people of America are going to their own papers in these days for the news and for their guidance in thinking. . . . . Wherever in all the land there is a considerable Negro population there is a Negro newspaper. . . . .

As for the prosperity of these periodicals, there is abundant evidence. As for their influence the evidence is no less. The Negro seems to have newly discovered his fourth estate, to have realized the extraordinary power of his press. Mighty as the pulpit has been with him, the press now seems to be foremost. It is freer than the pulpit, and there is a peculiar authority in printer's ink. His newspaper is the voice of the Negro.[1]

An indirect but valuable criterion of the influence the Negro press is exerting is the attitude taken by members of the white group. Sometimes this is one of startled curiosity, as is shown by the *Mountain Eagle* of Birmingham, which prints a double column under the head: "*Chicago Defender a Negro Newspaper Widely Circulated.*" Occasionally a white editor will essay an argument with a colored editor. Sometimes a Negro editorial will be quoted by a white man's paper, as in the case of "Who's Afraid?" a challenge flung out by the *Chicago Whip* and printed entire by the *Chicago Tribune* under the caption, "Editorial of the Day." Some publishers write that the white press is friendly and notices favorably the occasional matter it chooses for comment. The *New York Age* gives space (November 20, 1920) to a letter of commendation received by Editor Fred Moore from Chair-

[1] *The Voice of the Negro, 1919*, New York, 1920, p. ix.

man Will Hays, of the Republican National Committee, for the former's successful publicity work in the presidential campaign of 1920. Of course there were several other colored newspapers so employed. In addition to these stray indications of interest, the *Annual* of the Associated Negro Press mentions the fact that many white dailies have asked for news service, and prints letters of commendation from the *New York World*, the *Cincinnati Times-Star*, the *New Orleans Times-Picayune*, and the *Detroit Free Press*. The *Wilmington Advocate* writes:

We cover the state of Delaware like a blanket and there is not a town in the state in which we do not circulate. Our paper is subscribed to by all classes of our people and by a considerable number of Caucasians. To indicate the interest Caucasians have in the *Advocate* would say that General Coleman du Pont subscribes to two copies each week. . . . . To no publisher could the white press in Wilmington be more kind than to us. . . . . The Sunday *Star* quotes us editorially nearly every week.

But the attitude of direct hostility sometimes exhibited toward the Negro newspaper speaks still more impressively of the influence attributed to it by the whites.

How important the Negro press has been in the process of the Negro's becoming politically articulate can be measured by the statements of white men. Magazines like the *Crisis* and *Challenge*, newspapers like the *Defender*, are cordially execrated among white men in the South. An article in the *Defender* was held responsible for the riot in Longview, Texas. Governor Charles Brough of Arkansas said he believed the *Crisis* and *Defender* were responsible for the Arkansas riots and announced his intention of asking the Postmaster-General to exclude them from the mails.[1]

[1] H. J. Seligman. *The Negro Faces America*, New York, 1920, p. 288.

There are several petty persecutions, some very violent attacks, and attempts to change the paper's expression by means of manipulating advertising. Certain towns have proscribed the buying, selling, or circulating of these race papers. The *Philadelphia American* (February 19, 1921) has this to exhibit as evidence of the importance white people attach to the Negro newspaper:

ATHENS, GA., Feb. 17.—John Lee Eberhardt, your staff correspondent here, was taken from the local jail and burned at the stake. Eberhardt had been arrested early yesterday as a suspect in the murder of a white woman by name of Lee.

It is believed by many here that advantage was taken of the situation to "get" Eberhardt for circulating the *Philadelphia American*. He had been warned on several occasions. More than five thousand took part in the lynching.

The *Richmond* (Indiana) *Blade*, a paper whose policy it is "to serve the people of the local community and to look out for their interests first," one that lives quietly enough in the "Quaker City" of Indiana was taken very seriously by white people in Sylvester, Georgia. There Macie Giddens was said to have been tried in a court which he was not allowed to attend until sentence was ready. Replying to the letter written from Georgia, the *Richmond Blade* gave vent to this editorial (April 1, 1912):

A brother writes to us from Sylvester, Ga., the home of Macie Giddens, and tells us in plain words that he does not like the letter that appeared in last week's *Blade* and warns us that if we do not stop "lying" on the south, we are liable to "git" a sample of the same thing Macie Giddens is going to "git" April 8th.

For the information of our "writin" friend in Sylvester, we beg to say that we live in the state of Indiana, thank goodness, in the city of Richmond (none better)— on Boyer street, it's easy to find. Here we are.

Come and see us. We believe in the law, and expect the law to protect us. But—let us also say this. What little "raisin" we got, we got in the state of Kentucky—fourteen miles from the railroad, and six miles from the big road. We used to be on very friendly terms with the old Kentucky Winchester. We have brought down many a "flyin" hawk and crow—have shot many a rabbit through the crack of rail fences, and, although sometimes we wear glasses, a rifle stock feels good in our hand yet. We have been our man since the age of twelve, and of course, have had to "tect" ourselves quite often. Here we are. . . . .

Naturally one expects this hostile attitude to be shown toward the *Chicago Defender*. The following has been transcribed from a facsimile of the original. It was written from Arkansas, where in the fall of 1919 there was a so-called riot of the blacks, but, according to the Negro version, the whites attempted a general massacre of the other race. The letter runs:

You are agitating a proposition through your paper which is causing some of your good Bur heads to be killed and the end is not in sight yet, but you have not got since enough to see it, go on.

You could be of assistance to your people if you would advise them to be real niggers instead of fools. Our Governor and also the mayor of Elaine has been receiving letters of threats and ect Gov. Allen of Kansas has been paid the price for Hill and you think you have won but the price is being paid still, and will continue as long as you Bur heads keep this up propaganda up. We are still in the saddle and some of your good niggers are paying the price of your ignorance go on nigger and keep this up.

This bitter hostility must mean that the white man fears the influence of the Negro press on the Negroes themselves. In 1919 the same fear seems to have existed in the federal Department of Justice when the attorney-general included the Negro magazines and newspapers in his investigations. "Neither is the influence of the

Negro press in general to be reckoned with lightly," says the report to the Senate.[1]

It is difficult to compare the press of the Negro group in any quantitative way with the same institution among other racial groups in the United States. There are indeed impressive achievements of this sort to be credited to our foreign-language press. These papers are read by people who do not habitually talk English. On these they really depend for their news and their advertising. The great dailies printed in English scarcely compete in this field. The Negro on the other hand is using the culture and language of English-speaking people. He reads his own paper and the white man's paper too. To be sure the Italians in the United States seem to have a newspaper circulation of approximately one-fifth their population, the Poles about one-third.[2] In these cases we have a healthier situation in that a large total circulation is divided among fewer papers. The Polish papers seem to reach a circulation in the neighborhood of a million—about the figure estimated for the Negroes—but print for this only about eighty papers as against the 492 of the latter. The contrast appears unfavorable to the Negroes. But it is to be remembered that the foreign-language groups are large, compact masses of city-dwellers, while the colored people are distributed over a wide geographical area, not to mention the millions who live in poverty, rural isolation, and illiteracy. The

[1] *Investigation Activities of the Department of Justice*, Sixty-sixth Congress, First Session, Sen. Doc. 153, Washington, 1919, p. 162.

[2] Figures taken from N. W. Ayer and Son's *Newspaper Annual, etc., 1921*, and estimate of populations (including, of course, more than those rated "foreign-born" in the census) in R. E. Park and H. A. Miller, *Old World Traits Transplanted*, New York, 1921, p. 225.

Negroes themselves are not satisfied with the progress their press has made to date.

With twelve millions of people within our race, it works out that we have only one publication for every 25,000. Making a fifty per cent reduction for illiteracy, we find that we have only one publication for every 12,500 readers.

This appalling state of facts proves to every open thinker that every colored newspaper should be a medium of high intelligence with diffused information on all matters that concern the race.[1]

When we compare the Negro newspaper with that of some other minority groups, the result is more favorable. Such groups often seize eagerly upon the press as a weapon in their struggle for recognition. It is, however, a commonplace that no minority group can maintain a press unless it is subsidized. Of the deficits universally expected one has an easy illustration to hand in Upton Sinclair's account of the *New York Call*.

I know few more heroic stories than the twenty-year struggle to establish and maintain the "New York Call." . . . . At last they managed to raise funds to start a daily, and then for ten years it was an endless struggle with debt and starvation. It was a lucky week when the "New York Call" had money enough to pay its printing force; the reporters and editors would sometimes have to wait for months.

The same attempt was made in Chicago, and there bad management and factional quarrels brought a disastrous failure. . . . .[2]

Another example can be found in the following editorial utterance of *Solidarity*, the organ of the I.W.W., published in Chicago (January 11, 1921):

Members of the I.W.W., who have had access to the financial report of the General Office, have known for some time that nearly

[1] *Chicago Whip*, January 15, 1921.
[2] *The Brass Check*, Pasadena, 1920, p. 411.

all our publications have for several years been running on a deficit basis. . . . .

Up to the present, the General Office has been meeting this deficit, and that of the other publications. . . . . But conditions just now make it imperative that we try to relieve the General Office of this extra draft on its finances. . . . .

If we claim the Negroes as a minority group in which the press is succeeding without being subsidized, it may be pointed out in reply that the Negro press is not all propaganda: it has a substantial basis in the everyday sort of news and advertising business on which the normal newspaper depends. Still there is enough of minority insurgency about it, along with the usual racial handicaps, to render its degree of success surprising. The *Crisis*, beginning with an organization behind it, was after five years self-supporting and out of debt. True there has been a considerable mortality rate. Eighty-four papers seem to have gone out of existence since their listing in the *Negro Year Book* (1918–19). In addition we may consult the enumeration of periodicals obtained with some care in 1910 by the Atlanta University Negro Conference. At that time there were found to be 288 Negro periodicals,[1] 163 of which are absent from the list in 1921. Some of these 163 may have merely passed into new hands and been given new titles in cases that cannot be traced. On the other hand the same set of figures tells of 105 periodicals that have been in existence since 1910 or earlier and are still doing business. More striking still, fifty-nine of these papers have achieved the success of a career reaching back to 1900 or farther.

[1] W. E. B. Du Bois, ed., *Efforts for Social Betterment among Negro Americans*, "Atlanta University Publications," No. 14, Atlanta, 1909, pp. 114 ff. Correction is made for two papers repeated on this list.

Eight of them date from some time earlier than 1880, seven being religious papers. This may be taken as a fair measure of economic success.

Glimpses of the struggle for existence show through the columns occasionally.[1]

We are appealing to your race pride, to your civic pride, and to the pride that you have as individuals, to foster, maintain and support this paper. You must do it. It is your organ. . . . . A dog that will not wag his own tail is a very sorry cur.

So many papers have failed here in the last twenty years that *we have permitted subscribers to owe us*, in order to secure their confidence in the stability of *"The Union"* which has ever been Cincinnati's *reliable race paper*. Thousands have paid us, but our list of *"Dead Ones"* will show quite a number who have stung us severely. . . . . We are compelled to adopt *business methods!* . . . .

"The Union," 16 years old, is *your own home town paper!* Your cooperation and influence will help it grow. Its success is yours.

Our present circulation is two thousand. In our advertising columns we have never sold one inch of space to a saloon for our policy from the start was only to advertise with legitimate enterprises.

Many of wealthiest and most influential citizens readers. Among them are capitalists, millionaires, Governors, United States Senators and Congressmen. Ministers, doctors, and educators. Fill out the blank below. Help us go over the top.

I was elected by the grand lodge of Good Samaritans and Daughters of Samaria, with not a dollar to begin with. . . . . My former contemporaries did not care to sacrifice their earnings, hence they failed each one of them. We began 1909 with one subscriber, and now we have about 1,000 or more. . . . . Yours for success. . . . .

[1] Some of the quotations which follow are from letters to this writer.

The *Informer* has enjoyed pretty fair sailing upon the sea of journalism, despite the efforts of several bodies of critics to destroy the paper by insisting upon white merchants withdrawing their ads. . . . . This was done thrice. . . . . but today the paper boasts of more paying advertising than any similar journal in America. . . . .

Our present circulation, in less than two years' time, is in excess of the 14,500 mark and it is still growing by leaps and bounds.

The *St. Louis Argus* is published by the St. Louis Argus Pub. Co. (a corporation). $20,000 capital stock. Publishes weekly in own shop. Circulation 22,500. . . . .

The *Bulletin* owns its own plant, giving employment to nine men and women daily. Has a circulation of over six thousand. Started from the ground with little encouragement and no capital. . . . .[1]

As several references have been made to the *Chicago Defender*, it is worth while to instance its economic success. A pamphlet issued about the time the paper went into its new building, which it owns entire with equipment, describes the mechanical possessions.

Four linotype machines, each one equipped with two magazines. . . . . The stereotype department is equipped with the most modern machinery. . . . . The press is a 32-page and color machine, made by the celebrated Goss Printing Press Company of Chicago, Ill. . . . . It prints, folds and counts the papers all in one operation at a speed of 35,000 copies per hour. . . . .

Forty tons of print paper are used for each edition. . . . . Five hundred and twenty-eight mailing sacks are used weekly for the transportation of the *Chicago Defender* to the post-office. . . . .

Vying with the *Defender* now is the *Florida Sentinel* with its new twenty-thousand dollar equipment at Jacksonville.

[1] From the *Tampa Bulletin*, Tampa, Florida.

To own and operate its plant is the great ambition of the Negro periodical. At least thirty-six papers are doing this. The African Methodist Episcopal Church publishes the *Christian Recorder* in its own plant at Philadelphia, putting out other publications at Nashville. The Colored Methodist Church owns and publishes both at Jackson, Tennessee, and at Nashville; the African Methodist Zion Church owns a plant at Charlotte, North Carolina; and the Baptists have a very imposing printing and publishing concern that occupies half a business block in Nashville. Of this last a favorite talking-point is the fact that it is run and manned entirely by Negroes.

The National Baptist Publishing Board's literature is produced from printer's devil to editor, even on the printing presses, by Negroes, and is therefore, head and shoulders above any other literature from this particular denomination.[1]

An attitude of "pardonable pride" like this is often in evidence. The publisher of the *Indianapolis Recorder* writes of his "cylinder press, ... linotype machine and all necessary machinery for the work," and speaks of giving employment to eight people, "all of the race." An advertisement of "The Pushkin Printing and Publishing Company, Incorporated," a $25,000 corporation organized in New York City to print colored newspapers, is in keeping with the same widespread attitude.[2] The sentiment involved is well indicated by the hero-worship surrounding the name of the great Russian poet, Pushkin, who had a Negro strain in his ancestry.

Where does the Negro newspaper get its news? There are reports from local churches and lodges, personal

[1] *Kansas City Sun*, April 2, 1921.

[2] *Brooklyn and Long Island Informer*, January 18, 1921.

items, letters from correspondents out of town, occasional letters sent in by interested parties after some exciting event, and contributions from occasional visitors. The papers also receive the service of a clipping bureau, and of course they clip from each other and from white newspapers. Beside this there are some organized services such as are referred to in this announcement from the *Western World Reporter*, Memphis (June 4, 1921):

The *Western World* can now guarantee to its many thousands of readers the best there is in news service from all sections of the country. With our special system of news gathering, the Reciprocal News Service of the National Negro Press Association, Nashville, the Associated Negro Press Service, Chicago, the Capital News Service and the Negro Press Syndicate, Washington, and our N.A.A.C.P. and Exchange News Service of New York and Boston, enables us to give to you, dear reader, all there is in general race news and happenings throughout the entire country. Send on your order now and keep posted. . . . .

There is also a Tuskegee Institute Press Service and one connected with Hampton Institute, this latter being directed by a white man, William Anthony Aery.

The Associated Negro Press was formed in 1919, with Nahum D. Brascher as editor-in-chief and Claude A. Barnett as director.

The Associated Negro Press is an organization of affiliated newspapers. It disseminates news to the papers comprising its membership, We gather, from the membership editors and through correspondents located throughout the country, happenings of every description of interest to the race which are national in scope. We act as a clearing house for the hundred and more papers which we serve.

Copy sent out by this Press contains both news and editorial matter. For instance, during the opening of the administration of President Harding, N. D. Brascher spent several weeks at Washington and sent in not only reports of what was going on but column-long articles commenting on the general state of political affairs. W. H. A. Moore contributes other editorial matter under the caption "Current and Otherwise." President Harding wrote under date of March 12, 1921:

In the last year I have had some opportunity to learn of the work of the Associated Negro Press, and . . . . it has seemed to me to be doing a useful work in the direction of establishing a sound understanding and really enlightened attitude of mind toward the race problem in this country. . . . .

The National Negro Press Association is primarily a means of getting colored newspaper men in touch with one another. Henry A. Boyd, editor of the *Nashville Globe*, is the corresponding secretary, and J. R. B. Whitney, in New York City, the advertising manager. According to Article 2 of the Constitution:

Its object shall be the moral, material and general betterment of the Negro press of the United States and the world, to bring the press and people into closer communion, and to increase the influence of the Negro newspaper as an agency for the advancement of the Negro millions on American soil.[1]

The Association met in Washington in the first week of March, 1921, a week felt to be significant for the nation-wide body of Negro people, in that a Republican administration seemed to promise a new era for the oppressed. As reported in the *Negro World* of April 2:

While the membership of the organization numbers over one hundred twenty, ... sixty-eight publications answered present to the roll-call. Among the items of interest taken up by the association were:

1. The perfection of their National Negro Press Service news, which is an improvement over the reciprocal news service and which will augment the inner circle telegraph service.

[1] Copy of this in *Proceedings*, Sessions of 1917–19, Nashville.

2. The enlargement of the advertising office located at 489 Fifth Avenue, and in charge of J. R. B. Whitney.

3. The appointment of standing committees. . . . .

There are also such bodies as the Manhattan Newspaper Men's Association and a National Capital Press Association, local gatherings of the newspaper men of a city.[1]

These indications of a growing group sense among the writers and publishers of Negro periodicals probably point also to a real *esprit de corps*. All this reacts again to enhance the importance of the press as an institution in the view of editors on the one hand and the readers on the other. There is a mixture of self-consciousness, self-criticism, and professional idealism in the way the newspaper talks about itself.

The value of our newspapers in the course of our race progress can hardly be estimated. They don't always come out on time, they are not always brim full of news, and they don't always wield the best of influence in times of heated excitement. But in spite of that they are generally there with the goods and usually furnish the whistle for the race to keep up its courage. They contend for that which is right for the race and their voice is usually heard whether everybody says so or not. The influence of the Negro newspaper is saying something and doing something for the most ignorant Negro in the fartherest [*sic*] off backwoods. But the tragedy of Negro journalism lies in the fact that it is more often found casting pearls before swine. . . . . The Negro race ought to wake up and give the most liberal sort of support to the Negro press.[2]

So much for a statement of the volume and influence of the Negro press in America. Many questions remain.

[1] See *New York Amsterdam News*, May 4, 1921. The *New Era* (Charleston, S.C.), in issue of December 3, 1921, urges a Palmetto Press Association for its state.

[2] *Baptist Vanguard*, Little Rock, Arkansas, April 28, 1921.

What lies back of the press of today? What is its history? Further, what are the newspapers like—what is in them? What is their contribution to the whole problem of racial aspiration and struggle? What is the Negro thinking? Such a study ought to shed light on Negro life. For, as Arthur Brisbane has written:

The newspaper is not, as Schopenhauer says, "a shadow on the wall," although many a newspaper is a mere shadow of what a newspaper should be. A newspaper is a mirror reflecting the public, a mirror more or less defective, but still a mirror. And the paper that the individual holds in his hand reflects that individual more or less accurately.[1]

[1] Quoted by James Melvin Lee, *History of American Journalism*, Boston and New York, 1916, p. 429.

CHAPTER II

THE NEGRO PRESS IN SLAVERY DAYS

Almost as far back as records go there were efforts toward self-expression on the part of the Negro people. Indeed, if we are willing to admit the folk-song and spiritual, these were more than efforts. Isolated from so much of social privilege and subjected to the place of cogs in the economic scheme, these people yet produced for themselves compensations that the most advanced Negro of today still claims as distinct racial contributions. In behalf of the spiritual, James Weldon Johnson sings:

> O black and unknown bards of long ago,
> How came your lips to touch the sacred fire?
> How in your darkness did you come to know
> The power and beauty of the minstrel's lyre?
> Who first from midst his bonds lifted his eyes?
> Who first from out the still watch, lone and long,
> Feeling the ancient faith of prophets rise
> Within his dark-kept soul burst into song?
>
> There is a wide, wide wonder in it all,
> That from degraded rest and servile toil
> The fiery spirit of the seer should call
> These simple children of the sun and soil.
> O black slave singers, gone, forgot, unfamed,
> You—you alone, of all the long, long line
> Of those who've sung untaught, unknown, unnamed,
> Have stretched out, upward, seeking the divine.[1]

[1] Poem, "O Black and Unknown Bards," reprinted from *Century Magazine* in the *Dunbar Speaker and Entertainer*, Naperville, Illinois, 1920, p. 167.

When and how this art form, which the Negro has so definitely made his own, took shape, is not known, although it is certain that as early as 1782 melodies ascribed to the American blacks were being printed in Britain.[1]

The eloquence of the orator, too, has long been characteristic of Negroes in America. "The greatest orator I ever heard," said John Randolph, "was a woman. She was a slave. She was a mother and her platform was the auction block." With that Randolph himself imitated the thrilling tones of this slave woman and said, "There was eloquence. I have heard no man speak like that."[2] The expressiveness of Negro preachers during slavery has often been commented upon. Negro newspapers today record the winning of prizes in oratory by colored men over white contestants. How interested these people could be during the twenties in this form of expression is hinted in the following:

The colored boys of the town had a custom of assembling every Sunday afternoon at a certain mineral spring in the suburbs of the place, and discussing, in imitation of the whites, the issues of the day. Some of them, especially the slaves of prominent men, could repeat with exactness speeches that they had heard during the week. The whites were often present at these meetings, and the master of a bright slave boy would feel a pride in the prowess of his negro and encourage him to improve. At last, however, they came to see that the effect of this was to turn the minds of the slaves toward freedom and they forbade the meetings.[3]

[1] Grove's *Dictionary of Music and Musicians* (J. A. F. Maitland), III (New York, 1907), 361.

[2] Booker T. Washington, *The Story of the Negro*, I (New York, 1909), 279.

[3] John S. Bassett, *Anti-Slavery Leaders of North Carolina*, Baltimore, 1898, p. 67.

No doubt this expressional activity with its feeling of self-expansion would encourage the slave to "improve his condition" in earnest.

There must eventually have been sporadic cases of educated Negroes who wanted to write. Only a few instances are accessible for the period before 1827. The real herald of the dawn for the colored race in America was Phillis Wheatley, whose first publication came out in 1770. Three editions of her poems were sold after her death. The fact that Jefferson spoke slightingly of her work, while Washington admired it, is not perhaps important. She can scarcely be taken as racially representative, having assimilated the Boston culture to the point of imitation, and revealing more of Pope than the American Negro. Still it is the example set by these occasional successes that has inspired the race in the same field of endeavor.[1]

Meanwhile there was a growing number of free Negroes in the North. The Revolutionary War resulted in a large number of manumissions. A few free Negroes were becoming economically successful and some managed to get education. From this class the impulse was to arise which would provide political discussion and the organization of effort, the very thing for which the press functions. It is significant that we have the names of leading colored men signed to several public petitions.[2] Alice Dana Adams, in a study entitled *The Neglected Period of Anti-Slavery in America (1808–1821)*,[3] says:

[1] See Benjamin Brawley, *The Negro in Literature and Art*, New York, 1918, chap. ii.

[2] G. W. Williams, *History of the Negro Race in America*, New York, 1885, I, 404, 462; II, 125, 126.

[3] Radcliffe College Monographs, No. 14, Boston, 1908, pp. 91 f.

Nominally the Negro at the North was free to express his opinions and to labor in behalf of his race, so far as it was allowed to any class of person. Yet their participation was small, considering their number; how small we can only understand when we remember how low was the position actually held by the blacks, even at the North. Few were educated sufficiently to write or speak publicly in behalf of their people; fewer still had the money or social position to put their sayings or writings into a form preserved to our day. Under the circumstances the fact that we have any record of such Negroes is wonderful. . . . . There were a few, however, who were educated and prosperous, and whose reputation has descended to our day. One of the best known was James Forten, of Philadelphia. He was spoken of in 1823 as a sail maker of good education and as prosperous in his business; he owned a country residence and kept a carriage. . . . . In 1813 he made an appeal to the Senate of Pennsylvania against slavery, claimed equality with the whites, and spoke of the "inalienable rights" of the blacks.

This James Forten was chairman of the first convention of free Negroes held in Philadelphia. To William Lloyd Garrison he was "the greatly esteemed and venerated sailmaker of Philadelphia," who helped him more than once to weather the financial difficulties of the *Liberator*. Another man of the class just mentioned, whose name will be found in 1827 attached to the first Negro newspaper, was Samuel Cornish, who seems to have lived in New York. Cornish sought to show, in an article printed in a New York newspaper, that the blacks were not any worse, but better, than the lower-class whites, since many of them had education, refinement, and wealth. What evils there were, were the results not of emancipation, but of slavery.

In 1827, then, Samuel Cornish and John B. Russwurm put their names to the first Negro periodical,

called *Freedom's Journal*.   Carter G. Woodson[1] thinks
that the general situation throughout the country at that
time was more favorable to literacy and education among
colored people than it was at the end of the period, or
about 1861, following the policy of widespread repression.
There cannot be a paper without some money and some
education, and so all these early efforts were confined to
the North and the free Negro there.

Irving Garland Penn writes:

The inception of the Journal was the result of a meeting of
Messrs. Russwurm, Cornish and others at the house of M. Bostin
Crummell . . . . in New York, called to consider the attacks
of the local paper mentioned . . . . a local paper published in New
York city . . . . by an Afro-American-hating Jew, which made
the vilest attacks on the Afro-Americans.[2]

The Negroes able to support such a paper and the white
abolitionists together were too few for its continued
success.   Its name was changed to the *Rights of All;* in
1830 it died.   Russwurm was of the educated group par
excellence, since, according to Woodson,[3] he was the first
college graduate among Negroes when he took his degree
from Bowdoin in 1828.   After his journalistic experiment
he taught school in Liberia, where he published the *Liberia
Herald* and later became governor of Maryland at Cape
Palmas.   David Walker, author of the famous "Appeal,"
also contributed to *Freedom's Journal*, and so did Stephen
Smith, a successful lumber merchant and agent of the
Underground Railroad.[4]

[1] *The Education of the Negro Prior to 1861*, New York, 1915, p. 228.
[2] *The Afro-American Press and Its Editors*, Springfield, Massachusetts, 1891, pp. 27 f.
[3] *Op. cit.*, p. 265.
[4] Washington, *op. cit.*, I, 292 f.

The issue of *Freedom's Journal* dated March 30, 1827, has on the first page three articles. One continues the "Memoirs of Cap. Paul Cuffee"; the second is an essay, also "to be continued," on "People of Colour"; the third a bit of news about a cure for drunkenness. As a sample of the phraseology, one may quote the second article:

> The law of God requires that all the provision should be made *by law* which the public welfare will admit, for the protection and improvement of colored subjects, as well as white subjects. *And this has not been done.* . . . . We must show that their rights are acknowledged, their protection secured, their welfare promoted, and that, in every particular, excepting that of involuntary servitude and its necessary attendants, they stand upon the same ground with their masters. When this is done we shall feel no guilt upon the subject.

A temperate plea certainly. Immediate emancipation is not mentioned here. "Righteousness exalteth a nation"—the motto—seems to be also the keynote. But the fight for freedom is there, too, although apparently subdued. The Negro press, taking its start from a situation of conflict, carries through its entire history this motive, the fight for liberation.

No Negro publication in all these ante-bellum days, however, so stirred the public as Walker's famous "Appeal," not a periodical but a pamphlet that appeared in several editions.[1] In 1827 David Walker, a free Negro from North Carolina, opened a second-hand clothing store in Boston and began holding meetings at which he addressed Negroes and attempted to lay plans for an

[1] Alice Dana Adams, *op. cit.*, pp. 93 f.; Williams, *op. cit.*, II, 553; Samuel J. May, *Some Recollections of Our Antislavery Conflict*, Boston, 1869, pp. 133 f.; Benjamin Brawley, *A Social History of the American Negro*, New York, 1921, pp. 155 f.

insurrection of slaves. He had received some education
and had already traveled widely among the states. While
still a boy in the South he said; "If I remain in
this bloody land, I will not live long. As true as God
reigns, I will be avenged for the sorrow which my people
have suffered. This is not the place for me—no, no. . . . .
Go, I must!" His pamphlet was called: "Appeal, in
four articles; together with a Preamble to the Coloured
Citizens of the World, but in particular and very ex-
pressly, to those of the United States of America." The
excitement caused by Walker's exceedingly able writing
is proved by the fact that as far south as Louisiana men
were imprisoned for being in possession of the pamphlet.
The mayor of Savannah demanded that the mayor of Boston punish the author, and the latter replied expressing his
disapproval of the work. The Virginia legislature almost
passed a measure prohibiting not only seditious literature but the education of free Negroes.

Occasionally other sporadic writings by free or
escaped Negroes were issued. William Wells Brown,
who worked as a boy in Lovejoy's printing office, wrote
several books, one of them called *The Black Man*. Mrs.
Frances Harper, school teacher, Underground Railroad
worker, lecturer, produced both prose and poetry.
H. H. Garnett, W. C. Nell, and M. R. Delaney made
the colored race their principal theme. Most interesting of
all, perhaps, were the many personal narratives of escaped slaves, among the best known of which are those
of Lunsford Lane, Bishop Loguen, Solomon Northrup,
Samuel R. Ward, Sojourner Truth, Henry Box Brown,
Frederick Douglass, William Wells Brown, and Josiah
Henson.

Including *Freedom's Journal* there are twenty-four periodicals whose names have been preserved as representatives of the journalism engaged in by Negroes before the Civil War.[1] Many of these appeared so seldom or irregularly that they can scarcely be differentiated from pamphlet literature. Penn's comment on many of them is simply, "It enjoyed but a brief existence," or as in one case, "It did not survive a long life." The titles are sometimes expressive. *Freedom's Journal* itself was soon changed to the *Rights of All*. Others were the *Mirror of Liberty*, the *Elevator*, the *Clarion*, the *Genius of Freedom*, the *Alienated American*, the *Ram's Horn*, the *Colored American*. The last mentioned, which existed between 1837 and 1842 in New York City, declares, "Its objects are, ... the *moral, social* and *political* elevation and improvement of the free colored people; and the peaceful emancipation of the enslaved." Most of these papers were published in New York City and state, but others came from Pittsburgh, Cleveland, Cincinnati, and San Francisco. Apparently the proportion of news, as compared with editorial argument, must have been very slight. It was only the anti-slavery agitation that made the press possible to Negroes in this period.

"Of the influence of the Anti-slavery Society upon the colored man, Maria Weston once said, it is 'church and university, high school and common school, to all who need real instruction and true religion. Of it what a throng of authors, editors, lawyers, orators and accomplished gentlemen of color have taken their degree.' "[2]

[1] Excepting three titles mentioned by Washington in his *Frederick Douglass*, these names are to be found in Penn's work.

[2] Williams, *op. cit.*, II, 79.

A few examples of this intelligentsia have been described to us. Garnett, born a slave in Maryland, escaped, took refuge with a Quaker in Pennsylvania, was put to school in New York, ridiculed when trying to study Greek and Latin at the age of seventeen, and mobbed in a New Hampshire seminary. He also traveled in Great Britain and Germany; was a missionary to Jamaica; chaplain of colored troops during the war; and finally pastor in New York City. Dr. James McCune Smith received his medical training in Scotland; and on returning to America contributed widely to newspapers and magazines. James W. C. Pennington, a slave in Maryland, learned there the trade of blacksmith. Later a Presbyterian minister, he studied in Germany and was made Doctor of Divinity by the University of Heidelberg. Dr. Delaney, chairman of John Brown's famous "Chatham Convention," a physician, traveler, soldier—whence his later title, Major—went with an exploring expedition to the Niger Valley and afterward lectured in England. The career of Frederick Douglass is well known.

Douglass has given us an insight into his motives in establishing the *North Star*. He had been discouraged from the attempt by his anti-slavery acquaintances, and himself admitted both the failure of previous Negro periodicals and his own lack of training for the enterprise.[1] But friends in England presented him with funds for the equipment of a paper, and he began. Perhaps this "determination to have his own way was his first declaration of independence."[2] At any rate:

[1] Frederick Douglass, *Life and Times of Frederick Douglass, Written by Himself*, etc., Hartford, Connecticut, 1882, chap. vii, and pp. 261, 262.

[2] Booker T. Washington, *Frederick Douglass*, Philadelphia, 1907, p. 126.

I told them that perhaps the greatest hindrance to the adoption of abolition principles by the people of the United States was the low estimate . . . . placed upon the negro as a man, that because of his assumed natural inferiority, people reconciled themselves to his enslavement and oppression, as being inevitable if not desirable. The grand thing to be done, therefore, was to change this estimation, by disproving his inferiority and demonstrating his capacity for a more exalted civilization than slavery and prejudice had assigned him. In my judgment a tolerably well conducted press in the hands of persons of the despised race, would, by calling out and making them acquainted with their own latent powers, by enkindling their hope of a future, and developing their moral force, prove a most powerful means of removing prejudice and awakening an interest in them.

"The *North Star* was a large sheet, published weekly, at a cost of $80 per week, and an average circulation of 3,000 subscribers." The change of name to *Frederick Douglass' Paper* was made, he says, in order to "distinguish it from the many papers with 'Stars' in their titles." It is difficult not to think that the change reflects also the increasing selling value of the name of the successful orator.

Among the losses Douglass incurred was the burning of his house and the consequent destruction of twelve volumes of the paper. There were obstacles to be met in the antagonism of the citizens of Rochester. They read in the *New York Herald* the suggestion that the editor should be exiled to Canada and his presses thrown into the lake—a sentiment they eagerly absorbed for a while. But gradually this attitude was overcome. The greatest obstacle was the constant shortage of funds. The "non-voting abolitionists"—among whom are mentioned Gerrit Smith, Chief Justice Chase, Horace Mann, Joshua Giddings, Charles Sumner, and W. H. Seward—

supported Douglass until he became a "voting abolitionist." They then gave up their practice of holding festi-
vals and fairs to raise money. He kept his "anti-slavery
banner steadily flying," however, until the emancipation
of the slaves and the union of the states was assured.
His especial gratitude was aroused by Mrs. Julia Griffiths
Crofts.

> She came to my relief when my paper had nearly absorbed all
> my means, and was heavily in debt, and when I had mortgaged my
> house . . . . to meet current expenses; and by her energetic and
> effective management, in a single year enabled me to extend the
> circulation of my paper from 2,000 to 4,000 copies, pay off the debts
> and lift the mortgage from my house.

In the motives leading to its establishment, in its
fight for freedom, and in its chronic financial difficulties,
Frederick Douglass' Paper is typical of the Negro press
as a whole. He had assistance at times from W. C. Nell
and Martin Delaney, but the success he achieved was
due to his own unusual personal powers. Samuel J.
May[1] spoke of the paper with respect, Garrison praised
it, and Edmund Quincy said its "literary and mechanical
execution would do honor to any paper, new or old,
anti-slavery or pro-slavery, in the country."[2]

The one periodical to persist from this period until
our own day is the *Christian Recorder*. It made its
success not as propaganda but as a carrier of news and
discussion in the group that subsidized it. No paper
existed at that time among Negroes that could succeed
as a paying proposition merely between publisher and
individual reader. Both educational and economic
advance had to come first; and when they did come the

[1] *Op. cit.*   [2] Washington, *Frederick Douglass*, pp. 125 f.

denominational organs, like the *Christian Recorder*, were lifted first on the wave.   The African Methodist Church, founded in 1816 by Richard Allen, in two years had started a publishing department.   But the most of the members were in slave states where they would not be allowed to go to school or to read books and papers. There was consequently little published besides a hymnal. In 1841 the New York Conference voted to start a monthly magazine and for lack of funds this had to become a quarterly.   Negroes wanted to read papers even before they could afford them, and the quarterly lived somehow.   For seven years or more it kept bringing the conference news to the church member.   Then it changed to a weekly and in 1848 it became the *Christian Herald*, Major Delaney's *Mystery* having been purchased for the purpose.   Finally in 1852 the present name was adopted.

This paper was looked upon by the slave holders of the South and proslavery people of the North as a very dangerous document or sheet, and was watched with a critical eye.   It could not be circulated in the slave-holding states. . . . . Through the aid of the Christian Commission it did valuable service to the freedmen throughout the South.   It followed the army, went into the hovels of the freedmen and also the hospitals, placed in the hands of soldiers, speaking cheer and comfort. . . . .[1]

Although suffering occasional intermissions and irregularities in time of publication, besides changes in editorship, the *Recorder* still lives and thrives.   In 1912 its circulation was 6,500.[2]

[1] *Economic Co-operation among Negroes*, ed. W. E. B. Du Bois, "Atlanta University Publications," No. 12, Atlanta, 1907, p. 60, quoting *Arnett's Budget*, 1900, p. 138.

[2] *Centennial Encyclopedia of the A.M.E. Church*, Philadelphia, 1916, p. 458.

In the absence of any press whatever among southern Negroes during this period, there are intimations that the slaves did get some reading matter of an abolitionist sort. Samuel J. May tells us that it was against the principles of the anti-slavery whites in the North to put any of their publications in the hands of slaves. Yet it was the reading of Walker's pamphlet by slaves that aroused the South to sterner repressive measures. In spite of this the southern Negro group presents the spectacle of a widely scattered body of people among whom were many who were endeavoring to get some idea of what the rest of the group was doing and some light on possible action.

When Nat Turner appeared, the education of the Negro had made the way somewhat easier for him than it was for his predecessors. Negroes who could read and write had before them the revolutionary ideas of the French, the daring deeds of Toussaint L'Ouverture, the bold attempt of General Gabriel, and the far-reaching plans of Denmark Vesey. These were sometimes written up in the abolition literature, the circulation of which was so extensive among the slaves that it became a national question.

Trying to account for this insurrection the Governor of the State[1] lays it to the charge of the Negro preachers who were in position to foment much disorder on account of having acquired "great ascendency over the minds" of discontented slaves. He believed that these ministers were in direct contact with the agents of abolition, who were using colored leaders as a means to destroy the institutions of the South. The Governor was cognizant of the fact that not only was the sentiment of the incendiary pamphlets read but often the words. To prevent the "enemies" in other States from communicating with the slaves of that section he requested that the laws regulating the assembly of Negroes be more rigidly enforced and the colored preachers be silenced. The General Assembly complied with this request.

[1] Of Virginia.

The aim of the subsequent reactionary legislation of the South was to complete the work of preventing the dissemination of information among Negroes and their reading of abolition literature.[1]

The close of the war brought with it problems of political orientation for the black man, complicated by poverty, illiteracy, and general social disorganization. Washington says:

Until freedom came the life of the Negro was so intimately interwoven with that of the white man that it is almost true to say that he had no separate history. . . . . It was after freedom came that the masses of the Negro people began to think of themselves as having a past or a future in any way separate and distinct from the white race.[2]

The first paper that started in the South, the *Colored American*, October, 1865, had, after six months, gone into the hands of its creditors.[3] It was followed by others that died as swiftly. The *Colored American* was published, while it lasted, in Augusta, Georgia. The *Anglo-African*[4] published a prospectus of this paper, including the characterization: "Vehicle for the diffusion of *Religious*, *political*, and *General Intelligence* . . . . to keep before the minds of our race the duties and responsibilities of freedom; and to call attention to the wants and grievances of the colored people." Another venture that ended in failure, although it was not quite so short-lived, was the *New National Era* begun by Frederick Douglass in Washington after the war. The associate editor of this journal, Williams tells us,[5] was Richard T. Greener,

[1] C. G. Woodson, *op. cit.*, p. 163.

[2] *The Story of the Negro*, I (New York, 1909), 7, 8.

[3] Penn, *op. cit.*, pp. 101 ff.

[4] Quotation made by Penn, *op. cit.*, p. 101.   [5] *Op. cit.*, II, 438, 440.

first colored entrant of Harvard, who took the Bolyston prize there for oratory, afterward well known as a teacher and especially as dean of law in Howard University. Douglass speaks briefly of the paper, concluding thus:

A misadventure though it was, which cost me from nine to ten thousand dollars, over it I have no tears to shed. The journal was valuable while it lasted, and the experiment was full of instruction to me, which has to some extent been heeded, for I have kept well out of newspaper undertakings since.[1]

One paper that formed an exception to this rule of quick failure was the *Elevator*, of San Francisco, edited and published by Philip A. Bell and W. J. Powell, which Penn calls (p. 95) the "Napoleon of the Colored Press." This was still alive in 1890. A little later, in 1871, a paper was published that made a record of unusual longevity. The *Progressive American*, in New York City, continued its career until 1887. But in general there was a uniformity in the situation thus described by Penn.

From the year 1866 on, Afro-American newspapers were being founded in almost every state, some of which died an early death, while others survived many years. . . . . These papers were started by some of the ablest men. . . . . They labored at a time when the Afro-American, just out of slavery, did not engage to any great extent in literary efforts, and consequently a support of their journals was obtained by the hardest efforts only.[2]

With regard to the character of the secular press after the war, Penn[3] agrees entirely with the statement of Hershaw:

When slavery was abolished . . . . the race began a new life, and the necessity for creating and organizing public opinion and for looking after the particular interests of the race became at once

[1] *Op. cit.*, p. 408.   [2] *Op. cit.*, p. 107.   [3] *Ibid.*, p. 112.

apparent. As this necessity arose in the midst of political change and revolution, the newspapers started under its spur were narrowly political and partisan. Most of them were the "organs" of county, district, and state committees. Their editors were politicians and office-seekers, rather than broad-minded men seeking to enforce eternal principles and to accomplish permanent results.[1]

These beginnings of race journalism after the war were accompanied by a flood of pamphlet literature. This is true to historical precedent. The strugglings of seventeenth-century England were marked not only with the growth of the press but of a great number of pamphlets as well. Other epochs of change show the same features, as for instance the French Revolution. The difficulties of sustaining a regular press immediately or soon after Emancipation can, of course, be readily granted. The "voice of the people," lacking other utterance, took some compensation in this occasional, fugitive form. Mr. T. T. Fortune says:

For many years before and after 1880, until our newspapers became established as vehicles of race news, hopes and aspirations, the thinkers of the race found an outlet for "their pent-up Utica" in pamphlets. I had a collection of some ten thousand or more of these pamphlets when I disposed of my newspaper property in 1907. Unfortunately the entire lot was destroyed, and I have always deeply regretted the loss, inasmuch as it had been my intention to present the bulk of them to the library of my favorite college.[2]

But more than political interests claimed a voice in the press. These were years also of church-building and denominational expansion. It is scarcely necessary to emphasize here what has been so often noted, the central

[1] "The Negro Press in America," *Charities*, Vol. XV (1905), No. 1, p. 67.

[2] *Favorite Magazine*, Autumn, 1920.

importance in Negro society of the church.   The third
Atlanta Conference approved these words with reference
to it:

Under the leadership of priest or medicine man, afterward of
the Christian pastor, the Church preserved in itself the remnants
of African tribal life and became after emancipation the center of
Negro social life. So that today the Negro population of the
United States is virtually divided into church congregations which
are the real units of race life.[1]

It will be remembered that the *Christian Recorder* dates
from 1852.   In the seventies came the *Southwestern
Christian Advocate* (Methodist Episcopal), the *Christian
Index* (Colored Methodist Episcopal), the *Star of Zion*
(African Methodist Episcopal Zion), the *Afro American
Presbyterian*, the *American Baptist*, and the *Georgia Baptist;* in the early eighties, the *Western Star* (Baptist), the
Baptist Vanguard, the *A.M.E. Church Review.*[2]   There
are about four and a half million church-members
representing these various denominations and supporting
their publications.[3]

The story of the National Baptist Publishing Board,
although this institution was not launched until 1896,
should be told here.[4]   Richard Henry Boyd was sold on
an auction block in 1859 for $700.   During the war he
remained true to his Texas master and after his death
took care of the details on the plantation.   Later a cow-
puncher, he finally became a minister.   In 1896 the

[1] *The Negro Church*, ed. W. E. B. DuBois, "Atlanta University
Publications," No. 8, Atlanta, 1903.   Foregoing report, 1898, p. 11.

[2] *Efforts for Social Betterment among Negro Americans*, "Atlanta
University Publications," No. 14, Atlanta, 1909, pp. 114 ff.

[3] *Negro Year Book*, etc., p. 240.

[4] Washington, *The Negro in Business*, Boston, Chicago, 1907, pp. 186 ff.

National Baptists in convention at St. Louis authorized him and a committee to undertake the printing of Negro literature for Negro Baptists. This involved breaking away from the leading-strings of the white American Baptist Publication Society, and after some difficulty was accomplished by securing reprints from the Southern Baptists of their Sunday-school literature, until Negroes could get to the point of writing their own copy. Beginnings of the National Baptist Publishing Board were made in a room on Cedar Street, Nashville. "This small room, 8 by 10 feet, one small second-hand table, two small second-hand split-bottom chairs, and one oil lamp, a small bottle of ink, two plain pen holders, five cents' worth of pen points, and fifty cents' worth of plain writing paper and envelopes, constituted the initial fixtures and furniture." The printed material used was put in special covers which were admired by the Baptists and the series was called the "Negro Backs." Secretary Boyd had acquired copies of all associational and Sunday-school proceedings and publications and otherwise secured names and addresses of all church workers who might be customers.

Then he prepared price lists, order blanks, self-addressed envelopes, and a circular letter which he had his printer set up in imitation of typewriting, on letterheads that he had already prepared. While the letter was in preparation, he secured the services of three young women and set them to work directing envelopes to addresses taken from these associational and Sunday School minutes. He mailed in one day 5,000 of these letters, addressed to superintendents, clerks, and pastors in every state in the Union where he knew there was a Negro Baptist church.

In thirty-two days the record revealed cash receipts of $12,000 from 750 Sunday schools that had been sent supplies. The first year's report to the National Baptist Convention showed that 700,000 copies of Sunday-school papers had been sent out, and cash receipts were over $5,000. Growth was rapid. The Baptists made the board a general publishing concern; books, hymnals, manuals, literature of all sorts, began to be printed. Many of the songs printed were those composed by Negroes. There came to be seven brick buildings, the latest machinery of all sorts, the additional business of general church supplies, including furniture, a chapel room where services were held each day in the forenoon and attended by the entire personnel, a pay-roll of $200,000 a year, and a mail business bringing in as high as 2,000 letters a day.[1] A fight over the control of this concern caused a split in the ranks of the Baptists that has not yet been closed. As a result of a court decision the National Baptist Convention, Incorporated, finding itself left without the plant which is still controlled by the Boyds, has resolved to build a large and complete publishing concern of its own.[2]

During the years since the Civil War there was a normal growth of papers representing the fraternal orders. These orders have been multiplying, as is well known, and have entwined their roots more or less among those of the church life, banking operations, social activity, and the undertaking businesses which have been carried on by Negroes for themselves. The Masons and the Odd Fellows had organizations in ante-bellum days. Of

[1] Clement Richardson, *National Cyclopedia of the Colored Race,* Montgomery, 1919, pp. 414–16; W. N. Hartshorn, *An Era of Progress and Promise,* Boston, 1910, pp. 517–27; *Negro Year Book,* p. 361.

[2] Dr. R. H. Boyd died in the fall of 1921, while attending a meeting of the National Baptist Convention (Unincorporated) at New Orleans; he was struck by a bullet fired at another man.

those organizations that are mentioned in the *Negro Year Book*, six were founded in the sixties, one in the seventies, three in the eighties, six in the nineties or thereafter, and some are undated.   Forty-five or more newspapers now exist representing the needs of these institutions.   Some of these papers—indeed most of them—are common carriers of the news, opinion, and advertising that belongs to a general newspaper.   Some, too, like the *Atlanta Independent*, which was started in 1903, have built up a considerable circulation and wide influence.

It is impossible not to picture the activity of the Negro press, while it was making such determined efforts to get a foothold after the Emancipation, as playing an important part in the process of educating a race.   Booker T. Washington is never more eloquent than in his description of the reading-hunger that possessed his people after the war.   He says:

I shall never forget the strange, pathetic scenes and incidents of that time.   I can recall vividly the picture not only of children, but of men and women, some of whom had reached the age of sixty or seventy, tramping along the country roads with a spelling-book or a Bible in their hands.   It did not seem to occur to anyone that age was any obstacle to learning in books.   With weak and unaccustomed eyes, old men and old women would struggle along month after month in their effort to master the primer in order to get, if possible, a little knowledge of the Bible.   Some of them succeeded; many of them failed. . . . .

The places for holding school were anywhere and everywhere; the Freedmen could not wait for schoolhouses to be built or for teachers to be provided. . . . . More than once, I have seen a fire in the woods at night with a dozen or more people of both sexes and of all ages sitting about with book in hands studying their lessons. Sometimes they would fasten their primers between the plough-shares, so that they could read as they ploughed.   I have seen

Negro coal miners trying to spell out the words of a little reading-book by the dim light of a miner's lamp, hundreds of feet below the earth.[1]

It was inevitable that as literacy increased there were still large numbers who depended on oral transmission of the news of the day.   A great deal of this has been going on in the South in more recent times as well, and those who read a paper or hear it read have straightway carried the news to someone else.   During the migration of 1916–17 this was quite common.   What illiteracy really means in a group that has begun to get a glimpse of higher standards of life has been well told in the case of the Russian peasants by O. M. Sayler, of Indianapolis, who spent some time in Russia in recent years.

The illiteracy of the Russian peasant is a deceptive and mis-leading thing.   It is no proof of ignorance.   On the contrary, the withholding of the normal means of intelligence has only sharpened the native mental eagerness to acquire knowledge, and the Rus-sian peasant mind, unhampered with conventional modes of thought, has in its simplicity reached out with avidity to the dreams and promise of the socialized state.   If the peasant cannot read, he can listen.   Many times I have seen an intense group of them gathered round the only one of their number who could read, eagerly drinking in the information and the ideas which they were incapable of gaining through the symbol of printed language. By this means news travels in Russia to the farthest village as rapidly as it does with us.[2]

[1] *The Story of the Negro*, II, 136 ff.

[2] Oliver M. Sayler, *Russia White or Red*, Boston, 1919, pp. 282, 283.

CHAPTER III

THE NEGRO PRESS IN FREEDOM

It is natural that throughout the eighties and later the papers that began to function normally in the growing social life of Negroes appeared first in the cities, where some substantial cultural and economic organization was possible. As early as 1879 we find the first issues of the *Washington Bee*, the oldest secular paper now surviving. About this time began the *Indianapolis World*. In 1883 came the *Cleveland Gazette*, in 1884 the *Philadelphia Tribune*, in 1885 the *Savannah Tribune*, and about the same time the *Richmond Planet*. The *New York Age* appeared in 1887, followed before the nineties by the *Freeman* of Indianapolis. Something of the character of these journals is evident from the personal careers of representative editors.

William Calvin Chase of the *Washington Bee*, who died in 1921, was born in Washington where he went to a school in the basement of the Fifteenth Street Presbyterian Church. He also attended public school and later the law department of Howard University, selling papers for a living. Admitted to the Virginia bar, and also to the Supreme Court of the District of Columbia, he became active as a lawyer, then went into politics, and won the reputation of a fighter. His fearless personality has done a great deal to sell his paper.[1]

Typical, like Chase, of the generation just passing, the editor of the *Philadelphia Tribune* died, too, in 1921.

[1] Hartshorn, *An Era of Progress and Promise*, p. 460.

53

54 THE NEGRO PRESS IN THE UNITED STATES

Chris J. Perry was born in Baltimore, but at the age of eighteen went to Philadelphia to attend its schools. He supported himself by serving in private families and cafés. His first encouragement toward journalism was the result of his success in getting news items accepted by daily papers and in editing a colored people's column for a local Sunday newspaper. Mr. Perry was faithful to his church (the Lombard Street Presbyterian), where he was trustee, Sunday-school superintendent, and teacher. The *Tribune* was launched in November, 1884. It prints its own paper and runs a job plant. Editor Perry was also successful with investments in securities and real estate.[1]

William H. Steward, of the *American Baptist*, founded 1879, was born of slave parents in Kentucky, who "hired their time" and removed to Louisville, where by 1865, when he was eighteen years old, young Steward had managed to get considerable education in private schools. He has been a school teacher, the first colored letter-carrier in Louisville, an active layman in his church, chairman of the trustees of the State University in Louisville, and vice-president of the National Negro Business League.[2] He has also served as chairman of the Board of Directors of the Louisville Colored Public School and Grand Master Mason. He "lives in his own home, a brick residence."[3]

John H. Murphy, who established the *Baltimore Afro-American* in 1892, was interested in religious work. He was known to travel a great deal holding Sunday-school

[1] Hartshorn, *op. cit.*, p. 471.

[2] *Ibid.*, p. 463.

[3] *National Cyclopedia of the Colored Race*, p. 175.

institutes and conventions, and his first journalistic venture was the *Sunday-School Helper.*[1] "Baltimore was then known as the graveyard of colored newspapers,"[2] but the *Afro-American* has become a substantial success.

There are several conspicuous names connected with the *New York Age.* In 1907, Booker T. Washington told[3] how T. T. Fortune was born of slave parents, worked as a lad at odd jobs in a southern newspaper office, and there picked up a great deal of information that served as a sort of practical education. Since that time he has studied and traveled. When a young man he was appointed mail agent between Jacksonville and Chattahoochee, and in 1875 became Special Inspector of Customs for a district in Delaware. In 1879 at New York, after again working in a composing room, he essayed a journal of his own, the *Rumor.* This became the *Globe*, which was followed first by the *Freeman* and later by the *New York Age.* Fortune says of these years:

When I entered upon the active work of journalism, in New York City, in 1879, my partner and I were the first to set the type of the *Globe.* At night we prepared the forms for the press, and in the day we worked as compositors. Mr. William Walter Sampson and I had worked together as compositors on a daily newspaper, now the *Daily Times-Union*, at Jacksonville, Fla. Through him I secured a position on the *Daily Witness* in New York. Here I found my previous experience of great value, for it had been my good fortune to have met and collaborated with such men as John W. Cromwell, Charles N. Otey and Robert Peel Brooks, among the most brilliant men that the race has ever produced. My acquaintance also included the great Frederick Douglass, the lion of them all. . . . .

[1] *An Era of Progress and Promise*, p. 418.
[2] *Philadelphia Tribune*, January 1, 1921.
[3] *The Negro in Business*, pp. 178 ff.

As I remember, when I entered journalism, there were only four other newspapers of the race in publication—the *New York Progressive American*, the *Christian Recorder*, the *Pacific Appeal*, and the *San Francisco Elevator*. The latter was edited by Philip A. Bell, one of the old-timers, who had fought the anti-slavery fight all his days, a grand old warrior, giving no quarter nor asking any of the enemy.[1]

T. T. Fortune has published poems and a book of essays called *White and Black*. He still contributes to Negro periodicals.

Fred R. Moore, the present editor of the *New York Age*, has identified himself with several professional and business projects, including movements for the general advancement of the race. At the age of eighteen, he was made a messenger in the United States Treasury Department, and later was given work in a New York bank. Finally he held a position in the New York National Bank of Commerce. In 1893 he organized the Afro-American Building and Loan Company, and in 1903 was elected national organizer by the National Negro Business League.[2] Since 1907, Fred Moore has been identified with the *Age*. Among his political activities may be mentioned his acceptance of the post of Minister to Liberia, his nomination for New York legislature, and his position on the Advisory Committee of the National Republican Committee in 1912 and 1916.[3] In 1920 he conducted publicity work for the Republican party in the East.

Those who, as editors and publishers, have become famous among Negroes are too numerous to be detailed.

[1] *Favorite Magazine*, Autumn, 1920.

[2] *The Negro in Business*, pp. 181 ff.

[3] *National Cyclopedia of the Colored Race*, p. 226.

Only a few others may be mentioned. Harry C. Smith, of the *Cleveland Gazette*, has been thrice elected to the Ohio legislature, and while there managed the passage of two laws that have meant much to his people: the Ohio Civil Rights Law, and the Ohio Anti-lynching Law.[1]

George L. Knox, since 1897 the editor of the *Freeman*, escaped from his master while in the southern army and came into the Union ranks. In the North he was a successful barber, and at twenty-six began getting an education under a private tutor. He has managed two barber-shops and owns considerable property in Indianapolis. He is prominent in his church, and has been a member of Republican political organizations, once running for Congress.[2] The *Freeman* is conspicuous today for its theatrical news and advertisements. Formerly this paper was distributed by Pullman porters.

Nick Chiles of the *Topeka Plaindealer* came to Topeka with only fifteen dollars in his pocket, but he now owns a $7,000 plant, his own building, a fine residence, and a large amount of other property.[3]

John Mitchell, Jr., is not only editor and owner of the *Richmond Planet*, but also president of the Mechanic's Savings Bank. Once, after denouncing a lynching, he received an unsigned letter with drawing of skull and cross-bones and a piece of hemp inclosed. Thereupon he went directly to visit the place whence this threat had come.[4]

"Ben Davis," as he is familiarly known, is thus spoken of: "When you think of Benjamin Jefferson Davis,

[1] *An Era of Progress and Promise*, p. 444.

[2] *Ibid.*, p. 430.   [3] *Ibid.*, p. 475.   [4] *Ibid.*, p. 437.

you think of three things—the *Atlanta Independent*, the growth of the Odd Fellows and the Odd Fellows' Block in Atlanta, Ga."[1]   By his efforts this organization in about ten years grew from a membership of 10,000 to 50,000.   The building mentioned is seven stories high and contains six stores, fifty-six offices, three lodgerooms and the roof garden.   Davis is generally appointed one of the "Big Four" delegates-at-large from Georgia to the Republican National Convention.   In his own paper[2] he likes to depict—as in a recent cartoon—his humble beginnings as a "friend of the common people," and his later success, still as "a friend of the common people."

From these brief accounts of newspaper men it will be evident that there has been an alliance between the press as a profession and the various occupations which have helped to support it.   Instead of viewing this as a simple lack of differentiation of function in a society not yet ready for it, Richard W. Thompson wrote rather sadly in 1902:

It is a stinging indictment of our much-lauded "race-pride" that the greater proportion of our Negro journalists are compelled to depend for a living upon teaching, preaching, law, medicine, office-holding, or upon some outside business investment.[3]

The close relation of the newspaper to the actual life and struggles of the people makes it a fair index of the common impulses and ambitions moving within the group. The desire to get up and get on in the world, a desire characteristic of this as of so many groups in modern

[1] *National Cyclopedia of the Colored Race*, pp. 115 f.

[2] *Atlanta Independent*, December 30, 1920.

[3] *Twentieth Century Literature, etc., Relating to the American Negro*, ed. D. W. Culp, Naperville, Illinois, 1902, p. 333.

America, would be reflected in just such history as the Negro press has been making. One example of the enterprising spirit may be cited:

The *Hot Springs Echo* came into existence 22 years ago, its present Editor who was then a youth of 19, starting his journalistic career with a second-hand press, a few cases of type and no experience in either business or printing. By hard work, study and grit, he had a $5,000 plant bought and paid for 10 years later. Lost plant and all worldly possessions in a disastrous fire which almost destroyed the city. Kept hustling and still publishes the only live Negro paper in the section.[1]

The eighties saw the beginning of many attempts to build up a Negro daily. Penn mentions the *Cairo Gazette*, which began in 1882 and ran as a daily for six months, that is, until it was destroyed by fire; and the *Columbus* (Georgia) *Messenger*, beginning in 1887, which was a weekly the first year, then a semi-weekly, and finally a daily. Naïvely, Penn adds: "The Daily Messenger would not have suspended publication, but the editor having accepted a position in the Railway Mail Service, he was necessarily compelled to close up his business enterprise for a time."[2] There was recently the *Daily Herald* in Baltimore, of which the *Crisis* for March, 1920, said:

We have had many attempts to start daily papers for Negro readers, but none lasted longer than a few months and most of them have died in weeks. We feared this same result for the *Herald*. . . . . But a colored daily paper that has passed its second birthday, that misses no issues, has strong editorials, and publishes news, is an accomplishment which deserved unstinted praise. Our hats off to William T. Andrews, of Baltimore![3]

[1] Letter to writer, April 12, 1921, from *Hot Springs Echo*.

[2] Penn, *The Afro-American Press and Its Editors*, p. 127.

[3] G. W. Gore, Jr., *Negro Journalism*, Greencastle, Indiana, 1922, p. 20, mentions the *Indianapolis Daily Standard* as beginning in April, 1922.

The existence of six magazines some time during these years was mentioned by Washington in 1907. Two of these were religious quarterlies, one, *Alexander's Magazine* of Boston, new at that time; others were the *Colored American Magazine* of New York, and the *Voice of the Negro* at Chicago.[1]   Mr. Alexander also speaks of having edited an earlier venture, the *Monthly Review*, at Boston.

Penn finds that there were ten newspapers in 1870, thirty-one in 1880, and, in 1890, 154.[2]   Williams names fifty-six periodicals as existing in 1882.[3]   Seven of these have continued to the present day: *New York Globe*, perpetuated in the *New York Age; Washington Bee; Georgia Baptist* (Augusta); *American Baptist* (Louisville); *Afro-American Presbyterian* (Charlotte, North Carolina); *Christian Recorder* (Philadelphia); *Baptist Signal* (Greenville, Mississippi), now the *Sentinel-Signal* at Lexington. T. T. Fortune makes this characterization of the press in the eighties and subsequently:

From 1880 to 1890 there was a rapid development of Afro-American journalism, colored journalism becoming negated in the latter designation which I employed and made popular with white and colored journalists. The number of newspapers not only increased rapidly, but the white papers of the country began to take notice of their existence and to quote extensively upon their news and opinions. . . . .

Like all good things Negro journalism was a gradual growth, a systematic development, from very small beginnings. The old journalism had few readers and advertisers, and payday was always a deathless agony to the editor. He, typically, was a man of one idea, the Afro-American journalist, who cleaved close to the line of race rights and loyalty, and could not be swerved from his

[1] *The Negro in Business*, p. 176.

[2] *Op. cit.*, pp. 112, 114.

[3] *History of the Negro Race in America*, II, 576 ff.

purpose by bribes or intimidation. He supported the Republican party because he despised the Democratic party, and those of his school who are living today are of the same mind they were then. The old journalism was a fighting machine which feared no man or combination of men. It refused to print anything that would damage the good name or morals of the race, and kept all scandal and personalities, however sensational the news might be, in the background.[1]

The more aggressive note in Negro journalism comes soon after the opening of the Great War. There had been, as Fortune says, a fighting spirit all along, but the newer race propaganda is very well marked by the entrance of the *Crisis* into the field in 1910.

Various elements in the total situation had been creating increasing tension. The laws passed by southern states for the restriction of the suffrage began in 1890. As early as this the new generation born since the Civil War was preparing the stage for new conflict. Illiteracy among Negroes was already registering spectacular decreases, from 70 per cent in 1880 to 57.1 per cent in 1890. The percentage dropped to 44.5 in 1900, and to 30.4 in 1910. There was increasing economic competence. The amount of gain in wealth-accumulation came to more than a billion in 1919.[2] Meanwhile the lynching record kept pace, reaching its highest record in 1892.[3] In 1901 William Monroe Trotter began publishing the *Guardian* at Boston, a paper that is now known as among the most aggressive—or (in a racial sense) "radical." A riot in Springfield, Illinois, in 1908, stimulated the

[1] *Favorite Magazine*, Autumn, 1920.

[2] These facts are all brought together in the *Negro Year Book*— illiteracy on pp. 277 f; suffrage restriction, pp. 202 ff; wealth, p. 1.

[3] *Ibid.*, p. 373.

birth of the National Association for the Advancement of Colored People in 1910. The *Chicago Defender* arose in 1905, and began its headlining policy in 1910. Finally, in 1914, the death of Booker T. Washington removed one of the greatest influences that might make for milder utterance.

W. M. Trotter, president of the New England Suffrage League and chief sponsor of the National Equal Rights League, received his Harvard B.A., in 1895 and M.A., in 1896, having been elected a member of Phi Beta Kappa as an undergraduate. Those of his own race have thus spoken of him:

Mr. Trotter. . . . selected a field after graduation in which he could express the sentiments of the oppressed race. Having felt keenly the vicious thrust of race prejudice he turned to journalism as the most effective means to combat the evil. . . . . Mr. Trotter's ability could easily win for him an easy berth by compromising the cause of the race. But he has steadfastly refused to be bought either in cold cash or through appointment to a political berth.[1]

Every issue of the *Guardian* contains a cut of Mrs. Trotter with an editorial caption as follows:

Geraldine Trotter, My Loyal Wife, who is no more. To honoring her memory . . . . I shall devote my remaining days; and to perpetuating the *Guardian* and the Equal Rights Cause and work for which she made such noble and total sacrifice, I dedicate the best that is in me till I die and ask the active aid of all Colored Americans and of all believers in justice, equality and fraternity and in the brotherhood of man. For the rights of her race she gave her life. William Monroe Trotter, October 12, 1918.

Trotter has lived up to his reputation for bravery. He led a delegation in a personal interview with President

[1] J. L. Nichols and W. H. Grogman, *The New Progress of a Race*, Naperville, Illinois, 1920, pp. 435 ff.

Wilson to protest against discrimination; and again, when a passport was denied him, he made his way across the Atlantic as a cook, at least to observe, if he could not attend, the Peace Conference at Paris. The *Guardian* is published not only for the group in and about Boston, but for a nation-wide circle as well.

The *Crisis* is a magazine of forty-eight pages and cover, furnishing the reader with what he would require from a literary magazine as well as the propaganda of the National Association for the Advancement of Colored People, whose organ it is. Begun in 1910, it reached a sale of 100,000 copies by June of 1919.[1] W. E. Burghardt Du Bois, its editor, tells in *Darkwater*[2] how he was led into that work, tracing his path from the Massachusetts town where he was born, through his school days, his college years at Fisk and Harvard, his student-experiences in Europe, his teaching first at Wilberforce and then at Atlanta, to what he calls the "great Decision."

At last, forbear and waver as I would, I faced the great Decision. My life's last and greatest door stood ajar. What with all my dreaming, studying, and teaching was I going to *do* in this fierce fight? . . . . I found myself suddenly the leader of a great wing of people[3] fighting against another and greater wing. . . . .

Away back in the little years of my boyhood I had sold the *Springfield Republican* and written for Mr. Fortune's *Globe*. I dreamed of being an editor myself some day. I am an editor. In the great, slashing days of college life I dreamed of a strong organization to fight the battles of the Negro race. The National Association for the Advancement of Colored People is such a body, and it grows daily. In the dark days at Wilberforce I planned a

[1] *Crisis*, September, 1919, p. 235.

[2] New York, 1920.

[3] The Niagara Movement seems to be meant.

time when I could speak freely to my people and of them interpreting between two worlds.   I am speaking now. . . . .

. . . . My salary even for a year was not assured, but it was
the "Voice without reply."   The result has been the National
Association for the Advancement of Colored People and the *Crisis*
and this book, which I am finishing on my Fiftieth Birthday.

In March, 1917, the *Crisis* told the story of its growing
circulation, adding that in 1916 the magazine was out of
debt and entirely self-supporting.   The present circulation is over 60,000.[1]

The story of the *Chicago Defender* symbolizes the
aspiration and enterprise of the race.   Robert S. Abbott,
the proprietor and editor, was born in Savannah and educated in Hampton Institute.   He has the degree of
Bachelor of Laws.   His first acquaintance with Chicago
came in the nineties, where his experience in seeking work
from white employers was dispiriting.   He knew what it
was to stand in the bread line of a prominent white
church and be told to step out and make way for a white
man; and again, to make way for a white man looking
for work, even though the latter were an immigrant who
could not speak English.   The first copies of the *Defender*,
which Abbott started in 1905, were handbill size.   These
he distributed himself.

His entire bankroll was a 25 cent piece, and the manner in
which he secured money enough to bring out the initial publication
will always remain a hazy page in his book of memories.   He had a
vision, however, he recognized in . . . . Chicago a field much in
need of an up-to-date, progressive newspaper . . . . week after
week he found it a desperate struggle to raise sufficient money to
bring out the current issue.

[1] *Eleventh Annual Report, N.A.A.C.P.*, New York, January, 1921.

In 1910 Abbott hired J. Hockley Smiley, whose ideas included the use of headlines, for which the *Defender* has since been remarkable. At first other papers of the race ridiculed this new departure, but later several followed the lead.

After the death of Smiley, Alfred Anderson was added to the staff as editorial writer, and more recently L. C. Harper has become managing editor. In course of time, the various departments of a metropolitan newspaper were introduced: drama, sports, and special features. The paper seeks to live up to its title of *Defender*. Colored people from all over the country turn to it when in trouble; the staff interests itself in securing legal aid and justice for individual Negroes. Over 100,000 copies a week are sold—the war and the migration from the South having greatly accelerated circulation. It was the mechanical equipment that visitors came to see on the grand opening day. Scores passed in under the sign, "The World's Greatest Weekly," to be shown through the new building. Said the issue of May 14, 1921:

The *Chicago Defender* entertained approximately 5,000 people at its formal opening in the new plant Friday, May 6. . . . . As one entered, two murals by W. E. Scott attracted the attention. One, on the left, showed a daughter of Ethiopia holding in one hand the *Defender*, or Light, and in the other the balance scales . . . . before the oppressed of all lands and climes. . . . . Under one painting the complete office equipment of the first *Defender* was exhibited, a small folding table, and a single chair. . . . . Guides met the incoming guests and escorted them through the plant. . . . . At 10 o'clock, when the doors were closed, the crowd was still coming in. . . . .

In its rôle of champion of the common people and in its aggressive advocacy of Negro rights the press has found in recent years a pronounced welcome from its people. This is evident from the volume and kind of letters written by its readers. When Negroes have trouble of any sort they write to the paper, sometimes, merely to utter their cry for justice. The *Indianapolis Ledger* (March 14, 1921), prints a letter from Louisiana where a company of colored actors was set upon, whipped, stripped, and driven from town. The letter closes: "No name given, for I fear the South. Yours in Christ for the Negro race." Another, from an Ohio town[1] recites the refusal of a physician to give treatment to colored patients: "I ask for this publication in your valuable paper. May other Colored papers also copy." The following reached the *Chicago Defender* from Arkansas:

Nov. 21st to the *Chicago Defender*

Please allow me to tell how mr. E—— was treated here [he came] from Helena ar. to haul timber he made $65.45 so monday after Payday He goes to the P.O. to Buy an money order and the Post master says to him how much you want to send mr. E——says $50.00 P.O. master say who to mr. E—— says to Mary E—— at leland miss. Then he say give me the money mr. E—— give him five ten dollars Bills at first and 50 cents in Silver after the Postmaster had Receive the money he Replyed to mr E——you must going to send your family north to Vote ant you mr E—— Said I dont know then the P.O.m. said Well Buy God you will know Before she get this $50.00 mr. E—— said you dont mean to take $50.00 do you he said yes what in hell you going to do about it mr. E—— said the thing I want to know What are you going to do and that time he struck mr. E—— and mr E—— knock him down and that time 5. more white Join in and mr E.—— fought them they sprain mr E Right leg and he Broke 2 of them legs and knock one eye out then the mob Begain so Mr. E—— was takeing away

---

[1] Letter dated, Canton, Ohio, March 14, 1921, probably written to the *Cleveland Call*.

By sone of the Better Class of white and members of our Race and kept untell he got well and we sister of the A.M.E. Church Paid his doctor Bill and sent him out of the state north and his whareabout now I dont know i seen him the 10th of this month and told me write his wife and mrs. ———— at Leland miss it was such shame tell none of the white papers said nothing about it

The fighting spirit of the press was naturally stimulated by all the conditions that went along with the Great War. There was a great stimulus given to the growth of newspapers that have arisen in or since that period. Possibly 100 periodicals have begun publication in this time. Some, of course, have been born and buried since 1914.

The combined result of Negro activities during the war was an increase in racial consciousness and desire for self-assertion. The white Americans have not been free from suspicions as to the attitude of Negroes in this emergency. If the patriotism of their press be taken into account, such suspicions would certainly be relieved. Robert Russa Moton says:

The Negro press was also found by the Government to be a very helpful factor in the prosecution of the war. It stood almost solidly back of such men as were appointed by the Government in all of their efforts for the country's good. And whatever happened they were most loyal to the Government, even when, as was sometimes true, they might have criticized with justification many of the things which took place. The attitude of these publications, numbering some three hundred or more newspapers and magazines, was a very important factor in determining the attitude of Negroes on many questions. . . . .[1]

Emmett J. Scott also testifies on this point. He was special assistant to the Secretary of War in the matter of welfare and morale of colored people.

[1] *Finding a Way Out, an Autobiography*, Garden City, New York, 1920, pp. 248 f.

An outstanding force that helped to win the war was the Negro press of the country. Aside from the efficient work done by this element of power through the conference of Editors at Washington, ... the press was an asset of incalculable value in pushing the war work among colored people by the regular publication of the bulletins of information the Special Assistant caused to be sent out from the War Department week after week, beginning shortly after the assumption of his duties. His mailing list embraced more than two hundred Negro journals and magazines having a large circulation in practically every State in the Union, ... besides the Speakers' "Committee of One Hundred" and many newspaper correspondents, special writers, heads of schools and colleges and men of influence and standing in the strategic centers of the nation. . . . . Our editors were conservative on all current questions, at no sacrifice of courage and absolute frankness in the upholding of principles. . . . .[1]

The newspapers did insist on the training of Negro officers, proper provision for the needs of the troops, and absence of discrimination. They had the "absolute frankness" Scott speaks of. The *Washington Bee* said:

But the Negro is willing today to take up arms and defend the American flag; he stands ready to uphold the hands of the President; he stands ready to defend the country and his President against this cruel and unjust oppression. His mother, sister, brother and children are being burned at the stake and yet the American flag is his emblem and which he stands ready to defend. In all the battles the Negro soldier has proved his loyalty and today he is the only true American at whom the finger of scorn cannot be pointed.[2]

In June, 1918, E. J. Scott, on behalf of the War Department and the Committee on Public Information, called together a group of Negro leaders, including thirty-

[1] *Scott's Official History of the American Negro in the World War*, Washington (?), 1919, pp. 361 f., 116, etc.

[2] Quoted in the *Crisis*, May, 1917, p. 23.

one newspaper men.[1] For three days they discussed
the relation of the Negro to the conduct of affairs, men-
tioning his special grievances and needs. Their recommendations, embodied in a "Bill of Particulars," follow.[2]
The special war correspondent appointed was Ralph W.
Tyler who had been more than thirty years a writer for
the white papers in Columbus, Ohio.[3]

(a) A message from the President in denunciation of . . . .
mob violence.

(b) The enrolment of colored Red Cross nurses for service
in the camps and cantonments of the army.

(c) The continuance of the training camps for colored officers
and the increase in their number and enlargement of their
scope. . . . .

(d) Betterment of the general conditions in the camps . . . .
and positive steps taken to reduce race friction. . . . .

(e) The extension to young colored men of opportunity for
special training in technical, mechanical and military science in
the various schools and colleges of the country.

(f) An increase in the number of colored Chaplains for army
service.

(g) The establishment of a woman's branch under the Council
of National Defense, with a colored field agent. . . . .

(h) Steps taken to recall Colonel Charles Young to active
service in the United States Army.

(i) The appointment of the first colored, regularly-commis-
sioned war correspondent, to report military operations on the
western front in France.

(j) The granting of a loan of $5,000,000 for the relief of the
Republic of Liberia.

In the first year of the war, indeed, the terrible events
at Houston, ending in the summary execution of "thir-

[1] Among them were W. E. B. Du Bois, R. E. Jones, Fred R. Moore,
B. J. Davis, John Mitchell, Jr., W. T. Andrews. *Crisis*, September, 1918.

[2] *National Cyclopedia of the Colored Race*, pp. 613 f.

[3] Died in 1921.

teen black soldiers"[1] and the imprisonment of many others, had provoked a bitter response.   Yet even in its bitterness the press maintained restraint.   Three illustrative comments may be given:

They "gave their lives a ransom for many."   While technically and legally they erred, still in the light of Ages and the eyes of the All-Seeing, they were more sinned against than sinning[?]. It is written: "They went to their death with heroic stoicism. There was neither bravado nor fear."—*Savannah Tribune*.

The Negroes of the entire country will regard the thirteen Negro soldiers of the Twenty-Fourth Infantry executed as martyrs. —*Baltimore Daily Herald*.

Strict justice has been done, but full justice has not been done. . . . . And so sure as there is a God in heaven, at some time and in some way full justice will be done.—*New York Age*.[2]

Typical of the sort of loyalty and self-restraint under which the press was doing its work in these days is an editorial that appeared in the *Crisis* (July, 1918), which, two months later, the editor felt called upon to explain. "Our Special Grievances" is his new caption.   There were many such, the constant burden of which was discrimination.   There was a limited number of higher officers, there was difficulty in accepting Negro nurses for service in France, and in many details there was room for irritation.   In spite of this Du Bois holds:

The leading editorial in the July *Crisis*, called "Close Ranks," has been the subject of much comment.   To a few it has seemed to indicate some change of position on the part of the National

[1] *Messenger* for October, 1919, has Archibald Grimke's poem by this name.

[2] Quotations taken from *Negro Year Book*, p. 53.

Association for the Advancement of Colored People and the *Crisis*. It is needless to say that it indicates nothing of the sort. . . . .

What the *Crisis* said is precisely what in practice the Negroes of America have already done during the war and have been advised to do by every responsible editor and leader.

The editorial was in exact accord and almost in the very words of a resolution written by the same hand and passed unanimously by the thirty-one editors of all the leading publications in America.

Did Negroes refuse to serve in the draft until they got the right to vote? No, they stormed the gates of the army for the right to fight. Did they refuse commissions because their army school was segregated? No, they were eager and diligent to learn. Have we black men for one moment hesitated to do our full duty in this war because we thought the country was not doing its full duty to us? Is there a single Negro leader who advised by word, written or spoken, rebellion and disloyalty? Certainly not. The *somebody* "forgot his special grievance" and fought for the country, and to him and for him the *Crisis* speaks. The *Crisis* says, *first* your country, *then* your Rights!

The feeling that the Negro press was not entirely loyal during the war is the result of a few sporadic utterances such as those of the *Messenger*, the *Crusader*, and others of New York. The former is frankly interested in socialism, the latter in similar ideas, including a free Negro state somewhere in the world. In August, 1918, the editors of the *Messenger* were jailed for two and a half days, and second-class mailing privileges were denied—the result of an article entitled "Pro-Germanism among Negroes," which the editors insist was ironic.[1] The associate editor, however, responded to the draft and served loyally in his place. The other charges of disloyalty center upon periodicals gathered up by the Department of Justice, apparently rather hastily, in 1919,

[1] Letter to present writer, March 19, 1921.

the war having been over a year and a half. The general tone of these papers is not different from that which now obtains. The *Negro World*, Garvey's organ, came into prominence only since the armistice, but has thrived largely because of conditions created during the war period.

The *New York News*, as recently as May 26, 1921, recounts the troubles that Negro newspapers underwent during this time of suspicion, and the difficulty in getting rid of that suspicion even now.

The migration to the North in which perhaps half a million colored people from the South had part, beginning in 1915 and continuing three years,[1] figures as both result and cause of increased activity on the part of the press.[2] The Negro newspapers were divided in their counsels, some being opposed to the migration, others in favor of it. The *Star of Zion* said, on July 19, 1917:

> While I concede the black man's right to go where he likes, for he has the right of liberty and the pursuit of happiness, yet I doubt the wisdom of such wholesale exodus from the South. There are some things which the Negro needs far more than his wages, or some of the rights for which he contends. He needs conservation of his moral life.

The *Christian Recorder*, in Philadelphia, wrote on February 1, 1917:

> If a million Negroes move north and west in the next twelve-month, it will be one of the greatest things for the Negro since the Emancipation Proclamation.

The *New York News* (September 17, 1916) gives this advice:

---

[1] *Negro Year Book, 1918-1919*, p. 8.

[2] Emmett J. Scott, *Negro Migration During the War*, pp. 160-65.

Yet a heavy responsibility rests upon every colored leader, moral and civic, in these northern States to take an especial interest in their newly arriving brethren. . . . . Urge them to get steady work and settle down. Urge them to become good citizens and better parents. Urge them to go to church, to lead patient Christian lives, and all will come out well in the end.

The newspapers also were one of the causes of the migration. This was true in the general sense mentioned by the *Dallas Express* (August 11, 1917):

Every Negro newspaper and publication in this broad land, including pamphlets and books, and the intelligent Negro pastor with backbone and courage are constantly protesting against the injustice done the Negro. And possibly these agents have been the greatest incentives to help create and crystallize this unrest and migration.

More specifically, the *New York Age*, in almost every mail "received letters from the South in which the writers make known their intentions of coming North in search of employment."[1] A sample is the following, from Florida, indicating the fact that advertisements in the *Age* suggested migration.

When spring opens we want to come North. We see through the columns of the *Age* very encouraging words for those who want work. We are enthused over this intelligence. Have been reading in the *Age* about employment offered at Holyoke, Mass., and in the tobacco fields of Connecticut. Let us know how we can get our tickets to come North, so we will be ready when the time arrives for our departure.

North Carolina was also heard from, and the following is from Alabama.

[1] Notes of Charles S. Johnson taken in connection with his work as special investigator of the migration for the publication of the work prepared for the Carnegie Endowment and mentioned above.

Please see to it that the Rev. Mr. Brown of Rochester, N.Y., gets this letter.   I saw an article in the *Age* that he is securing positions for colored girls.

The *New York Age* article directly stimulating the first of these letters was a lengthy one headed, "Opening of Northern Tobacco Fields to Negro Proves a Boon to Race."   The same paper, according to its issue of August 16, 1916,[1] received a letter from a body "representing the influential colored citizens" of Florida asking for advice on the whole situation.   The letter says, in part:

Our———has been asked by the white and colored people here to speak in an advisory way, but we decided to remain silent until we can hear from reliable sources in the North and East, and you have been designated as one of the best. . . . . Please give the benefit of your findings and reasons for your conclusion.

As to the part played by other newspapers, R. H. Leavell writes: "Single copies I have seen of Negro papers published in New York, Washington, and Indianapolis have been more self-contained"[2]—thus indicating the penetration of Mississippi by several northern sheets. Leavell does not mention the name of the *Chicago Defender* in the report cited but he means it certainly.   He speaks of "a weekly published in Chicago, whose editor knows clearly what he wants for his people and why he wants it."

[It] makes skillful use of a recent lynching in which the head of the dead man was severed from his body, so it is alleged, and thrown into a crowd of Negroes on the principal Negro street.   A photograph of what purports to be the head as it lies on the deserted

[1] *Negro Migration During the War*, pp. 43, 44.

[2] *Negro Migration in 1916–17*, U.S. Department of Labor, Division of Negro Economics, Washington, 1919, pp. 29, 30.

street is published under the telling caption, "Not Belgium—America.". . . . This publicity is all the more effective, because there is a natural tendency on the part of this Negro press to minimize such justification as may exist. . . . . One little Negro boy formerly had trouble in disposing of 10 copies a week, so that he was often late at Sunday school. Now, since the exodus has begun, he has had no trouble in selling his papers in time to get to Sunday school, and many other small boys are doing a lively business selling additional copies.

In July of this year a circulation of 80,000 in the United States was claimed for this weekly, and I was told recently on what seems unquestionable authority that the circulation is now 93,000. A reputable Negro in Louisiana to whom I was directed by a prominent white leader, said of this paper: "My people grab it like a mule grabs a mouthful of fine fodder."

It was reported to this investigator that the Negroes did not trust the loyalty of their southern press as much as they did that of the North. It was asserted by a southern business man that through advertising he was able to influence the expression of one of these local papers. The following are but two samples of the many letters received during this time by the *Defender:*

———Texas

I have read the *Defender* and I have put my mine on it and I wood lik to know mor abot it and if yo pleas send me a letter abot the noth. I will thenk uo becaus we have so miney members of the Race wont to come and live up thear and all they is waitin on is a chanch and that is all and they will say fair wel to this old world and thay all will come. some is railroad some is shop and anythong thay can gets to do. With hold the name.

I remain yors, ...

———Georgia

Enclosed you will finde stamp to envelop. Please accomodate me with a few good firms or the names howery and Lowcations so

I can instruct some of my people as to where is the best place for them to locate. I want to get every one away from this hell hold that I can. If this is too much truble you can please put it in next weeks ishue for I am a reader of your paper and also injoy reading it. I am also going to write to some of those Farm countries in the west for this is no place for the colored.

No longer than last week two white men knocked and beet a colored man and then the police walk up and put the colored man under rest and let the white man go free, so your Hon. please favor me with the knowledge as to where to go for the us to go.

Resp. yours.

As typical of recent adventures in the world of Negro journalism I shall set down briefly, using extracts from personal letters, the circumstances connected with three of these.

C. F. Richarson, editor of the *Houston Informer:*

I saw that the pulpit and the teacher could not do all the work of bettering, advancing, enlightening and solidifying our racial group; I also saw the potent factor of the white press was . . . . in the development, progress and expansion of their race. . . . . I finally dedicated and consecrated myself to the task, asking Divine guidance and protection and thus today I have nothing to regret. Many of my class and school mates have apparently made better headway, financially, than I have, but when the poor and down-trodden members of my race come to me and shake my hands and compliment me on my position for righteousness and fair and square deal in church and state, I feel that such encomiums and expressions of gratitude excel all monetary considerations.

In recent years, financially, I cannot complain, for the paper has afforded several of us a nice and decent living; for our people appreciate and liberally support all movements, ventures, and undertakings that mean for their progress and uplift.

This is one case among many of the connection of college-trained Negroes with the more radical type of the present-day journalism.

The *Murfreesboro* (Tennessee) *Union*, a very recent paper, has Mary Vaughn as business editor. Her experience may indicate the fact that all newspapers are not radical, and perhaps would not be expected to be such in the smaller cities of the South.

What caused me to be so deeply interested in the newspaper world, I thought in this way I could help more of my people and get them interested in reading more and reading good books and good newspapers. . . . . Some of the best people of my race got together and thought it a fine movement, so I worked it up myself· . . . . I put in $100 to start our paper and we have now 300 subscribers, so you can see that there is nothing to be realized out of it as yet. . . . . I struggle from day to day canvassing the town with my pad and pencil trying to meet the printer's bill. . . . . I went straight to the white folks in this section and knocked at the door of their conscience and they received me, and assured me of their loyal support.

The *Crusader* is one of the more radical magazines. It is published in New York.

The *Crusader* was started September, 1918, with the first edition of one thousand copies. Apparently—like the Garvey movement only in lesser degree and necessarily divergent manifestations—it struck the hidden chords of the Negro Heart with its new ideas and bold ideals of aspirations. . . . . Within three years, its circulation had climbed to the average of 33,000 per month. The *Crusader* came as a result of well laid plans following the donation of a sum of money by J. Anthony Crawford, president of the Inter-Colonial Steamship Co., Inc., to Cyril V. Briggs, then editorial writer of the *Amsterdam News*. The purpose of the donation being to give Mr. Briggs an organ of his own to carry on propaganda which he had begun for a Free Africa, A Strong Negro State (in Africa or elsewhere), etc. The publication had few early difficulties, meeting as it did with almost instant approval. . . . .

In 1920 the Associated Negro Press estimated that the previous five years had seen a growth of circulation from 100 to 300 per cent, and advertising patronage from 50 to 200 per cent.[1]   With this substantial advance there has been likewise a growing new spirit among Negroes, according to the *Promoter* (August, 1920):

New Negro publications are not only expressive of the new spirit that has seized the race, but they are exerting a tremendous influence in inspiring the people with the highest racial ideals and aspirations.   They are inculcating into every Negro a sense of race pride and determination which is without parallel in the history of the race.

[1] Kerlin, *The Voice of the Negro*, p. 4.

CHAPTER IV

FAVORITE THEMES OF THE NEGRO PRESS

In its news of current events, expression of advice and opinion, contributed articles of a more general character, and advertising, the Negro press contains what one expects to find in the press anywhere. Its small-town and metropolitan papers somewhat resemble those of a corresponding class published by white people. But there is a difference. Through all the Negro press there flows an undercurrent of feeling that the race considers itself a part of America and yet has no voice in the American newspaper. Members of this group want to learn about each other, they want the stories of their successes, conflicts, and issues told, and they want to express themselves in public. Thus the *Kansas City Call* (April 16, 1921):

Oh, if you could see the story of your struggles honestly and fairly related in the newspapers, if you could find your heart yearning after good will with all men, if your aspirations were met with applause as are those of your neighbors, this would be a wonderful world! But no! You are denied what other men are freely granted and to get your wants you must plan and work.

The newspaper, printer's ink and white paper are the best lever to win a fair deal from the world. The Race press needs you and you need the press. The press ought to do your publicity and you must keep it up.

Occasionally it is recognized that only the nature of the case is responsible for the absence of Negro stories from the white press. Thus the *Portland* (Oregon)

Advocate (May 7, 1921), quoting *Method*, of Richmond, Virginia:

In order to get Negro news in full, you must read Negro newspapers. There are many friendly white dailies and other periodicals, but their columns are so crowded with the business of their own people (and justly so) that they have little time and space to devote to Negro activity as such. You owe it to yourself to know what your race is doing. You can know it but one way—the way of the Negro press.

"We cannot hope," says N. D. Brascher, of the Associated Negro Press, "to have the daily newspapers give our viewpoint and the aspirations and struggles that we are making."[1] R. R. Moton, principal of Tuskegee Institute, is quoted by the *Norfolk Journal and Guide* (December 18, 1920):

The Negro law breaker has easier access to newspaper columns than the fifty-two Negro bank presidents in the South, one of whom is a woman; than the fifty thousand Negroes who are conducting business enterprises; than the thousands of physicians, dentists, and other professional men, who in a quiet but effective way are contributing to the educational, moral and material advancement not only of their own race, but also of the South and of the nation.

A statistical study of Negro newspapers shows that the amount of space devoted to news and opinion seems to average 60 per cent. For the most part the advertising represents local business, generally business carried on by Negroes. To the white reader advertisements of cosmetics appear rather prominent. Some papers, generally those from smaller communities, have a large amount of plate matter supplied by a syndicate

[1] Report to the Chicago Commission on Race Relations, unpublished form.

and similar to plate matter everywhere.   This consists of miscellaneous and innocuous information, comic cartoons, and advice for home and farm.   The casual reader of the Negro paper is impressed by the large proportion of opinion as over against news, but this is due largely to the tone of the news-writing.   The editorials as such take an average of 4 per cent of the space.   About one-seventh of all goes into out-of-town news.   Events of general interest having nothing to do with race matters scarcely appear.   As for special pages dealing with sports or the theater, these belong only to the newspapers in larger cities.   Such are the results of an analysis of forty typical periodicals.[1]

[1] Murfreesboro (Tenn.) Union
Red Bank (N.J.) Echo
Cadiz (Ky.) Informer
Palatka (Fla.) Advocate
Hopkinsville (Ky.) New Age
Danville (Ky.) Torch Light
Robbins (Ill.) Herald
American Star (Sheffield, Ala.)
Pike County (Ala.) News
Morrillton (Ark.) Voice
Shreveport (La.) Sun
People's Recorder (Columbia, S.C.)
Star of Zion (Charlotte, N.C.)
Raleigh (N.C.) Independent
Watchman-Lantern (Muskogee, Okla.)
Newport News (Va.) Star
Rome (Ga.) Enterprise
Rising Sun (Pueblo, Colo.)
Progressive Citizen (Texarkana, Ark.)
Phoenix (Ariz.) Tribune
Times–Plain Dealer (Birmingham, Ala.)
Baptist Leader (Birmingham, Ala.)
Denver (Colo.) Star
Washington (D.C.) Bee
Savannah (Ga.) Tribune
Michigan State News (Grand Rapids)
Louisville (Ky.) News
Dallas (Tex.) Express
St. Luke Herald (Richmond, Va.)
East Tennessee News (Knoxville)
Pittsburgh Courier
Philadelphia Tribune
Cleveland Advocate
New York News
Boston Chronicle
Buffalo American
St. Louis Argus
Afro-American (Baltimore)
Chicago Whip
Detroit Leader

The first ten of these papers come from towns of less than 10,000 population; the next ten from cities between 10,000 and 50,000; the next group from those between 50,000 and 500,000; the last from the largest centers.

In addition to these forty papers examined, twenty-four more were taken, and the entire sixty-four gone over for an analysis of topics treated. Editorials were analyzed along with the news as indicating the attitude of the paper toward the subjects handled. Sporting news, theater writeups, local and social happenings, as well as local reports of meetings—these were taken for granted and not counted. The remainder, eight hundred and seventy-nine articles, were noted with the following result:

On the subject of racial wrongs or clashes, 151 news items, 71 editorials.

On race progress and pride, 124 news items and 12 editorials.

On welfare efforts, including education etc., 92 news items, 15 editorials.

On the work of movements (such as the N.A.A.C.P., etc.) directed to the solution of racial problems, 59 news items, 4 editorials.

On negro crime (chiefly in city papers), 85 news items, 2 editorials.

On all other subjects, 194 news items, 70 editorials.

A large number of the articles, especially in the news, have to do with local or national politics, and frequently there are articles on Africa, Brazil, or other parts of the world toward which Negroes are now looking. The outstanding fact is, however, that when you add together the figures in the first four groups, you have 528 articles, or almost three-fifths of all devoted to the characteristic racial struggles of the Negro group. Sample articles on these subjects will be quoted.

Let the reader ask himself, as he glances over the following items, whether he finds this sort of news in his daily paper, or whether news of this sort, when it does appear, is so written and placed as to make more than a fleeting impression upon the white reader. In the most cases it will be discovered that so far as the dailies are concerned these matters are not mentioned.

I.   RACE WRONGS AND RACE CLASHES

We have never been able to see anything but evil in any Jim Crow Law. We have always been ready to lend a hand to any measure that tends to elevate any people and instill in them a higher degree of self respect and personal conduct and behavior. A Jim Crow Law, instead of helping to improve any people, is rather a strong aid to make degradation permanent. A Jim Crow Law is an abomination, and at the same time let it be known that a Jim Crow People are a scandal. Hardly a train, or other method of public service passes but what one can see how poorly many have the correct idea of their own conduct and appearance. This condition will hardly be removed as long as there are laws providing especially for such conditions.—*Florida Sentinel* (Jacksonville), December 4, 1920.

TUSKEGEE, ALA., March 18.—Armed with revolvers, bludgeons and ropes, and within sight of the famous institution founded by the late Booker T. Washington, a mob of white farmers charged the cabin occupied by Robert West, age 88, seized him and his son, George West, and forced Mrs. Duckie West, age 50 and Agnew West, 23 years old, to flee to the woods for safety. A search of the woods was made by members of the mob, but the woman and her son, after wading through creeks, escaped and hid in a barn on the outskirts of the city. Shots were fired at them as they left the rear door of the cabin.

Nine children adopted by George West, ranging in ages from 2 to 5, were left in the cabin at the mercy of the mob. It is not known what has become of them. Robert West, with his son George, was placed in jail, and while there W. E. Haust (white) is said to have gone to the West farm and removed 15 bales of cotton, 8 mules, 2 wagons, 23 head of cattle, 5,000 bundles of fodder, $75 worth of barbed wire, corn, sugar cane, cottonseed and a large amount of peas. When questioned regarding the removal of this

property, Haust is said to have remarked that it was too much for "a darkey to have," and that West owed him a debt of $200. . . . .
—*Chicago Defender*, March 19, 1921.

JACKSON, MISS., April 13.—Sandy Thompson, slave on the peonage farm of E. B. Dodson (white) and his mother-in-law, Mrs. Rachel Moore, were lynched by a mob of crackers here last week.

Thompson's body was found Monday of last week swinging from a limb of a tree.   He had been stripped by a mob after being shot in the leg his body quickly strung up and riddled with bullets.

Mrs. Moore had been missing from her home for the past ten days but it was only on Sunday that her body was found hanging to the limb of a tree in Rankin County, 15 miles from here.

A year ago Thompson bought a hog from Dodson with the agreement that he was to make payment for it by working on Dodson's farm.   According to Dodson's system of bookkeeping, Thompson had worked for a year without cancelling the debt.

Thursday afternoon Dodson went to the slave's home and declared his work unsatisfactory and demanded his hog back.   In desperation Thompson drew a gun and shot his master dead, after which he escaped to the woods where he was found and lynched.—*Afro-American*, April 15, 1921.

The prison system in this state [Texas] has long needed a reform.   The Harlem incident that occurred on one of the big state farms, where prisoners were worked, was a blot on the pen system of the state and on civilization.   Several Negro convicts were thrown into an air-tight dungeon and were left to smother to death.   They pleaded for air and water, but their pleadings were ignored by the human(?) guards.—*Beaumont* (Texas) *Monitor*, February 19, 1921.

NEW YORK CITY, Feb. 19.—Following the announcement a few weeks ago that the Pace Phonograph Corporation of New York had been organized to reproduce Negro Music, using exclusively Negro voices, notice was served on the Pace & Handy Music Co., of which Mr. Harry H. Pace was president, by two large white phonograph record companies that it need not expect any more of its published music to be reproduced by them. . . . .—*Cleveland Call*, February 19, 1921.

HAITI, MO.—There are some conditions in this section which ought to be corrected. The system of working Negroes is in some instances, no doubt, borrowed from states farther south, in a number of cases never getting a just settlement for their labor, and it will be remembered that it was in Cape Girardeau County a number of years ago where a number of peonage cases were uncovered. It is believed that now there are some such cases in this section.

Near here there is a farm known as Taylor farm, comprising something like 300 acres of land. If reports hereabouts are to be believed, and they come from good sources, on this particular farm, the work bell is rung at 4 a.m. and the wage paid for a day's work is $1.00, but the workers never get a settlement. At 11 a.m. the women are called from the field to work in the house, and at 1 p.m. they return to the fields to finish the day with their husbands. Workers are not permitted to have hogs, chickens, etc., and the reason, presumably, is to force them to patronize the store; the foreman gives as his reason for not allowing the help to have chickens, cows and the like is that they will get mixed up with his.— *Houston Informer*, May 28, 1921.

[Editorial] Where we live, move, and have our being is neglected, and as we must live in filth, move around in mud and mire, and have our being in fevered mires and miasmic quarters, we have a most holy and just right to complain, and until our prayers are answered, they shall continue to be prayers of complaint.— *Newport News Star*, April 21, 1921.

The truth about the origin of the Tulsa riots is now definitely known. Mr. Walter F. White, who went to Tulsa to investigate the Tulsa riots, in a special dispatch to the *New York Evening Post* says that the immediate cause of the riot was the claim of a white girl, Sarah Page, that a colored young man, Dick Rowland, had attempted to assault her. The girl operated an elevator in the Drexel Building in Tulsa. She stated that the colored boy had seized her arm as she admitted him to the car.   Rowland claims that he stumbled and accidentally stepped on the girl's foot.   She screamed.   Rowland ran.

On the following day the Tulsa "Tribune" painted the whole story in yellow.   The Chief of Police, the sheriff, the Mayor of Tulsa and a number of reputable citizens all stated that the girl had not been molested and that there had been no attempt at criminal assault.

Victor F. Barnett, managing editor of the "Tribune," stated that his paper had since learned that the original story, that the girl's face was scratched and her clothing torn, was untrue.   It was a crime on the part of the Tulsa "Tribune" that it did not find out that the story was untrue before publishing it.   If it had done so it is most likely that Tulsa never would have been the scene of murder and arson that it was.   Of course, the Tulsa "Tribune" felt that the story of a colored man assaulting a white girl would make good reading matter and sell a few more copies of the paper, but there ought to be some way to bring home to the Tulsa "Tribune" and other papers like it the fact that they are criminally responsible for publishing unauthenticated stories which are likely to lead to lawlessness.

And yet just the sort of thing done by the Tulsa "Tribune" is being done every day all over the country and especially by the South. . . . . [An example given from *Florence* (Alabama) *Daily News*.]

The bald truth of the matter is, the life of any colored man may now be put in jeopardy by any hysterical white woman.   She hasn't got to be violated; she hasn't even got to be touched. All that is necessary is for her not to like the looks of some Negro who is approaching and raise an outcry.   This is sufficient to put the man's life in danger.   This is what democracy and law and order come to in the United States.—JAMES WELDON JOHNSON, in the *New York Age*, June 18, 1921.

The final exhibit of this attitude in the Negro press is an editorial from the *Samaritan Herald* (April 15, 1921), a small fraternal paper in Sumter, South Carolina, with scarcely more than 1,000 circulation.

Nothing Is Settled until Settled Right

Failure, neglect, or refusal to comply with the unchangeable dictum of this maxim is, in our humble opinion, the, or one of the main causes for the delay in the settlement, and solution of our, so-called, race problem.

The great need, as we see it, is the standardization, not of the laws, but their administration. No intelligent man will, we take it, deny that there is, as practiced, a double standard, one for white and another for colored people. Naturally this causes dissatisfaction, friction and complainings, mutterings deep, if not loud.

The Negro does not want, ask or desire that mythical bugaboo, social equality upon which demagogues ride into prominence and office. What he does want and asks for is, what the late Col. Roosevelt called "a square deal." If our friends, the overwhelming majority, of whom we hear so much, would interest themselves, and by their influence and numbers, make that possible, even they would be surprised at the ease and dispatch with which the clouds would roll away.

II. RACE PROGRESS AND INDIVIDUAL ACHIEVEMENT

In an address before the United States Senate last May, Senator Spencer, of Missouri, brought together a large amount of information concerning the Negroes. . . . .

Since they obtained their freedom from slavery they have acquired property worth more than $1,000,000,000.

They have acquired lands exceeding 21,000,000 acres—an area greater than the entire State of South Carolina—and they cultivate as much more. In fact, they either own or rent about two-thirds of the cultivated land of the South.

The Russian serfs during the first fifty years of their freedom accumulated about $36 apiece, an aggregate of about half a billion dollars. During the first fifty years of their freedom the American Negroes saved nearly double that sum, or $70 apiece, an aggregate of $700,000,000.

A large part of the savings of the Negro is in lands and houses. . . . . Doubtless, now at least 600,000 homes are owned by Negroes. Negroes . . . . have established more than 50,000 prosperous business enterprises. They own 100 insurance companies. They own and conduct banks with a capitalization of nearly $2,000,000 and an annual business of $20,000,000.

In 1910 there were 27,727 Negro teachers. Three hundred counties are employing Negro industrial teachers. Today there are more than 40,000 Negro teachers presiding over schools in which 2,000,000 Negro children are enrolled.

As to church work, there are 34,962 Negro ministers, and out of their poverty the Negroes have put $68,000,000 into church buildings.

Negro physicians and surgeons numbered 3,400 in 1910; Negro dentists, 478; and there were 7,056 in other professions.

The Negro is not lacking in inventive power, and more than a thousand patents have been issued to him. He is not lacking in literary power, but edits and publishes 500 newspapers and other periodicals. He is patriotic. The Negroes gave $225,000,000 for Liberty Bonds and for war work activities. Two Negroes were the first soldiers of the American army to be decorated for bravery during the World War, and four entire Negro regiments received the Croix de Guerre for heroism in action. In addition, about 400 individual Negroes received medals of honor for bravery. It is a most striking fact that 74.60 per cent of the Negroes examined for the draft were accepted, and only 69.71 per cent of the whites. . . . . —Quoted from the *Christian Endeavor World*, by the *Washington Bee*, November 20, 1920.

NEW ORLEANS, LA., Feb. 10.—Eighty colored women were given certificates last week to practice nursing. The certificates were issued by the New Orleans Chapter, American Red Cross. More than six hundred have received certificates to practice the profession of nursing in this city.—*Shreveport* (Louisiana) *Sun* (by the Associated Negro Press).

WASHINGTON, D.C.—Announcement has been already made of the decision of a group of Colored men, representing Colored banking institutions and Negro business, to put under way a national banking program looking to closer affiliation with metropolitan banking interests. . . . by the opening of the new year a new one million ($1,000,000) dollar concern will have been launched by the strongest group of Negro financial interests ever joined together in an allied movement.—*Kansas City Sun*, December 11, 1920.

[Editorial] More than 100 varieties of products from peanuts, ranging from the purest of milks for the sick room, mothers and infants, to ink useful for writing and sketching have been discovered by George W. Carver, Negro professor of Tuskegee Institute. He showed them to the Ways and Means Committee and delivered a discourse on them—was greeted with applause from the members and spectators—the first demonstration of the sort that the tariff hearings have known.

His discoveries exhibited ten kinds of milk, five kinds of punches, cherry, lemon, orange, blackberry and plum; salted peanuts; two grades of flour; two grades of meal; five breakfast foods; new flavorings for ice-cream, cakes, gingerbread, cookies and various confections; chocolate coated peanuts; peanut candy bars; crystallized peanuts; three relishes; nine wood stains ranging from malachite green to fumed oak; black ink; face powder and face cream; Worcester sauce; four different kinds of stock foods made from the vine; ground hay with Chinaberry added as a tonic, and various kinds of oils.

There can be no doubt but that such scientific discoveries will place Prof. Carver among the leading scientists of America. The fact that he is a member of our group is especially pleasant since it may be truthfully said that he is without an equal in that particular line. . . . . —*Dallas Express*, February 12, 1921.

Orlo South Who Is Hailed as the Phenomenal Track Man of Commercial High School Established New Record at Indoor Inter-Class Meet at Municipal Auditorium and Is Awarded Gold Medal as Individual Point Winner, Scoring $20\frac{1}{4}$ for Seniors.

The Colored Lads Certainly Scintillated as the Particular Stars of the Inter-Class Track Meet. South Was Winner in Four Events. Crawford Pulled the Sophomores Out of a Hole and Put Them in Third Place. This Was Done in Spite of Lack of Training Facilities. . . . .

After the meet when the special reporter sent by the *Monitor* to cover the event was congratulating South on his wonderful work, South said, "You know, if I had the chance these white boys have I'd call myself an athlete, but I haven't. Here after this meet all the white fellows are going over to the 'Y' and take a shower. I've got to go home and take a bath. I surprised myself by doing what I did because I didn't do a bit of practising. You know how bad the weather has been outside and I couldn't practice at the 'Y.' "—*Omaha Monitor*, April 14, 1921.

TRENTON, March 30.—For the first time in the history of New Jersey a Negro today occupied the chair of Speaker of the House of Assembly. . . . . Speaker George S. Hobert . . . . was called [away] and appointed him in his place. . . . .

Dr. Alexander is the first of his race to be elected to the New Jersey Legislature. . . . . —*New Jersey Observer*, April 1, 1921.

NEW ORLEANS, LA., May 4.— . . . . The State Supreme Court handed down a decision in the suit by Lillie G. Taylor versus the State of Louisiana, Angelina Allen and George West, decreeing to the plaintiff, a vast tract of land in the southwest section of Claiborne county, the land being rich in oil and gas deposits.

The case turned on Lillie Taylor's relation to her mother who took the estate as daughter of Ison McGee. . . . .

The estate is estimated to be worth no less than $20,000,000, and it makes the litigant the richest colored woman in the world.— *Washington Colored American*, May 5, 1921.

CAMBRIDGE, MASS., April.—Miss Eva B. Dykes of Washington, recently passed her examination for the degree, Doctor of Philosophy in English at Radcliffe College, Cambridge, Mass. Miss Dykes is the first colored woman to be recommended for such a degree. . . . . —*East Tennessee News*, May 12, 1921.

Frederick Ernest Morrison, who appears on the screen as "Sunshine Sammy" in the Harold Lloyd and Snub Pollard comedies, is now about nine years old. It is reported that his salary is $700 a week, regularly. He is the highest salaried colored person in the world today. He started in working occasionally at $5 a

day.   Now, no Harold Lloyd or Snub Pollard comedy released by
Pathe would be considered complete without him and he is beloved
by all the white players. . . . . Sunshine isn't much impressed
with his own importance.   He will forsake any press agent living
for a vanilla ice-cream cone.—*Richmond* (Indiana) *Blade*, April 15,
1921.

Charles Gilpin, the actor, and Jack Johnson, the prize
fighter, are also favorite heroes of the Negro press.

It is characteristic of the Negro newspapers that a
great deal of space goes for various sorts of welfare and
uplift effort.   It is a group that keeps on saying: "Tell
them we are rising."

DALLAS, TEX., Dec. 1.—The annual convention of the Texas
Congress of Mothers and Parent Teachers' Association for Negro
Women, which has been in session at the Munger Avenue Baptist
Church since Wednesday, was brought to a close Friday with a
mass meeting in which final business for the coming year was
transacted. . . . .

An interesting program was presented by the children of the
Home-makers' Industrial and Trade School, of which Mrs. Josie
Brigg Hall is president.   This school has drawn the attention of
Dallas civic workers for the splendid work it has done for the
young Negro girls of the city. . . . . —*Progressive Citizen* (Tex-
arkana, Ark.), December 4, 1920.

. . . . According to the report from the secretary of the
Child's Welfare Association, out of 160 counties of the State there
are only 80 Juvenile Courts at present, notwithstanding the law
passed in 1916 requiring each county to have a Juvenile Court.
Very often the officers of the law, according to this report, have
been found to be over ignorant regarding this law or grossly indif-
ferent with reference to its administration.   It is encouraging,
however, to note the disposition of the regular constituted authorities to co-operate with the Welfare Board in establishing Juvenile
Courts when sufficient public sentiment has been crystallized to
substantiate the need.

The colored people are asked to co-operate with this Welfare Board, reporting to Mr. Burr Blackburn, Secretary State Department, Public Welfare, Atlanta, Ga., wherever there are children under the age of 16 on the chain gang or imprisoned with adult criminals.   We would also urge that wherever we can we secure the co-operation of the local authorities in each community toward throwing around your wayward boys corrective influences, as well as an effort to get them out of contact with seasoned criminals. . . . . —*Atlanta Independent*, April 4, 1921.

We have a plenty to do for our Race, both here at home and abroad.   One thing we need badly—and something we can get if we try hard enough—is a first class Community House, or Center, exclusively for ourselves.   We should have a building, like the Y.M.C.A. has, but always open for the benefit of both sexes.   In this building be an auditorium for public and social gatherings, a swimming pool, gymnasium, and dining rooms and rest rooms for both sexes, and all should belong to us.   Right now some steps should be taken toward getting it.   This is a job for the Colored Citizens Civic League to tackle.—*Richmond* (Indiana) *Blade*, February 18, 1921.

The State Federation of Colored Women's Clubs, whose president is Mrs. M. M. Bethune, of Daytona, is making a strong appeal for the sum of five hundred dollars to close a wonderful bargain for a site for delinquent girls of the state.   At the last session of the federation, which was held in Mt. Zion A.M.E. Church in this city, this measure was given careful attention and specific steps were taken to that end.   The present appeal is made with all haste and seriousness, and clubs and individuals are asked to make immediate response.   There can hardly be any doubts of the proper management of such a home in the event of its establishment, and whereever this appeal may come it is worthy of favor. . . . .—*Florida Sentinel* (Jacksonville), February 12, 1921.

One may also note in connection with this general subject, a front page such as the *Savannah Tribune*, for February 12, 1921, which treats the following:

Conference Held to Discuss Improvement Negro Rural Life (Tuskegee)

Suit to Be Brought by Negro Farmers [Against White, for Peonage]

Urban League Holds Meeting

Farmers' Meeting Here Next Week

Negroes Changing in the South [Sociological Item]

Health Organizations Hold Meeting

Douglas-Lincoln Day at the "Y"

Exercises Were Held at School Yesterday

Du Bois Lecture and Banquet

Here is an indication of a welfare movement that hints at more than local uplifting.

The 17th annual session of the South Carolina Race Conference will convene in Columbia Feb. 16th and 17th. All agencies and forces will be united to make the 1921 Race Conference a success. Let every organization in South Carolina that hopes to become Statewide, hold its annual meeting in Columbia at the time the Conference meets. The Race Conference program will be broad enough to cover every phase of racial development. The program will be published later. Let every preacher, teacher, farmer and leader in every part of the State use his or her influence toward helping to carry the news of this great Conference to the people so that we may assemble and give first hand information upon the subject that is so much needed at this particular time in our racial development. . . . .—*Standard* (Columbia, South Carolina), January 18, 1921.

Examples of press news of movements working toward amelioration of race relations will include more news of the National Association for the Advancement of Colored People than of other organizations, since this body constantly forwards its matter to the press. Other bodies heard from will be the National Equal Rights League, the National Race Congress, and the Universal

Negro Improvement Association ("the Garvey movement").

III.   RACE MOVEMENT

WASHINGTON, D.C., Jan. 14.—For the first time in a number of years, Congressmen from the South, who are holding their memberships because of the disfranchisement of Colored Americans, "had their feelings hurt," and became noticeably peeved, in the hearing before the Congressional Committee. . . . .

Among those who have offered evidence before the committee are James Weldon Johnson, William Pickens, Walter F. White, ... all officials of the National Association for the Advancement of Colored People. . . . .

Secretary Johnson says: "The following information was laid before the committee:

"1. That uniformly in the southern states it took fewer voters to elect representatives to Congress than in northern and western states, 11,000 votes electing a representative in Georgia against 61,000 required in New York.

"2. We presented the names, addresses and registration certificate number of 941 persons who were denied the vote in the city of Jacksonville, Florida, and informed the census committee that 3,000 other names accompanied by affidavits or sworn statements would be forwarded.

"3. We presented photographs showing long lines of colored people who stood all day without being permitted to vote.

"4. We presented evidence of the cold blooded murder of upwards of 30 colored people in the election riots of Ocoee, Florida."—*Shreveport Sun* (by the Associated Negro Press), January 15, 1921.

Boston Authorities Thanked for Barring Southern Race Prejudice and Propaganda from Boston—Satisfaction Voiced over "Birth of Nation" and Blair Case—Rousing Welcome Home to Trotter —Rev. McClane Made Local Treasurer Defense Fund—Big Audience.

The audience which assembled Monday night with the Equal Rights League filled the big auditorium of the 12th Baptist church, overflowed around the walls, out in the vestibule and down the front stairs where some sat all the evening. This was the "Victory Meeting," one long to be remembered by the big crowds. There was joy and there was enthusiasm galore.

The choir sang, Rev. Plaatje of So. Africa prayed, Mr. E. T. Morris opened and explained the meeting was to signalize the victory in race protection by stopping the "Birth of a Nation" and by convicting to a time sentence the Southerner at Harvard who slashed a Colored policeman, Officer Blair, also to welcome home from the West Wm. Monroe Trotter.

Rev. Shaw began with a tribute to the marvelous persistence and consistency of Mr. Trotter. He approved the N.A.A.C.P. as the whites had a duty to perform working for and with us, but that to foster and execute nothing of ourselves, weakened race stamina and lent credence to the criticism by the whites that we Colored people are all right as imitators and followers but have no ability to initiate or carry through. The Equal Rights League is starting to raise a big national defense fund for and by the race for rights and justice. . . . .

After his appreciation of the most kind greeting and tributes, Mr. Trotter spoke, telling in an even thrilling manner of his travels to the Pacific. What he saw was represented by this "Birth of a Nation," everywhere the South was pushing its prejudice into the North and by surrender and indifference and staying out of public places the Colored people were losing every public right of service and accommodation. His remedy was to spend some time mixing and mingling with the rest of the Americans to keep them used to our presence and to insist upon service firmly when we enter public places. Don't let the South triumph over us, was his appeal.—*Guardian* (Boston), May 28, 1921.

President Harding received the Delegates of the Sixth Annual Session of the National Race Congress of America, Inc., in the Executive Office May 5, 1921, when the following Memorial was filed with the President in behalf of the Colored Citizens of America.

To the President of the United States of America by the National Race Congress of America, Inc., Sixth Annual Session, May 4, 5, and 6, 1921, Washington, D.C.

Mr. President:

We come to you today, bearing the aspirations of 12,000,000 of God-fearing American citizens of unquestioned loyalty. Our group, suffering from traditional civil, social, and industrial handicaps, as well as a striking difference in racial type, is compelled to resort to the constitutional right of petition as long as unrighted wrongs, unrequited toil, unmasked lawlessness, and uneven justice stain the flag and dim the glory of democracy. . . . .

The burden of our petition is: Equality of opportunity as well as equality of responsibility. . . . . Mr. President, we complain of the following:

1. Lawlessness manifested in lynching, riots, peonage, and discrimination in the administration of justice.

2. Unjust restriction of suffrage.

3. The direct violation of the Constitution in the transportation of interstate passengers.

4. The un-American practice of discrimination and segregation on account of color in the Government Departments in Washington. . . . . —*Dallas Express*, May 21, 1921.

There seems to be some difference of policy with regard to the treatment of crime. The *New York Dispatch*, a new publication, endeavored to initiate a crusade against the prominence in the Negro press of such news. In its issue for January 7, 1921, it says:

More than two months ago the *New York Dispatch* started a campaign against the Screaming of Crime in Newspapers and made a canvass among the master minds of the country. . . . in order to get an expression of public opinion with the result that each week has brought letters from men and women in every walk in life supporting the stand taken by the Dispatch . . . . such persons as ex-President Taft, John Hope of Morehouse College, Dr. Gregg of Hampton, Prof. Smith of the University of Pa., President Hadley of Yale University, Dr. J. Stanley Durkee of Howard University, Dr. McDonald of Storer College and a host of others have all registered their opposition against such methods. . . . .

That this paper has adopted a new policy or has not entirely succeeded in the old is apparent from its front page of May 27, the same year.   Fully three columns are here given to the following subjects:

Mrs. Monta Clarke . . . . Killed by an Enraged Jealous Husband

Colored Man to Hang for Love of White Girl
Mother Zion Sunday School Teacher Robbed
Alonzo Crowell Charged with Rape is Freed
Colored Dentist Unsexed by Mob Down in Texas

Meanwhile some papers like the *Defender* and *Whip* of Chicago have deliberately made Negro crime prominent.   For including an item of the same nature as the one last mentioned in connection with *New York Dispatch*, the *Whip* was excluded from a Texas town by authorities there.   The *Defender* often uses its red type to add prominence to news of crime.   But most of the papers are not generally marked by a very large proportion of criminal reports.   The *New York Age* is as free from this as any.   Its front-page material is more typically such as in the issue of December 18, 1920, where the page-wide headlines read:

National Board, Y.W.C.A., Hostess to 19 Colored Women
Brooklyn Opens Campaign Supporting Anti-Lynching Bill

Of course, the presence of crime items in a Negro newspaper would be expected, since this is a normal part of the white man's press.   Crime has always been recognized as valuable news.   It is not the usual, but the unusual thing in the life of a community, and the publication of it certainly makes it possible for that community to exercise criticism on its own life.

Among the articles otherwise unclassified were mentioned those dealing with politics and those on Africa. A few illustrations may be indicated.

COLUMBIA, MO., Feb. 12.—What was called the Lincoln-Douglass-Moore celebration was held in this city last night at McKinney's hall on Broadway. This was the largest gathering ever seen at the hall. Not only was every available space occupied but many were turned away being unable to get to the doors.

The attraction of the occasion was the presence of the Hon. Walthal M. Moore of St. Louis, representative in the Fifty-first General Assembly of the Missouri Legislature. . . . . —*St. Louis Argus*, February 18, 1921.

WASHINGTON, March 17.—The unannounced entrance of a representative of the *Afro-American* into the office of Senator Weller, in the State Office Building, this Thursday morning threw consternation into a coterie of colored men gathered there to tell the white party chieftains what they regarded should be the program for all the colored people of Maryland.—*Afro-American*, March 18, 1921.

WASHINGTON, D.C., June 25.—Daily newspaper comments, special writers, Congressmen, Senators and "every day citizens," besides the press of the Race, have filled the air on the subject of the adopted report of the Republican National Committee. . . . .

Attorney Nutter says: "In my opinion the Republican National Committee made a tremendous tactical mistake in cutting down Southern representation in the Republican National Convention. It smacks of 'Lily White' tendencies, and impresses me as being an ungrateful attitude for the loyalty that we have given to party welfare in the face of overwhelming odds. This move is particularly distasteful in the face of Congress being painfully silent on boasted disfranchisement in the South." . . . . —*Charleston* (S.C.) *New Era*, June 25, 1921 (by the Associated Negro Press).

Discrimination at Washington, the distribution of political plums by the Republican administration, efforts for political rights, local agitation for political effort on behalf of needed improvements, factional discussions, criticism of leaders from President Harding down, the relation of race advancement to larger issues such as the League of Nations, the Japanese exclusion policy, immigration and the Irish question—all these matters are touched upon.   Here are two articles on Africa:

Harry Foster Dean, returned Adventurer and Explorer, gives thrilling lecture on Africa which every Race person should see.

Churches open your doors and let the people have this information concerning Africa, the country on which the eyes of the world are centered.

There never was a Negro in Africa.

No cannibals make their abode in the "dark continent."

Every tribe in Africa is civilized, though not according to standards of anthropologists.

The Africans are going to get rid of European domination by any means necessary.

It is ridiculous to hunt the brontosaurus in Africa because that is the youngest continent.

There is no proof that Africans are sons of Ham.

Africa has a population of between 600,000,000 and 700,000,-000 persons though statisticians give the number as only from 150,000,000 to 250,000,000.

These are assertions made in Denver Friday by Harry Dean, who is said by some to be the most extensive explorer of "Darkest Africa" now living.

Thirty years ago Dean was reading law in this city. He returns after 21 years of world explorations, including many years spent in Liberia. . . . . —*California Eagle* (Los Angeles), February 26, 1921.

PHILADELPHIA, PA.—An elaborate observation tour for Colored Americans is being planned here for the early fall.   The goal of the cruise is Liberia, Africa, and will take forty-five days. During the latter part of September and the early part of October the Republic of Liberia will celebrate her One Hundredth Anniversary with an exposition and convocation of native chiefs. The Liberian Plenary Commission now in this country with President King as its chairman, indorses the cruise. The steamer chartered is commodious and elegantly appointed and the reservations are limited to three hundred. The tour will be under the personal direction of Dr. W. H. Jernegan of Washington, Dr. Henry J. Callas, Dr. L. G. Jordan, Dr. R. R. Wright, Major William H. York, Miss Nannie Burroughs, Dr. Frank Bishop, Bishop W. H. Heard, Miss Maggie Walker and Major R. R. Wright, Sr. Arrangements are being carried on from 529 South 19th street, Philadelphia, Pa.—*Omaha Star*, June 11, 1921 (by the Associated Negro Press).

CHAPTER V

WHAT IS IN A NEGRO PAPER

A great many Negro papers may be recognized as such at a glance even by one who is unacquainted with them. This is generally due to the prominence of pictures of colored people, emphatic news headings, or a special type of advertising. Sometimes one finds a poor quality of printing or an apparent absence of classification of material on the page. But as papers attain economic success they are likely to show decided improvement in these matters. And the leading news-papers and magazines will stand favorable comparison with those of white people in make-up and general attractiveness. On the one hand, the reader may note the front page of a paper as well established as the *Richmond Planet*, containing, as in one instance, twenty-two separate items, including letters, poetry, social items, news of all sorts, no large headings and no apparent principle of arrangement on the page. On the other hand he will find the studied symmetry of the *Philadelphia Tribune* or the *Norfolk Journal and Guide*.

When we turn more specifically to scan the pages for local news, we come upon personal and society items similar to those found in all papers. For instance, from "Society News," *Dayton Forum* (February 11, 1921):

Jaymes Pierce, Albert Hand and George DeMarr of Ohio State University spent their mid-semester vacation with relatives and friends of this city.

Mrs. E. E. Lucas of Leroy St. was called to Louisville, Ky., on account of an accident sustained by her grandmother, Mrs. Bettie Arnett.

Mr. and Mrs. Thompson of Chicago, Ill., spent a few days in the city as guests of Mr. and Mrs. L. J. Rice of E. Fifth St. Mrs. Thompson was a former resident of this city and her many friends were glad to welcome her and husband.

Out-of-town correspondence produces items of the same type, such as this (*Negro Star*, Wichita, Kansas, April 15, 1921):

Pine City, Ark., News

Special to the Negro Star:–

Please let me have space to say a few words through these wonderful columns about our community, owned and controlled by Negroes, with exception of a saw mill which belongs to whites. We have a colored postmaster in person of Mr. J. E. Copeland of whom we are very proud.

Mr. G. H. Watson is doing a respectable business here at Pine City Junction, he is also ticket agent.

On the night of April the 11th, Mrs. Susie Stewart, our teacher and well prepared instructor of our race, gave a grand commencement for her students and this community; the many different kinds of work exhibited was great work.

Our Easter program was something rare, conducted by one of our teachers in person of Mrs. C. Parker and our beloved superintendent, Bro. W. M. Harris. Mrs. Parker is another one of our wide-awake workers. She knows what to do with children.

I will tell you later of our district work in June.

(Mrs.) MARY DARDEN, Box 47.

It may be remarked that the large number of letters beginning "Please allow me space in your paper," indicate not only a ritual of dignity attaching to the highly honored newspaper, but also an urgent desire to get an audience for group achievements. Reports of church meetings are often sent in according to this formula. Organizations are naturally the most responsive news sources. The *Newport News Star* (see issue of January 20, 1921) is under necessity of inhibiting their response:

Dear Agents:—

Many of you have failed to read and obey the rules about memoriams, programs, marriage write-ups, and announcements. Some do. Every one that is sent they send extra pay for them. There are others who send them in right along without a particle of remittance. . . . . Space in the *Star* is very valuable, material is very expensive, and in order to pay our agents for their services we must have some profit from some source. . . . .

Without any further notice, when this matter is sent us, with no money to cover cost of the same, it will be left out in the future.

A typical "announcement" is this one (*Boston Chronicle*, May 14, 1921):

The Colored Smart Set of Providence, R.I., will hold a big holiday dance Decoration day night, May 30th at Altair Hall, Elmwood Ave. and West Friendship St. . . . . The music will be by Worthington's Jazz Orchestra, Rhode Island's society entertainers, pep music "tell the world." Dancing 8–12. Admission 55c, tax paid. Much hospitality to one and all, strictly polite in every particular. . . . .

Lodge notes are also "copy," but churches are the best source. The *New Era* of Detroit (February 26, 1921) says:

Those who read *New Era* two years ago know of its popularity when it started printing the news of Detroit. When we failed to print the news we lost popularity—people like news—we are unable to keep up and had to fall back on our specialty—opinion. . . . . U know that to get the news U must visit the churches. Had we kept up it was inevitable that we must criticise the preachers strongly and it is not a pleasant job.

There are frequent references in church news to sermons preached. All is described most enthusiastically. Four clippings will indicate, on the one hand, the comprehensive way in which the church among Negroes represents their life, and, on the other, the readiness of the press to speak for the church. The first clipping, reports a lecture on "A Rooster with Two Dead Heads," and says:

Where in the world Dr. Somerville got hold of that matter without being divinely inspired is a greater puzzle than his Greek "Enigma."[1]

The second is the *Brooklyn and Long Island Informer's* item:

Rev. B. T. Harvey, Jr., of Trinity Baptist Church, Williamsbridge, took as his sermon last Sunday night Prof. Albert Einstein's "theory of relativity." This . . . . was hailed by those present as a fine example of the expanding "breadth of vision" of Colored ministers.[2]

In the third the *Chicago Enterprise* reports the raising of all indebtedness on the Pilgrim Baptist Temple of Chicago and shows a cut of a substantial stone church. The amount of money raised in one day was $157,780. There is no fulsome praise of any of the principals.[3] The fourth, from the *Washington Colored American*, reports the

National Race Congress of America, a movement which conceived in the mind of Rev. Dr. William H. Jernagin, pastor of Mount Carmel Baptist Church of Washington . . . . was held in the Mount Zion Baptist Church.[4]

[1] *Vigil*, Portsmouth, Virginia, March 31, 1921.

[2] Issue of May 14, 1921.

[3] *Enterprise* of May 14, 1921.   [4] Issue of May 6, 1921.

It is in the larger papers, of course, that we look for special pages on sports and the theater. The *New York News* has four pages for these subjects, the *New York Dispatch* a page for each. The *Public Journal* of Philadelphia has a page each, and a woman's page as well—something that is also found elsewhere. The *Norfolk Journal and Guide* has separate pages for church news, for society, and for the amusements and sports. The *New Age* of Los Angeles has church, society, sports, on separate pages. The *Afro-American* has featured serial stories in their second section. The *Negro World* gives extra space to contributed articles and poetry. The *Freeman* of Indianapolis is noted as a theatrical news medium and sometimes gives two pages to this institution. Chicago papers also have separate pages for these subjects, the *Defender* having two pages of each with special staff writers. The *New York Age*, beside its page on stage and athletics, has two columns regularly set aside for music.

As for comprehensiveness in dealing with all news matters that affect the group, no more striking exhibition could be given than the *Hephzibah Herald*, a paper published in Hearne, Texas, which might be described as violently religious, and in its own words, "an uncompromising defender of the Negro race."

This paper will carry sport news every week. Basket ball, lawn tennis, baseball, social items and state lodges, hay rides, fishing parties, bicycle races, horse races, auto races for those who love it will be able to see it. Old reliable Jack Johnson who has made a record in the sporting secret is now spending a term in prison which will end on the 4th of March, and will be free again. He has made thousands of dollars on baseball and local prize fights in prison.

Another item in the same issue:

The churches of Austin are calling for unsaved people. Last Sunday we noticed hundreds of people, white and colored, going to their different churches, morning and afternoon services. When you read this paper thank the Lord for the good things that has reached you through this paper.

While, as stated above, a few Negro publications can be found that have no editorials, it is true that editorial expression of opinion is for the most part insisted upon. This is apparent from the mottoes chosen.

'Tis More than a Mere Race Paper, 'Tis a Voice that Asks for Justice.—*Cleveland Advocate.*

Independent in All Things, Neutral in Nothing.—*Afro-American* and *Raleigh Independent.*

A Journal Published to Create Racial Interest and Inspire Young People to Higher Ideals.—*Richmond Voice* (Virginia).

Unbridled Servant of the People.—*Washington Eagle.*

Ye Shall Know the Truth and the Truth Shall Make You Free.—*East Tennessee News.*

The *Gary* (Indiana) *National Defender and Sun* ("A Journal of Education and Uplift") says, September 4, 1920:

In reading the *Defender and Sun*, remember the editor writes not to please anyone—not even himself—but to tell the truth about men and affairs, to defend justice and right and to fight for liberty. You may not agree with all that appears in the *Defender;* we do not expect you to; but bear in mind that our fight is not for the present but for generations yet unborn.

The *Dallas Express* carries this every week:

The *Dallas Express* has never hoisted the white feather, neither has it been disgraced by the yellow streak. It is not afflicted with the flannel mouth. It is a plain, every day, sensible, conservative newspaper, which trims no sail to catch the passing breeze; flies no doubtful flag; it professes a patriotism as broad as our country. Its love of even handed justice covers all the territory occupied by the human race. This is pretty high ground, but we live on it and are prospering. Boys of the press come up and stand with us. This ground is holy.

Among those papers whose editorial policy is that of definite and regular statement may be mentioned the *Houston Informer:*

THE INFORMER'S PLATFORM

1. Democracy, both domestic and foreign.
2. Playgrounds for colored children.
3. Better educational facilities, both teachers and physical properties, for colored youths.
4. Educated, consecrated ministry.
5. Development of the Houston Ship Channel, thereby making Houston the South's premier city.
6. Co-operation between the white and colored races on all matters of vital importance and less racial animosity and antagonism.
7. Good streets, better drainage and sanitary toilets for entire urban population.
8. Federal investigation of, and Federal legislation to suppress lynching.
9. Equality before the law for all men and equal railroad accommodations for all passengers.
10. Racial co-operation, teamwork, advancement, betterment and solidarity.

The *Vigil*, Portsmouth, Virginia, has a more succinct statement, "Religion, Land Getting, Missions, Education," being its watchwords. The *Charlottesville* (Virginia) *Messenger*, published recently a series of editorials on "Vital Needs." "Vital Need II" was that of a Young Men's Christian Association. "Vital Need IV," a future burying-ground (issues of March 19, May 28, 1921).

That Negroes can write editorials as well as make orations, is evident from the fluency of many of these, for example (*St. Luke's Herald*, Richmond, Virginia, May 21, 1921):

The thing that we need most is to get ourselves straight. We have among us four kinds of Negroes . . . . Wishbone Negroes, Jawbone Negroes, Funny-bone Negroes, and Backbone Negroes.

The Wish-bone members of our Race are those who sit down with sighs and wishes for things to go better with us. They feel discouraged over the conditions and pray or prate about "the downtrodden Race."

This [There] is the Jaw-bone division that sputterates, froths and foams at the mouth and jaw-bone and when it comes to a showdown that class of the Race is never present.

The Funny-bone Negroes are those who grin and cringe at every insult or pun that the white man chooses to poke at him or his Race.

THE BACK-BONE DIVISION are the Negroes who are making naught all such piffle as Williams talks and who resent silently or vocally every insult or affront that is perpetrated upon them and their race.

The following is by William Pickens (*Brooklyn and Long Island Informer*, April 23, 1921):

THE SUB-CONSCIOUS SLIGHT

An armed and murderous white bandit was in the act of holding up a place of business in Pittsburgh. A black policeman came along and wounded and captured the bandit. The Director of Public Safety presented a medal of honor to this brave black man, and said many fine words of praise. Among these fine words were the following, equally fine, so far as intentions go, but which display unconsciously the subconscious attitude, not of the Director of Public Safety, but of the group to which he belongs:

"Although you are black on the outside—I want to announce that you have no yellow streak in your makeup."

And then the Director breathed a chest-filling breath of magnanimity and perhaps of—generosity! As if to say: "I am not too narrow to recognize something good in a black man, when that exceptional thing does happen."

That is exactly what that "*although*" means. It means that, in the subconsciousness of the man speaking, it is inconsistent to be both black and brave. Is not this a strange thing in the face of all the great and open records of Negro soldiers, Negro policemen and Colored officers of every kind? . . . .

It reminds me that long ago Solomon or some other wise man said: "I am black *and* comely," and then all the white scholars who have since translated his words have phrased it: "I am black *but* comely." They have done with their "*but*" just exactly what the Director did with his "*although*." . . . .

Other features in the press that are more or less allied to the editorials are the cartoons, people's letters to the editor, and welfare departments. The *Atlanta Independent*, the *Afro-American*, some New York papers, and those in Chicago, along with occasional others, have cartoons. Several weeklies have health talks, and occasionally there is a column for legal advice. Many papers print letters from readers, and in a few cases these letters thresh out some quarrel before the public. The *Dallas Express* gives advice to girls through the person of "Aunt Pat," besides having a Priscilla Art Club. Other papers give advice on etiquette and hints for neighborhood improvement.

More pungent criticisms of the various aspects of everyday life are offered in a column in the *New York Dispatch* headed "The Meddler." Thus (November 26, 1920):

> All that glitters is not gold,
> Black sheep dwell in every fold,
> Stocks turn out to be but logs,
> And some editors only inflated frogs.

This feature is strongly similar to the *Chicago Whip's* "Nosey Sees All Knows All." For instance (July 2, 1921):

> Every time the clock strikes in that bungalow "love nest" on Eberhardt Avenue, someone leaves the front door. . . . . Nosey put his head up to one of the windows and discovered men stirring things in big pots and others were putting things in little jars. The men who left with those packages were taking off the products of their labors. . . . . In other words, the simple little residence was not a love nest but was a manufacturing plant. . . . . Some day Nosey is going out and get a job in that beautiful little bungalow—it smells oh So Sweet.

Readers of the paper in Chicago's Second Ward are still wondering who Nosey is. The *Pueblo* (Colorado) *Rising Sun* has an "Uncle Eph" (January 21, 1921):

> Yo unkle was down ter Denver, en Attorney S. E. Cary sed dat out 18 months dat he was out 12 times widout his wife. Dis am de stuff. As sho as Ise borned yo old unkle knows dat he es some *lawyer*.

> Dey tell me dat A. J. Seymore wus de nite man et de undertaking parlor en de gals has never ceased to call over de phone. Jes think of a young *girl* calling a feller at 12:30 A.M. because she loved him so. Ise jes not gwine ter call yo names dis time.

> De quil pushers is gwine ter meet in Denver Friday and Saturday and look de law makers over. Many of de boys air hiding from yo unkle kase dey don't want dey sins ter find dem out.

The *New York Amsterdam News* (as January 12, 1921), has a place for "Rubberneck Recollections." The *Afro-American's* "Old Timer" is more serious.

Occasionally poetry finds a place. It ranges from humble attempts on local subjects to more ambitious verse. In the *Texas Freeman* (May 30, 1921), there is a poem on "Some Professions of the Negro," by Cora L. Dawson:

> The Negro is a working race,
>   And so with circumstances
> Does try to reach some noted place;
>   In general he advances.

Then there are mentioned, in a stanza each, the preacher, teacher, speaker, inventor, doctor, lawyer, editor, poet, merchant.

> The poet, with a share of verse,
>   Attracts the reader's eye;
> In quality 'tis somewhat terse,
>   And cannot pass it by. . . . .

Profoundly moving is "The Sad Appeal"—a long poem meant to be set to music, printed in the *Public Journal* of Philadelphia, February 19, 1921. This is a sample of the feelings and attitudes of Negroes and of their desire for expression in verse. It was "composed and given tune by Rev. G. W. Dickey, preacher, poet, and divine healer." The men referred to were condemned for rioting near Elaine, Arkansas, and are believed by the race to be innocent.

A song dedicated to the twelve men condemned to be electrocuted at the State Penitentiary, Little Rock, Ark.: Coleman, Knox, Jelus, Wildon, Hicks, Martin, Hicks, Hall, Fox, Moore.

> We are the twelve poor Negro men,
> Incarcerated in this awful pen,
> We, like our Christ, His burden must share,
> We can do nothing but sit in prayer.

Every stanza ends with "prayer," "pray," or "praying."

> Can you see any justice in our sad case?
> Nobody made to suffer but members of our race—
> Will any one say that we are then treated fair?
> Oh, God will you fix it by answering our prayer?

CHORUS

> Then for ourselves we do not care;
> Fate and prejudice has brought us here;
> Our families are wandering from door to door—
> Oh God be with them wherever they go.

The *Negro World* regularly gives considerable space to poetry on such themes as Africa and its beauty.

The *Chicago Enterprise* (January 29, 1921) has a poem by Maurice Mays, a young Negro of Knoxville on trial for murder and held by his race to be innocent. The poem asks for financial aid in his legal struggles.

> Doomed to die without a crime
> My hope is Public Aid
> Who will volunteer, and help
> To save me from the Grave?
>
> Oh, listen to my tender cry
> I am dying in despair
> Please won't you lend a helping hand
> To save me from the chair.

There are, however, some acknowledged poets who contribute to the newspapers. Lucian B. Watkins, who died February 1, 1921, as a result of war service, has been very frequently noticed. The following was printed in the *Afro-American*, February 4, 1921:

LOVED AND LOST

> My fallen star has spent its light
> And left but memory to me,
> My day of dream has kissed the night
> Farewell, its sun no more I see,
> My summer bloomed for winter's frost,
> Alas, I've lived and loved and lost!

What matters if today should earth
   Lay on my head a gold-bright crown
Lit with the gems of royal worth
   Befitting well a king's renown?
My lonely soul is trouble-tossed,
   For I have lived and loved and lost!

Great God!   I dare not question Thee—
   Thy way eternally is just,
This seeming mystery to me
   Will be revealed, if I but trust:
Ah, Thou alone dost know the cost
   When one has lived and loved and lost!

The greater part of the advertising in these papers is secured from local business people. For the most part this is natural. But it ought to be emphasized in view of some conspicuous exceptions which excite comment. How much white patronage comes in this form cannot be determined. Reference has already been made to the change in editorial policy effected in a paper by manipulation at the hands of white men of the advertising of white merchants.   Some papers resist this influence, like the *Houston Informer*, which fights on.

Nevertheless there are certain sorts of advertising that strike the reader as unusually prominent. First among these come the cosmetics. The persons and firms who do hairdressing or sell skin bleaches and hair straighteners are legion. One paper[1] presents to us "the Hawaiian system of hair growing, ... guaranteed to grow the hair 3 inches in 6 months"; another[2] prints a testimonial to the following effect: "I started using her treatment in

[1] *Indianapolis Ledger*, March 26, 1921.

[2] *Brooklyn and Long Island Informer*, April 23, 1921.

September, 1920.   My hair was then five inches in length. My hair is now nine inches . . . . and it has thickened wonderfully."   A religious paper[1] recommends "Climax King" to make "hair straight to stay straight."   While these are examples of rather extreme statement, yet the largest and most successful papers are not free from the policy.   A famous metropolitan weekly announces Mona Marvel Compound as "the most wonderful bleach on the market today."   The most successful Chicago paper had twenty-five advertisements of this character in a random issue.   A Memphis paper had twenty-two in one issue. Another city paper gives 40 per cent of its advertising to this business, two others in large southern cities give just about half, and a religious paper more than half of all its advertising.

It is of especial interest to note the career of Madam C. J. Walker, who was, among colored people, a pioneer in the profession of hairdressing.   Evidently here was a substantial and constant demand on the part of Negro people not so much for copying the white woman's complexion, as for making themselves neater, more comfortable, and more attractive to each other.   It has been pointed out that kinky hair calls for a greater amount of attention than the white person realizes.   At any rate Mrs. Walker set out to make a serious profession of this art, not only manufacturing the necessary applications but giving courses of training to hairdressers.   She thus developed the Walker "system of hair-culture"— there are now other systems—and grew to be very wealthy as well as highly esteemed.   Her "villa" on the Hudson is described as magnificent.

[1] *National Baptist Voice*, December 4, 1920.

The volume of advertising business related to this type of activity is, however, so great as to attract unfavorable comment from Negroes themselves. There are some newspaper men who deprecate the large amount of space thus used, although themselves unable to stop the practice. Certain undesirable features in the advertising are passing away—such as rude pictures of "before and after using." The extravagant claims and suggestions that a Negro can lighten his skin and straighten his hair are less frequent. Present tendencies in the direction of race pride are also leading people away from any suspected imitation of the white man's looks. The emphasis will in the future no doubt be placed more largely on the fact that all people use toilet preparations. The white man, too, reads papers and magazines in which preparations for softening and beautifying hair and skin are well represented. One Negro magazine, the *Crusader*, says: "We do not accept face and skin bleaching advertisements, hair-straightening, etc." But another attitude is evident in a startling message displayed by several weeklies, among them the *Washington Eagle* of December 4, 1920—"Hair-Vim is Growing Hair Around the World." The *Washington Colored American* (May 3, 1921) writes thus:

WOMEN WHO MAKE OTHER WOMEN PRETTY

There has been a commendable increase in pride of appearance, which will show its effects in the effort put forth to maintain the income by which the appearance is made possible. . . . . .

The manicurist, hairdresser, or dressmaker is more than an artisan, she is an artist and often a friend and adviser.

When you look for the cause of the rapid increase in self-confidence among the women of today, you must look for the women who make other women prettier.

Other things represented by the cheaper class of white periodicals are advertised in the Negro press. Among these are wonderful mail order bargains. For instance,

Send No Money—Genuine $12.00 imported Velour Hat, $6.89. A Stunning, Stylish Hat, Full of Jazz and Pep. . . . . Write quickly for this amazing bargain. . . . . A hat you can wear, season after season, for years. *Don't send a penny*—Pay only $6.89 C.O.D.[1]

Patent medicines, too, are present. The *Chicago Defender* tells the reader (July 9, 1921):

If You Suffer from

Malaria, Chills and Fever, Loss of Nature, Catarrh, Dropsy, Ulcers, Prickly Heat, Tired Sleepy Feeling, Headache, Pain in Neck, Sides, Shoulders, Back or Hips; Sick Stomach, Kidney and Bladder Trouble, Female Diseases and Women's Troubles, Bad Colds, LaGrippe, Stomach Ulcers, Fever; Mean, Tired Feeling, by all means take a bottle of Aztec Indian Kidney and Liver Medicine. It has made hundreds well and strong again.

The *New York Amsterdam News* of May 4, 1921, has thirteen advertisements of patent cures and so-called specialists on page 11, with two more on page 12—an extreme case. It is difficult to estimate the proportion of advertising space occupied by this class of business, but it can be said that the larger proportion of what is called "foreign advertising" is covered by the display of cosmetics and medicines. Very few of the larger papers are free from patent medicine advertisements.

One may find several announcements of clairvoyants. There seems to be nothing distinctive about such advertisements unless it is the suggestion of grounds for belief in the superstition of Negroes. The *Richmond*

[1] *Christian Recorder*, June 9, 1921.

(Indiana) *Blade* (April 22, 1921) introduces to us Rev. Leo S. Osman, who says:

My incense and my parchment prayers are proclaimed most wonderful. Charges only made for the incense. My work is free to you. Parchment prayers also free. I have benefitted many thousands. . . . . Price of the Sacred Scripture Temple Incense $1 and 10 cents extra for tax and mailing.

The *Washington Eagle* of February 12, 1921, advertises four fortune-tellers. "Madame Leona . . . . reads your past, present and future life. . . . ." "Madam Mavis, the great Egyptian palmist," tells us that "her clients are both white and colored." The same human nature is appealed to in a long and quaint advertisement carried in *Vigil*, Portsmouth, Virginia, March 31, 1921, and several other issues. Only portions of this can be quoted:

Why suffer, or Use Poisonous Drugs, when nature in her wisdom and beneficence has provided in her great vegetable kingdom and laboratories the fields and forest a cure for most of all ills of mankind. We have over 1,000 different varieties of herbs, roots, barks, seeds, leaves and flowers in stock, and can supply any herb grown in any part of the world. . . . .

Lesser Periwinkle—Dr. Culpeper, an old English herbalist, writes of the herb as follows: "The leaves of Lesser Periwinkle, if eaten by man and wife together will cause love between them." . . . .

Buckeye—Also called Kenker and Bongay Tree. The fruit of this tree is a hard nut and is carried around in the pocket to overcome and avoid rheumatism; also to bring good luck. . . . .

Devil's Shoe String—. . . . An old colored mammy explained to me that this root if placed around a baby's neck will drive the evil spirits away and stop it from crying, especially during teething. . . . .

After several statements of this nature, the advertiser concludes as follows:

The writer wishes it understood that these articles are merely described and sold for their medicinal values and as curiosities and are not recommended for their evidently impossible magic properties. He is not of a superstitious nature himself and does not believe in magic of this brand.

A startling example of the appeal to superstition is spread on the pages of the *Christian Recorder*. This highly honored religious periodical advertises patent cures among its church supplies, invites business investments, handles many advertisements of cosmetics, and, in the issue of June 9, 1921, tells us that:

Madame Jefferson . . . . can cure any disease that you were not born with, in fact, she can locate any disease in your human body, and tell your complaint by your writing to her when other doctors have failed. . . . . She has a supernatural gift. God has given her power to heal and lead her people. Her advice on business problems is worth more than you will ever be able to pay. Madame Jefferson has discovered a wonderful hair restorative. It grows hair on bald heads. . . . .

One advertisement has been found calling on "ladies and gentlemen interested in racing" to address someone who evidently wishes to assist them in placing bets. There is very little advertising of this nature. Advertisements of dice, although rare, occur.

That the press is not oblivious to moral standards in the whole conduct of the advertising is indicated by occasional statements as to advertising policy. The *Competitor*, a magazine in Pittsburgh, writes, "This magazine has but one policy—It will not carry any fake or spurious advertising knowingly." The *Cleveland Advocate* uses almost the same words.[1]

[1] Letters to this writer, 1921.

During election campaigns, and in some papers more than others, political advertising appears, generally occupying large display space, such as a half-page. This is generally supplied by white candidates and is of the usual sort. Large space is given to theater announcements. The theater offers its attractions—write-ups appearing in due form as accompanying news matter—movies are also represented, dance-halls and cabarets display their events, companies that engage actors are advertised, calls are put in for actors and musicians, and stock in theater organizations is offered for sale. Lodges, too, announce dances and cake-walks. Advertisements of schools and colleges occur only sporadically in the weeklies but the *Crisis* carries several of them. Often there is a directory of churches, and "special services" have display space. "Baptizing" is an attraction frequently mentioned.

Some esoteric book may offer itself for sale, as, for example (*Richmond Planet*, February 26, 1921):

The Book of Seven Seals by Lucinda Young, who in the year 1890 laid on her bed for twenty-four days and saw dreams and visions, was commanded by God to write the wonders she saw into a book. . . . . The book is sold at 60 cents and is on sale at Mrs. Davenport's, 710 N. First Street, also at Mr. O. R. Robinsons's Wonderful Hair Grower and Restorer, 1103 W. Leigh Street, Richmond, Virginia. Address all communications to Mrs. Lucinda Young, R.F.D. No. 4, Box 73-d, Richmond, Virginia. Agents Wanted.

More compelling still are such prophetic demonstrations as this:

THE KINGDOM OF GOD

Looms Up All Over the World In a Day And All Nations Tremble! *the man:*—Spoken of in Isaiah 32, the Prophet of God, whom

God Almighty has chosen and qualified and commissioned. *To set up the Kingdom of God all around the whole earth in 1921:*—will make a world-wide call for the True Elect of God, and the true Righteous, of Every Race and Nation, Not later than June the 30th, 1921. . . . .

Now everyone who wants to secure a copy of it, and a copy of the *Kingdom of God*, they must apply for a copy of it *now*, with a volunteer offering to the expense fund of $1.00 or more by registered letter, and One Million and Four Hundred Thousand (1,400,000) Righteous Agents will be given a life time Employment in the work of Introducing and Training all People in the Ways of its Everlasting Glory.

S. A. HICKS, Secretary.[1]

A similar sort of advertisement in the *Freeman* of Indianapolis, concludes by saying, "I the Writer, am the Supreme Speaker for God the Almighty, and the Founder of the Almighty Church," and asks all who want to escape destruction to contribute "$1.00 and up" to the $7,000,000 expense fund.

One will discover in the advertising other and more substantial enterprises. There are many notices of fraternal societies and insurance companies. In the *Richmond Voice*, February 19, 1921, the Southern Aid Society of Virginia, Incorporated, displayed its twenty-seventh Annual Statement of assets and liabilities, showing gross receipts for 1920 of $857,724.52. A Kansas City, Missouri, paper announces the formation of a new life insurance company by men of the race. The *Chicago Whip*, June 25, 1921, advertises the Liberty Life Insurance Company of Chicago, a new race enterprise. Then there is the Interstate Benevolent Association of Helena, Arkansas. The *San Antonio*

[1] *Richmond* (Indiana) *Blade*, June 17, 1921.

Inquirer, February 19, 1921, gives space to the Supreme Order of the Golden Rule of the World, and an advertisement in the *Newport News Star*, February 10, 1921, represents the Knights and Daughters of Tabor's Hall.

Significant of recent tendencies toward labor organization is a four-column advertisement, in the *Chicago Defender*, of the Railway Men's International Benevolent Industrial Association (issue of March 19, 1921). The *New York Age* for September 18, 1920, advertises the work of the Harlem Tenants' and Lodgers' League in providing employment for Negroes. Another strong tendency—the interest of colored people in acquiring real property—is witnessed by appeals to invest money in real estate subdivisions, lots for farms, land in Brazil, or homes in the suburban areas about the large cities.[1] The *Pittsburgh American* of December 31, 1920, offers for sale shares in a five-story apartment building. In the same issue it implores its readers: "own a share in your race bank, ... the Steel City Banking Company." Many investment opportunities are offered. There is a Thermocomb Corporation of America,[2] a Gate City Feature Film Company, of Kansas City—to make motion pictures of Negroes[3]—the Douglass Square Savings Bank of Boston,[4] various co-operative enterprises, such, for instance, as the Richmond (Indiana) Grocery Company,[5] the Chicago Realty Association,[6] two

[1] For instance as in one column, the *Chicago Defender*, March 19, 1921.

[2] *New York News*, April 14, 1921.

[3] *Kansas City Call*, May 14, 1921.

[4] *Guardian*, February 12, 1921.

[5] *Richmond* (Indiana) *Blade*, June 17, 1921.

[6] *Chicago Whip*, June 25, 1921.

branch banks of the Tidewater Bank and Trust Company of Norfolk, of which Editor Young, of the *Norfolk Journal and Guide* is president,[1] and the Harlem stock Exchange, Incorporated.[2] There is even an occasional "Oil and Gas Company" inviting stock subscription. One of these asks: "How did Rockefeller make his millions?" and exhorts: "Put a Bet on Yourself."[3] All these occur at random, some more significant than others. And all give testimony to the economic advance of the Negro people.

Occasionally a project comes to light that suggests not only business enterprise but an attempt to link this with newer racial schemes. The *National Baptist Voice*, November 6, 1920,[4] has the following:

A Ship Direct to Africa Our Fatherland

The African Steamship and Sawmill Co.

A Million Dollar ($1,000,000) Corporation Chartered March 16, 1919, Under the Laws of Delaware

The United States Government is anxious to have a great big Merchant Marine Fleet, because it is a paying business. The African Steamship and Sawmill Company is going after the Palm Oil, ... Coffee, Mahogany, Ginger, Ivory and Gold trade in Liberia.

The A. "SS." & S. M. Co., is no one man affair, but is owned by the Stock-holders and managed by a Board of Directors.

The Company is in a Great Drive for $350,000 to Complete Their Plans by July 26, 1920, Liberia's Natal Day for Launching Our First Ship, etc.

[1] *Norfolk Journal and Guide*, December 18, 1920.

[2] *Philadelphia Public Journal*, February 19, 1921.

[3] *Western World Reporter* (Memphis, Tennessee), June 4, 1921.

[4] Notice discrepancy between this date and the one mentioned in the advertisement.

Advertisements such as this may, as in this case, present no evidence of financial reliability.[1] This "Back to Africa" notice is quoted because it occurs in some other periodical than the *Negro World*, the organ of the Garvey movement. This paper gives the greatest part of its advertising space to the projects related to that organization.

Illustrations of a different sort of racial aspiration are occasional bits of miscellaneous advertising such as the following:

$100,000.00 Bargain in Soaps of all kinds, beautiful Negro pictures, post cards, calendars and colored dolls.   Large and small sizes. . . . .[2]

Six Remarkable Lectures on Negro race and culture . . . . under the Auspices of the Frederick Douglass Literary Society. . . . .[3]

The Delaware Negro Civic League, ...
The object of the League is to unite the Negro population for co-operative effort to advance the economic, educational and moral interests of the race.[4]

The National Capital Code of Etiquette. . . . . Learn how to dress and conduct yourself on any and all occasions. . . . .[5]

Evidences that the advertising function generally is taken seriously appear in such indications as the "Advertising Chats," printed in the *New York News*[6] or the

[1] The same company has a similar advertisement in the *Washington Eagle*, December 4, 1920, and includes names of several persons as officers and directors who are supposedly well-known Negroes.

[2] *Negro World*, February 26, 1921.

[3] *New York News*, February 7 (?), 12 (?), 1921.

[4] *Wilmington Advocate*, January 15, 1921.

[5] *Washington Eagle*, August 28, 1920.

[6] As, e.g., in February 10, 1921, issue.

exhortations to readers to support the colored advertisers, which are fairly frequent. A constantly recurring theme in the news columns is the progress of business enterprise in the race, a theme treated with all the warmth of race pride. The *Washington Eagle*, April 23, 1921, referring to an event it was planning, offers its

Congratulations to the Business Men, Promoters and the General Public on the Progress made and to be demonstrated in the *Washington Eagle's* Auto Floral and Commercial Parade and Masquerade Mardi Gras, held to Advertise the Progress of the Colored Race Commercially, May 6, 1921.

Quite comprehensively the advertising of the Negro newspaper covers the field of interests within its group. As one instance, the *Charleston* (South Carolina) *Messenger*, February 2, 1921, advertises the Lincoln Café, the Lincoln Theater, Building Lots, Lecture announced by the local branch of the N.A.A.C.P., the People's Baptist Temple, a savings bank, an undertaker, a hairdresser.

Among advertising agencies that represent colored papers are J. R. B. Whitney of New York, acting for the National Negro Press Association and the W. B. Ziff Company of Chicago. It is generally recognized that remunerative advertising of the best sort, representing firms that do a nation-wide business, is hard for Negro papers to secure, the feeling still existing that they are class periodicals. The purchasing power of the Negro group is significantly referred to in a booklet gotten out by Albon L. Holsey.

"Who is Mr. Spaulding?" questioned the salesman for the Multigraph Company.

"Why he is the General Manager of the North Carolina Mutual Insurance Company, one of the oldest and most successful business enterprises operated by the colored people.   And you never heard of him?" I inquiringly replied.

"No," said the salesman.

"Well," I added, "you had better drop in to see him while you are in town, for I am sure they could use one of your machines in their office."

He saw Mr. Spaulding and after a very brief interview sold him a Multigraph and equipment amounting to about $600.00.

The incident recited above occurred about two years ago in the city of Durham, North Carolina, and since then I have been thinking of other similar instances which have occurred. It appears to me that it would be a profitable investment for sales managers and salesmen to get acquainted with this undeveloped field among the colored people. . . . . Quite recently I was discussing this same question with a man identified with the advertising department of one of the oldest and best known advertisers in the country, and I asked him very frankly why it was that national advertisers seemed not to be aware of the existence of the 200 colored newspapers. . . . .

He hesitated for a moment—"I suppose most of the fellows are just about like I am—never thought of it."

The leaflet of the Associated Press on the same subject argues:

Their home owners have increased in the period of freedom by 588,000; their farm owners by 980,000; . . . . accumulated wealth to $1,080,000,000. . . . .

The W. B. Ziff Company advertisement in the Advertisers' Directory of Leading Publications,[1] says:

A big advertiser who spends over $400,000 a year in advertising . . . . did a prodigious business in the Southern States. He consistently threw out all orders, as many advertisers did and do, which appeared to have been sent by a Negro.

Several months back they . . . . engaged a new credit agency. The New Credit Agency, a bit more thorough than

[1] Charles H. Fuller Company, Chicago, Vol. XXXI (1920–21), p. 432.

the Old, reported on the race of the customer in addition to other things.

The astounding discovery was made that 40% of the customers of this particular advertiser had been Negroes. In addition it was found that these Negroes were more regular in their payments than the whites!"

As to the response which these insertions bring from colored readers, there is no doubt that they are worth while. It is said that one firm bought from another the letters sent in response to one advertisement and, in paying $270.00 therefor, figured that each letter had cost them only two cents, reckoning the number of responses at over 13,000.

With regard to magazines a brief statement should suffice. Some thirty-one publications may be so classed. Perhaps the eighty-two school periodicals should be included. These of course are meant not only for the benefit of actual students but to serve as bulletins of information and inspiration to the entire constituency. The periodicals so issued by the larger schools, such as Howard, Atlanta, Wilberforce, Hampton, Tuskegee, Fisk, Talladega, are well printed and attractive, stressing genuine culture. The *Southern Workman* of Hampton Institute, on account of its organization and the publishing personnel, can scarcely be adjudged a Negro publication. Besides the *Tuskegee Student*, the Tuskegee Institute sends out a monthly called the *Rural Messenger*, sixteen pages "devoted"—as the title-page tells— "to every phase of rural life and its betterment." It speaks of itself also as the "only Negro farm journal in the world," and a "source of helpful information for the farm and garden." A copy of this for February,

1921, reports the thirtieth annual Negro Farmers' Conference at Tuskegee, Professor Carver's address to the Congressional committee, suggestions for child welfare, accounts of agricultural extension as carried on by district and county agents, of a local federal farm loan association in North Carolina, and of special conferences held for betterment of country life.

The fraternal magazines include two representing college fraternities, *Sphinx* and *Kappa Alpha Psi Journal*. The *Fraternal Advocate* of Chicago (twenty-four pages and cover) gives news from various secret and insurance orders or labor organizations, besides general "race-news." The *Pullman Porters' Review* is for the most part taken up with articles of general interest, including poetry and stories. Church magazines with religious articles, along with the ever-present racial literature, are exemplified by the *A.M.E. Zion Quarterly Review*. Business magazines include a house organ of the Poro Institute, St. Louis, a *Commercial Journal and Business Men's Bulletin* of Chicago, and *Method* of Richmond, Virginia. These were all less than two years old in 1921.

Of the five music magazines,[1] indicative as they are of the present vogue of Negro musicians among whites as well as blacks and the race's ever present love for music, the *Musician* thus announces its objects in its first issue:

> Pride in Achievement, Stimulus to Progress;
> Molder of Taste; Organ of Fraternity.

[1] *American Musician* and *Master Musician*, Philadelphia, *Negro Musician*, Washington, D.C., *Encore*, Cambridge, Massachusetts, and *Music and Poetry*, Chicago.

It has departments for piano, voice, organ, theory, community chorus, church chorus, orchestra, and violin. The *American Musician Magazine* has twenty-eight pages and cover, and is for "masters, artists, teachers, scholars and music lovers." It includes a few pages of music score. *Music and Poetry* also publishes Negro composition and betrays a particular interest in the adaptations of the "Spiritual." In the last two publications we come upon news of the National Association of Negro Musicians. *Music and Poetry* (March, 1921) has the following by Clement Wood:

AN OLD-TIME NEGRO MELODY

As I climbed the gentle hillside
In the earliest morning hour,
The April moon's waning crescent
Hung, rounded, keel to the east, uncertainly balanced,
Below the morning star.

There I heard an old-time Negro Melody,
Crooned by the wind in the leaves above me,
Or by the waning moon and the morning star,
Or by some mysterious singer—I could not tell from where.

The *Brownies' Book* is a magazine for children which attempts to bring to them:

1. The best in pictures and stories of Negro life.
2. The life and deeds of famous men and women of the Negro race.
3. The current events of the worlds told in beautiful language which children can understand.[1]

Other literary publications include Fenton Johnson's *Favorite Magazine*, a fifteen-cent periodical not greatly different in character from such a one published by whites: stories, poetry, articles of home interest, attract-

[1] From advertisement in the *Crisis*, June, 1921.

ive cuts, design on the colored cover. The *Half-Century Magazine* is one whose object is similar. The name is in celebration of the half-century of freedom. The *Up-Reach Magazine*, meant to be a "journal of education and social work," also published in Chicago, is edited by Willis N. Huggins, a teacher in the Wendell Phillips High School. It is specially "devoted to the interest of Negro teachers and social workers," as well as to "the promotion of the study and teaching of Negro history." In Memphis the *Negro Outlook*, edited by M. V. Link, began with the new year 1921. A distinctly pretentious effort is the *Competitor*, a general literary magazine published by Robert L. Vann, editor of the *Pittsburgh Courier*. It has eighty-four pages with illustrated cover. Of *The Black Man*, a monthly published in Vicksburg, Mississippi, the editor writes:

It's widely read and recognized by all classes and races. Highly literary in make up, carrying only clean "ads." Republican politically speaking, Methodist in belief—but liberal to all sexes and christian denominations.

The Journal of Negro History, edited by C. G. Woodson, for the Association for the Study of Negro Life and History, is a recognized contribution to learning.

There are other magazines, which represent not only general literary culture but also race propaganda of a distinctive type. Of these one naturally mentions the *Crisis*, "a record of the darker races," and the following four in New York City: *Promoter, Challenge, Crusader, Messenger*. What Negro radicalism is and just what papers like this stand for will be our inquiry in a subsequent chapter.

CHAPTER VI

THE DEMAND FOR RIGHTS

PRAYER OF THE RACE THAT GOD MADE BLACK
Lucian B. Watkins[1]

We would be peaceful, Father,—but when we must,
Help us to thunder hard the blow that's just!

We would be prayerful: Lord, when we have prayed
Let us arise courageous, unafraid!

We would be manly—proving well our worth,
Then would not cringe to any god on earth!

We would be loving and forgiving, thus
To love our neighbor as thou lovest us!

We would be faithful, loyal to the Right,—
Ne'er doubting that the Day will follow Night!

We would be all that Thou hast meant for man,
Up through the ages, since the world began!

God! save us in Thy Heaven, where all is well!—
We come slow-struggling up the Hills of Hell!

AMEN! AMEN!

The keynote of Negro militancy is struck in these lines. They suggest, too, what Negroes mean by "the race problem." With them it is not so much problem as struggle, a struggle that breaks out in open clashes at various points along an extended front.

[1] Quoted by Kerlin, *op. cit.*, p. 183, from the *Guardian*, Boston, August 30, 1919.

It is to be expected that the Negro's press will re-echo this conflict. In fact it is in the atmosphere of conflict that the white man's press took its start and went on to grow and thrive. This is true of the history of the newspaper in England, France, and America. It may almost be said that the revolutionary agitation of the seventeenth and eighteenth centuries breathed into the pamphlets, broadsheets, corantos, and mercuries, the breath of life and they became our modern press.[1] Not only in revolutionary times has conflict been important. Not only Mazzini, working at night to smuggle literature into Italy in packing-cases, but reformers, like Garrison with his *Liberator*, the Socialist Liebknecht—happy, as Bebel says, in his new editorship because now he could write whatever he wished to write—even "old Greeley" with his *Tribune* and many a partisan editor, have been set going and kept going because they were fighting for something.[2] So, too, with the Negro's newspaper. We have seen that *Freedom's Journal* arose in 1827 out of conflict, that the colored man's press since the Civil War

[1] For England: J. B. Williams, *A History of English Journalism, etc.*, London, 1908, and—the best treatment of this period—Roger P. McCutcheon, *Book Reviewing in English Periodicals, 1640–1712*, Harvard Doctor's Thesis, 1918. For France: E. J. Lowell, *The Eve of the French Revolution*, Boston, 1892, p. 333; F. C. Montague, *Cambridge Modern History*, New York, 1898, VIII, 168, etc. The contemporary journals themselves. For America: Frederic Hudson, *Journalism in the United States*, New York, 1873; G. H. Payne, *History of Journalism in the United States*, New York, 1920.

[2] For Mazzini, see for instance Bolton King, *Mazzini*, London, 1902, chap. iii. For Bebel, *My Life*, Chicago, 1912 (?), p. 93. For Garrison, *Liberator* (especially January 1, 1831), as quoted in *William Lloyd Garrison, 1805–1879, the Story of His Life Told by His Children*, New York, 1885. These are only a few illustrative hints out of a great many that are accessible.

has thrived on it, and that the fighting spirit is more vigorous than ever at the present day.

It is not surprising, then, that we have such titles as *Advocate, Protest, Challenge, Contender, Defender, Protector, Crusader, Whip, Hornet, Blade.* "We propose," says the *Rising Sun* of Pueblo, Colorado, "to wage a relentless warfare against everything that prevents us from being recognized as full fledged citizens of America." This emphasis on citizenship with the political and civil rights attaching to it is common to the great majority of the papers. The *Rising Sun* presents details, on which the press is generally agreed:

> We propose to contend for our complete rights before the law, just representation in politics; meritorious consideration in labor, no discrimination in education or public accommodation, no domiciliary restrictions, and a repeal or prevention of the enactment of any statute or ordinance by either state, municipality or nation in contravention to the constitution of the United States of America.

The aggressive tone is likely to be more marked in the North than in the South. Besides this there are differences among the papers as to immediate policies for the race to adopt. There is some difference of opinion, for example, as to the movement for organization of interracial committees now spreading in the South. There is some difference of opinion as to the amount of recognition that ought to be given to the nationalist movement headed by Marcus Garvey, and occasionally there is a slight interest in the possibilities for Negroes of the radical and labor movements. But economic radicalism is represented almost entirely by a certain clearly marked group of magazines and papers—not a large proportion of all. And the Garvey movement is represented actively by very few advocates outside the pages of the *Negro World*.

In treating of these various policies one may classify them thus:

The policy of securing civil rights in the existing American régime. .

The policy of economic radicalism.

The policy of nationalism and colonization.

The policy of lessening the struggle—the ignoring of it, advocacy of interracial co-operation, or "reconciliation."

The first of these, as already suggested, is that of the newspapers generally. Yet it is not a clearly defined line of constructive action. It is, rather, a practice of protesting against individual injustices when they occur. Says the *Fraternal Monitor* (Cincinnati, May 1, 1921):

Never let go unnoticed an expression in favor of the race. Write a letter of thanks to the President, the Senator, the Congressman or to any citizen for any kind of expression in our behalf Whenever an unfriendly expression is made, write the offender your protest. Let it be known that we are not asleep when our rights are protected nor when assailed.

The various race-conscious members of the group live always on the *qui vive*. They read the white newspapers carefully and note points of possible protest. The *Crisis* (March, 1920) mentions the launching of a "Correspondents' Club":

Holding ourselves bound together by a common impulse to resent and resist all efforts in public or private, by speech or writings, to misrepresent, defame, or discredit our race, we have organized "The Correspondents' Club." . . . .

We propose to accomplish our object through letters addressed to individuals, organizations, and publications, protesting with firmness against wrongs, and appreciating with gratitude what appears in our favor.

The press itself is just this sort of organization. Several papers quote the words of Ella Wheeler Wilcox:

To submit in silence when we should protest makes cowards out of men. The human race has climbed on protest. Had no voice been raised against injustice, ignorance and lust, the inquisition yet would serve the law, and guillotines decide our least disputes. The few who dare must speak and speak again to right the wrongs of many.

What specifically is the editor's complaint? The answer is difficult only because of the extreme abundance of the material. Lynchings are first likely to attract our attention. In one paper we are told: "Colored boy lynched for no special cause—trying to get ride, taken from jail by mob, at McGhee. Arkansas list of horrors is growing."[1] Another tells an "unspeakable brutality— how the Arthur boys were lynched and three sisters outraged," and exclaims, "Southern Chivalry!" This is the transcript of a letter giving all the gruesome details: "There was a regular parade of 17 cars and a truck with white men crying aloud—'Here are the barbecued niggers; all you niggers come out and see them and take warning.'" The letter ends with these words: "You are at liberty to publish what you see fit of this, only keep secret my name."[2] The Tuskegee Institute Press Service sends out at intervals of a year and less a record of lynchings for the whole country, and this is always given wide publicity in the newspapers.

[1] *Richmond* (Indiana) *Blade*, June 11, 1921.

[2] *Cleveland Gazette*, September 18, 1920.

Besides lynchings, cases of unusual cruelty or injustice are reported in full and commented upon. A clipping from a white paper in Georgia tells the story of a black preacher who was stripped, laid over a log and lashed with a wagon trace, because he had set the other Negroes "a bad example" by going about "dressed-up" and wearing a white collar. The white men took off the collar and cut it into souvenirs.[1] Of the same sort is this editorial in the *New York Amsterdam News* (June 15, 1921):

Justice appears to have gone crazy in North Carolina. . . . . Jerome Hunter has just been sentenced to eight years in the penitentiary, and six others for shorter terms, by Justice Kramer, at Warrenton, for participation in a riot. . . . .

A white merchant sold a basket of bad apples to an Afro-American, and, in the protest that followed, whites and blacks got badly mixed up in a riot. After it was over, the blacks who were in the mix-up were rounded up and placed in the Henderson jail. Soon after two of their number were taken out and lynched. His companions were then taken to Raleigh for safe keeping, and have just now been sentenced.

Not a white man connected with the rioting over the bad apples, or the lynching of the two blacks, has been arrested or prosecuted. That sort of justice in North Carolina, or anywhere else, is surely crazy. If white men expect that black men are going to stand for it always without fighting to the last man unto death, he must be a fool whose eyes have been blinded by their Lord.

There is a God in this Republic, and he, too, is flesh and blood.

The Negro press is especially on the alert for cases of assault by white men upon colored women. These are always played up. The *Cleveland Gazette* already quoted carries such an instance. These headings occur: "Burly White Brute Assaults Pretty Colored Girl,"[2] "Big Burly

[1] *Dallas Express*, December 25, 1920.

[2] *Philadelphia American*, February 12, 1921.

Brute Attempts a Criminal Outrage upon Colored Girl in California";[1] "An uncivilized white skinned curr [sic] on Monday afternoon . . . . the coward struck the woman down. . . . . *Race leaders will demand that the culprit be punished.*"[2] These three are all from various journals, but of the same date.

Cases of discrimination in public places or common carriers are also played up. The *Washington Bee* (April 2, 1921) under caption, "Victory Still Ours," makes common cause—note the "ours"—with all the race in a court decision to the effect that "State jim-crow cars are unconstitutional as applied to interstate colored passengers, even though they are riding on a local train moving between two points entirely within a jim-crow-law State." The *Crisis* for March, 1920, says, "Here is a good story from the Oklahoma City, Okla., *Black Dispatch*," and quotes that journal's account of a street-car incident. This is made to close with the words, "*The Law, the Law of Fair Play, of the Square Deal and Justice.*"

This policy includes a reinterpretation of any racial clash already reported by the white man's press. After each riot the "real truth" finally comes out, on the basis of the reports finally gathered from the terror-stricken Negro survivors. One who scanned the issues of the *Springfield* (Ohio) *Daily News* for the ten days covering the disturbances that took place there in March, 1921, would find nothing but the orthodox reports, the usual story of assault, of the police officers' disarming of the colored men, the city's being placed under martial law, and final quiet restored. On March 26, however, the

[1] *Houston Informer*, February 12, 1921.

[2] *Hephzibah Herald*, same date.

Cleveland Gazette printed an entirely different version of the matter under the head, "Springfield Riot Truth, the First Time Given to the Public by Any Publication. Veterans of the World War Were on the Job and Our People Were Ready—Chicago and Washington Their Precedent."

It will be noted here that there is no disposition to deny the armed resistance on the part of Negroes, rather to justify it. With regard to the Tulsa riot the same is true. A reinterpretation of this affair has been quoted above[1] from the *New York Age*. But the *Afro-American* of June 10, 1921, has the following significant item:

NEW YORK, June 4.—Negroes in New York were urged to arm by Hubert H. Harrison, president of the Liberal League of Negro Americans, at a meeting yesterday at 135th street and Lenox avenue to ask for contributions to a fund to relieve the suffering caused to the Negroes of Tulsa. He denied that the Negroes of Tulsa were in any way responsible for the rioting, and charged that the police and troops took sides with the whites until restrained by the authorities.

"It is not only these negroes, but those everywhere in the country, of whom we are thinking," Mr. Harrison said in asking for funds. "I am not making any predictions, but I should not be surprised if we saw three splendid race riots by next September. There may not be any in New York, but I advise you to be ready to defend yourselves. I notice that the State Government has removed some of its restrictions upon owning firearms, and one form of life insurance for your wives and children might be the possession of some of these handy implements. And it is absolutely necessary for your protection to join the Liberal League, which is carrying on a wide campaign for the interests of our race."

The attitude of Negroes in view of clashes such as these has been carefully indicated by Robert T. Kerlin

[1] Chap. iv.

in his work on *The Voice of the Negro*. Here he has quoted newspapers as published during four months following the Washington riot of 1919. In chapter v Kerlin gives extracts on the whole situation that are still typical of the Negro's reaction. Significant points are the insistence that the charge of assault on some white woman is generally unfounded and due to the white press, that the riots are begun by the whites, that the Negroes are compelled to resist with firearms, that the police and militia aid the rioters against the Negroes, and that the judicial investigations following the riots condemn Negroes almost wholesale while letting the whites off easily. The new attitude is armed resistance. All this is in striking contrast to the older doctrine, of which Booker T. Washington was the spokesman. At the time of the Atlanta riot Washington wrote in the *New York Age* (September 27, 1906):

I would especially urge the colored people in Atlanta and else-where to exercise self-control and not make the fatal mistake of attempting to retaliate, but to rely upon the efforts of the proper authorities to bring order and security out of confusion. If they do this they will have the sympathy of good people the world over.

Colored people near the scene of one of these affairs make strenuous efforts to get their side of the case into the hands of the Negro editor so that "the truth" may be known. Mr. Walter F. White, so light-complexioned as to pass easily for white, an officer of the National Association for the Advancement of Colored People, reported the Tulsa riot after having been sworn in on the spot as deputy sheriff. The result was not merely material for the Negro papers but an article in the *Nation* of New York (June 29, 1921) as well. The extreme caution with which others find it necessary to work is exemplified in such a letter as that quoted in the *Cleveland Gazette:*[1] "only keep secret my name." After the Elaine riots in Arkansas[2] not only was a detailed account of them sent out by the National Association for the Advancement of Colored People under Mr. White's signature,[3] but this report came to the office of the *Chicago Defender:*

SPECIAL TO THE CHICAGO DEFENDER

Your special correspondent, detailed to investigate the recent wholesale killings of Negroes in Phillips County, Arkansas, quietly dropped into Helena and visited the scenes of the recent troubles, talked with scores of Negroes, overheard the conversation of many whites, read the leading Arkansas newspapers, asked and got information and opinions and left the state without disclosing his identity and even being suspected of being a news writer.

The reason for this is obvious. We did not know whom to trust. We wanted to get the news—the whole truth, not to be lynched. For in the present state of mind of the white people of Phillips County, any Negro is as good as dead if he be even suspected of writing for a Northern Negro publication. . . . .

Here is the real truth about the whole matter. . . . .

After a fairly lengthy report, the communication ends as follows:

Dear Editor:

Please publish the above. You will understand that I do not dare to disclose my name. I have to give you the facts as I have obtained them, and that from the best and most reliable sources. Publish this just as if it came from your own special correspondent, so as to prevent any attempt to investigate the source of your news. I know you and wish you well. God bless our Race and

[1] See above, p. 134.

[2] Kerlin, *The Voice of the Negro*, pp. 87 ff., describes the situation.

[3] Printed for instance in the *Chicago Whip*, December 27, 1912.

our Negro Newspapers of the North. You are doing a splendid work. Tell the truth, cry aloud and spare not.[1]

That such caution is not entirely misplaced is evident by what William Pickens tells in the *New York Age* (September 25, 1920). A Negro in a southern town wrote an article about the wrongs of his people and sent it to the *Philadelphia Press* (white), which published it. When a white woman in the man's home town read the article, she turned it over to the "authorities." The chief of police with other officials and citizens summoned the Negro and on threat of lynching him compelled him to write another article contradicting the first one. He wrote the second article and it was published.

It is his own newspaper that offers a welcome to the Negro's cries and protests. Protest is the constant inspiration of the editorials. Peculiarly bitter are those editorials directed against other colored people who do not protest. The *Chicago Defender* (June 25, 1921) tells of a Negro who blamed his own people at Tulsa for resisting the whites and includes him in the following characterization:

Never was there another group that had in its ranks such spineless, ignorant, disloyal semi-human beings as these. . . . . We do not expect modern Judases to follow the example of the Biblical betrayer and hang themselves, but we do expect that, when they see the error of their ways, they will at least hang their heads in shame.

To be sure this policy of "crying out" is not always very definite. Peculiarly pathetic, for instance, is an outcry like this, from the *Mobile Weekly Press* (February 19, 1921):[2]

[1] Transcript from original.
[2] Possibly a service shared by other papers.

March 4th,—less than a month away.
It won't bring Heaven, but it may bring a change.
Anything, anything, Lord! but what we've got, anything!

But there are times when the policy can be stated as
definitely as in the following extract.[1] Note that here
the hope of a solution within the Constitution still abides·

This accomplishment is easy, if the people will meet the problem in the spirit of representative government. Just protect the
Negro in the south from Ku Kluxism, mob violence, peonage,
Jimcrow laws, disfranchisement and hurtful discriminations.
Encourage him to buy homes and farms. Guarantee him political
equality, protect his churches, schoolhouses and lodge rooms from
the torch of the midnight marauder, and make him happy and
contented where he is. Let him feel that the strong arm of the law
—state and federal—is stronger than any mob, Ku Klux Klan or
any disorderly band of citizens, and that when they approach him,
he must lean on the law for perfect security for protection of life,
property and happiness. Give him better wages; help him become
a tax payer; teach him to register and vote for the best men and
measures; let the white pulpit thunder against mob violence as it
does against whiskey and the Negro pulpit preach the saving of
men as well as the saving of the soul, and that an abundance of
grace in the heart, grit in the craw and greenback in the pocket is
the only equipment a man needs to succeed on earth in the enjoyment of the privileges of a man or to enter heaven and enjoy the
glories prepared for the righteous.

And we reassert that the government is all right, but the people
are wrong, and cause the world ofttimes to denounce our form of
government for its failure to protect its citizens at home. . . . .
Our government is all right, but the people are wrong, and we
speak of the people and not of the government.

It will be observed that words like "no discrimination" and "equality" are ambiguous. At least they go
beyond the line of what could be called civil rights and

[1] *Atlanta Independent*, December 2, 1920.

ask for the absence of prejudice, the acceptance of a friendly attitude on the part of whites, and the allowance of some recognition or status. This is a sphere that cannot of course be controlled by law and cannot be called a constitutional right. Strictly speaking there are only a few papers that seem to demand any more than the civil rights that are supposed to be guaranteed by the Constitution. They do not consider it possible to expect abolition of prejudice as between man and man, at least not by any political action. For this they wait upon the slow processes of education, religion, and general progress. But somewhere in the discussion of the Negro's program seems to lurk the ill-defined shape of "social equality." On this delicate subject Kerlin sums up the evidence as follows:

This is the crux. Almost the first question raised regarding the colored press is, "Does it preach social equality?" An unqualified monosyllable cannot be given in answer. First, because the colored press, while generally united in its purposes and efforts, does not hold to one manner of speech on all subjects. Secondly, because the question requires interpretation. It is capable of different meanings and implications. Thirdly, the question is so dangerous in the South that the colored papers there either keep away from it or pooh-pooh the idea. A very few papers without being specific on this question, demand "absolute equality."[1]

The quotation from the *New York Age* which Kerlin adds represents at least the conservative utterances on this subject:

The *St. Luke Herald* [Richmond, Va.] of which Mrs. Maggie L. Walker is the managing editor, rises to remark: "All the talk about the colored press encouraging social equality is a Southern made lie, invented and copyrighted that the South might have an

[1] *Op. cit.*, pp. 65 f.

excuse to justify it in the maltreatment of our race." Mrs. Walker hit the nail on the head. Social equality is a "homemade bugaboo," invented by Southern demagogues for domestic consumption chiefly.

Doubtless, if one could banish all the misleading connotations of the term, the words, "social equality," in the sense of justice and equity, or access to the same privileges others have, seems like a good phrase for the goal toward which, unconsciously or consciously, the Negro self-expression is moving. The black man does not—so he says—desire amalgamation with the white race. But he will not be satisfied with any social order that makes him feel inferiority. The caution commanded by their condition makes it imperative for southern papers to abjure so dangerous a term, and they avoid it. Another method of handling this *enfant terrible* is to give it an innocuous interpretation, as is done by the *Houston Informer*.

What the colored man demands is "social equity," "social sameness." He wants the same rights of society that other men and races enjoy; but he does not ask the association and companionship of men and women of other races. Social companionship can not be regulated by laws. If Bill Smith wants to associate with John Jones all the laws in the genius of mankind cannot keep them apart.

On the other hand if they do not desire each other's companionship . . . . no law can be enacted that will have sufficient force to compel these two men to be pals or social associates. . . . .[1]

But behind "social equality" crouches the still more terrible suggestion of miscegenation. And the *Informer's* editorial proceeds to disabuse the southern mind of its fears on this matter. The contention is that miscegena-

[1] *Ibid.*

tion has in the past and present been desired by white men more than by Negroes.

What the Negro really wants and what sort of content can be put into his conception of "social equality" appear still more definitely in the *Guardian* and the *Crisis*. The *Crisis* is evidently made up with a view to an impression upon whites as well as blacks, an impression not only of a group crying for rights but also of people who are interested in culture. It provides an artistic cover, often a sample of Negro feminine beauty; attractive cuts and drawings; items about race achievement and men and women of note; stories, drama, poetry; advertisements that include a large number of announcements of educational institutions; news notes and miscellany; editorials on the race problem; and articles. It said of itself in the first issue:

> It will first and foremost be a newspaper: it will record important happenings . . . . which bear on the great problem. . . . .
> Its editorial page will stand for the rights of men, irrespective of color or race; for the highest ideals of American democracy; and for reasonable and persistent attempt to gain these rights and realize these ideals. . . . .[1]

Political and civil rights are meant here. For such are the terms used in the article which, exactly ten years later, elucidates the troublesome issue of "social equality." Dr. Du Bois, the editor, is the writer of the article. It agrees substantially with the utterance of the *Houston Informer*.

> We were continually being "accused" of advocating "social equality" and back of the accusations were implied the most astonishing assumptions; our secretary was assaulted in Texas for

[1] November, 1920.

"advocating social equality" when in fact he was present to prove that we were a legal organization under Texas law. Attempts were made in North Carolina to forbid a state school from advertising in our organ, the *Crisis*, on the ground that "now and then it injects a note of social equality." . . . .

We believe that social equality . . . . means moral, mental and physical fitness to associate with one's fellowmen. In this sense the *Crisis* believes absolutely in the Social Equality of the Black and White and Yellow races and it believes too that any attempt to deny this equality by law or custom is a blow at Humanity, Religion and Democracy.

No sooner is this incontestable statement made, however, than many minds immediately adduce further implications: they say that such a statement and belief implies the right of black folk to force themselves into the private social life of whites and to intermarry with them.

This is a forced and illogical definition of social equality. Social equals, even in the narrowest sense of the term, do not have the *right* to be invited to, or attend private receptions, or to marry persons who do not wish to marry them. Such a right would imply not mere quality—it would mean superiority. . . . .

On the other hand, every self-respecting person does claim the right to mingle with his fellows *if he is invited* and to be free from insult or hindrance because of his presence. . . . . The late Booker T. Washington could hardly be called an advocate of "social equality" in any sense and yet he repeatedly accepted invitations to private and public functions and certainly had the right to. . . . .

The *Crisis* . . . . most emphatically advises against race intermarriage in America but it does so while maintaining the moral and legal right of individuals who may think otherwise and it most emphatically refuses to base its opposition on other than social grounds. . . . . The *Crisis* advises strongly against interracial marriage in the United States today because of social conditions and prejudice and not for physical reasons. . . . .

The *Crisis* does not for a moment believe that any man has a right to force his company on others in their private lives but it maintains just as strongly that the right of any man to associate privately with those who wish to associate with him and publicly with anybody so long as he conducts himself gently, is the most fundamental right of a Human Being.

An open letter to the president of the United States in the issue for March, 1921, makes plain that the policy of the *Crisis* follows that of the Negro press in general: it stands for political and civil rights. To President Harding the appeal is made:

WE WANT THE RIGHT TO VOTE.

WE WANT TO TRAVEL WITHOUT INSULT.

WE WANT LYNCHING AND MOB-LAW QUELLED FOREVER.

WE WANT FREEDOM FOR OUR BROTHERS IN HAITI.

The magazine is outspoken as a champion of these things because they seem to be the first necessities. It has been known as a fighting paper. In the issue for June, 1921, the editor rejoices over the exposure of mob law and peonage in Georgia made by the retiring Governor Dorsey inasmuch as his statement substantiates the charges the *Crisis* has been making all along.

One of the criticisms . . . . which has been hardest to bear has been that of deliberately exaggerating the mistreatment of Negroes . . . . far from exaggerating we were more often consciously suppressing and concealing the horrors of southern oppression. Month after month we go through the sordid and horrifying details—the letters, the newspapers, the personal visits and appeals —and say in despair: if we publish all this—if we unveil the whole truth, we will defeat our own cause because the public will not believe it, and our own dark readers will shrink from our pages. And so we have fed the world the atrocities we knew of in carefully regulated doses, often incurring the censure of members of our own race, who knew of particular incidents, for our failure to mention them.

While the *Crisis* is uncompromising, it does not want us to think it is opposed to racial co-operation. It bids

Godspeed to the Amity Convention of May, 1921,[1] and it approves the Inter-Racial Committee organizations in the South.[2] It is not so enthusiastic about the inter-racial movement, however, that it can refrain from pointing out what seem to it possible pitfalls and warning the colored members to keep out "'white-folks' niggers' like Isaac Fisher" and "'pussy-footers' like Robert Moton." Robert Russa Moton, Washington's successor at Tuskegee, has succeeded also, in the opinion of the colored people, to Washington's policy of gentle dealing with the white people. Du Bois, who only recently headed the Niagara Movement and, along with Du Bois, the aggressive newspaper men of the North have turned their backs decisively on "pussy-footing."[3]

The *Guardian*, representing the National Equal Rights League of which the editor, William Monroe Trotter, is the secretary, will go out of its way to cast a slur on Moton and all his works, just as Trotter did to Washington in the latter's lifetime.[4] The *Guardian*, like the *Crisis*, is racially aggressive. While it accepts virtually the same program, yet it lays emphasis on those ends that are characteristic of a northern, or shall we say a Bostonian Negro, who is galled by the petty inequalities of social life among his white fellow-citizens. The

[1] July, 1921.

[2] May, 1921.

[3] The *St. Paul Appeal* (March 26, 1921): "It is nauseating to read the rot given out by R. R. Moton . . . . and every time he opens his mouth the colored people of the entire country sink lower in the minds of those who read."

[4] His active opposition was shown in attempts to break up meetings addressed by Washington by such devices as throwing pepper about. See, in regard to Moton, the *Guardian* for December 18, 1920.

attitude of the movement as of the paper is well seen in the following bit of an article (July 3, 1920) sent in by a woman:

I am a Bostonian. Boston is the city of my birth. Here have I lived and breathed on the air of liberty and enjoyment of privileges freely offered alike to white and colored. In all my varied experiences in Boston I have yet to recognize the need of separate educational institutions for white and colored in this city. Above all there is absolutely no need of a colored Y.M.C.A. There is absolutely no call for one. . . . .

I would howl like a wolf and growl and show my fangs, even as a wolf, if I saw that enemy beast Segregation daring to make her lair in our fair city, and I should expect the howl to be taken up in every corner of the city of Boston, by every self-respecting colored citizen, until *the thing* was run under cover.

There are many items in the *Guardian* detailing the experiences of Trotter and others in contending for equal service in barber-shops or at soda fountains. There is an item (July 3, 1920) telling of an old man in the South who died of a broken heart because he was always hoping against hope to be allowed to vote. The Boston branch of the Equal Rights League appointed a special committee to see that an objectionable calendar was removed from sale in a department store, the calendar showing the picture of a Negro baby drinking ink instead of milk (January 1, 1921, issue of the *Guardian*). In an editorial headed "Japs and Jews out for Status," Editor Trotter thus brings in his characteristic message:

Peonage, disfranchisement, lynching are the grosser evils. Any grade of people would object to them. Our race shows its quality in so far as it resents civil displacements, disabilities and discriminations. These things are badges of inferiority of status and chiefest of these is every form of civic segregation. . . . . Refuse to be a party to segregation in the free North and you raise

your grade among the races of the world.   Stand fast for equality
of status.[1]

Included in the policy of general and continual protest
is the attitude of consistent suspicion toward the white
man's press.   There is a conviction that scarcely any
white dailies can be trusted to tell the truth about the
Negro and that many deliberately place him in an unfavorable light.   The Associated Press particularly comes
in for bitter reproach.   Thus:

Every newspaper editor of our group in the country knows that
the Associated Press, the leading news distributing service of the
country, has carried on a policy of discrimination in favor of the
whites and against the blacks, and is doing it daily now.   The
Associated Negro Press is in receipt of correspondence from
editors in various sections of the country decrying the way in
which the Associated Press writes its stories of happenings where
Colored people are affected.[2]

Certain obvious replies to this out-and-out condemnation may occur even to the uninitiated.   It is of course
true that the most of the news will have to be given to
the Associated Press by people who belong to the community where the news originates, and it is natural that
this should reflect the facts as seen by the dominant group
in that community.   Leading Negroes, who see how
unlikely it would be for a minority group to have its case
really stated by a majority press, take this as a matter of
course.   The Associated Press does not lack voices
uttered in vindication of its essential fairness.   To this
effect James Melvin Lee, in his *History of American
Journalism*,[3] quotes Oswald Garrison Villard and Mel-

[1] December 18, 1920; printed also in the *Denver Star*, January 1, 1921.

[2] *Wichita Protest*, October 31, 1919, quoted by Kerlin, *op. cit.*, p. 4.

[3] Boston and New York, 1917, p. 416.

ville P. Stone. In the present discussion we are not so much interested in the truth or untruth of these charges; it is sufficient to point out the feeling of the Negro people that the organized press of the nation is against them.

But apart from the Associated Press, there are specific charges against individual newspapers. The charges are in substance this: When anything evil is reported to have been done, the race of the culprit is not mentioned if the individual is an Irishman, Greek, Russian, or member of some other "white" race; but when he is a Negro the fact of his race is played up. Then when any Negro does something praiseworthy the world never hears of it through the press. William Pickens says:

Booker Washington used to tell with great amusement how he entered a little town and spoke to a large gathering, making as good a speech as he was capable of. The next morning he picked up the town paper, expecting to see himself and the meeting given considerable and prominent space, but found only an inch or so of recognition on the last page. He had made a successful speech, but the whole front page was given to a Negro who had made an *unsuccessful* attempt to snatch a woman's purse.[1]

The Negro papers are continually referring to this practice. Sometimes, as in the *Omaha Monitor* (April 21, 1921) it is pointed out that the same white paper will give four times the space to a crime alleged to have been committed by a black man that will be given to a similar crime by a white. The principle operates in such pronounced form that when some racial clash, such as a riot, arises, the Negro papers are kept busy giving their views of the events, that is, "the real truth." On the part played by the white press in "fomenting city

[1] *The New Negro*, New York, 1916, p. 230.

riots," there is unanimity of opinion among Negro editors. Kerlin[1] quotes the strictures of the *Crisis*, the *Omaha Monitor*, and the *Southwestern Christian Advocate*. With regard to the riots near Elaine, Arkansas, in October, 1919, the accusations of unfairness are loud and emphatic. It is true that the white papers gave out news indicating that the blacks were planning an insurrection. The *New York Times* is a conspicuous instance.[2] It reported a threatened massacre of whites by the blacks. The *New York Tribune* allowed itself to say, "Negro Plot to Massacre All Whites Found," and so "throughout the United States the impression was created . . . . that Negroes had organized against white men and had planned to murder and rob."[3] This report was in due time contradicted by the National Association for the Advancement of Colored People, and in self-defense measures were suggested by the whites in Arkansas looking toward better publicity in their favor. "There should be organized and systematic effort to answer each and every publication that fails to give a true account of the recent troubles," said the *Arkansas Gazette* (white) of Little Rock (October 19, 1919). Negroes, being told that the original story was false,[4] looked more and more to their own press to fight their news battles.[5]

[1] *Op. cit.*, pp. 5, 7, 79.

[2] Reference has been made to the files.

[3] H. J. Seligman, *The Negro Faces America*, pp. 224, 225.

[4] As may well be the case, judging from testimony presented at the trials of alleged offenders (see brief in the *Crisis*, December, 1921, and following month).

[5] A pamphlet entitled "An American Lynching" issued by the N.A.A.C.P., gives facsimiles of two Memphis newspapers announcing lynchings that had been definitely planned.

There are exceptions to this in the South, where there are Negro papers that report a friendly attitude on the part of the white press, naturally enough in cases where the black man dare not speak out. There are also occasional gleams of appreciation when some large city paper will print articles on Negro race progress. To this effect the *Indianapolis Ledger* quotes the *Detroit Free Press*, the *Chicago Defender* mentions the *San Francisco Call* and *Post*, the *New Orleans Searchlight* quotes the *Philadelphia Public Ledger*.[1] The *Chicago Daily News* also is recognized as true and friendly, and its articles on the Chicago riots written by Carl Sandburg are still remembered.[2]

Another characteristic of the conflict over race rights is the active antagonism of the whites, particularly in the South. The *Houston Informer* has already been referred to. Three times white merchants withdrew their advertising. The printing office was raided, "the entire edition of the paper, which was ready for the mails, together with the subscription and advertising books and other important documents, were stolen over night." The editor got out an extra edition only one day late, scoring his enemies, whom he took to be the Ku Klux Klan, with an editorial, "They Shall Not Pass." White editors and others commended his bravery.[3]

The *Dallas Express* also received a letter as follows:[4]

[1] Dates of the Negro papers above, respectively, March 19, 1921, April 23, 1921, February 12, 1921.

[2] Reprinted, New York, 1919 ("Chicago Race Riots").

[3] See *Savannah Tribune*, December 25, 1921, and *Houston Informer*, December 10, 1921.

[4] *Chicago Whip*, February 19, 1921.

We are rapidly organizing the Famous Ku Klux Klan in this City to keep forever inviolate the Constitution and make this a white man's country—also to protect both Races humble and ignorant. We are Convinced that Negroes like yourself & staff are Enemies of Poor ignorant Negroes trying to incite them to Rebellion no one pays any attention to it but ignorant Coons like yourself now we propose to let you do business provided you tell the truth and cut out trying to incite trouble between the Races if you Keep it up there will be a Negro massacre now don't think We Don't Know you—We are here to keep Order, and much better hand Coons like you than kill thousands of ignorant Coons Don't let Us hear of any more boasting lies in your paper the Press of the Country has not taken it up yet but We have and believe us We've been Coon hunting before—Yours for Law & Order even though it takes Death.

"Ku Klux Klan."

The *Dallas Express* answered by printing the letter and with it a defiant statement of its own. The following item appearing in the *Chicago Defender*, March 19, 1921, gives a similar instance:

BIRMINGHAM, ALA., March 18.—Members of the local Ku Klux Klan invaded the office of the *Baptist Leader*, official organ of the Alabama Baptist denomination, and notified the editor, Rev. R. N. Hall, that unless the publication ceased making attacks on the notorious order harm would be done. . . . . Rev. Hall announces that the articles would be continued. . . . .

Efforts made by local authorities to suppress the circulation of northern newspapers have been very common in widely separated parts of the South. The *Crisis*, the *Chicago Defender*, the *Crusader*, and other papers of this sort have been forbidden by law to be circulated. For instance the *Crusader* (July, 1920) prints a letter in this form:

IN THE LAND OF "THE FREE"

(Somewhere in the South. Names are deleted for safety of the writer.)

The Crusader Magazine,
2299 Seventh Avenue, N.Y.

DEAR SIR: We here in the South are not allowed to sell Northern newspapers. We have to slip the paper into the hands of our friends, and I am trying to induce my friends to subscribe by the year for the *Crusader*. Every public school teacher is closely watched, also the Negro preacher. I give you this Dot and you can read between the lines. You will please send me the magazines as I notify you. I will be responsible for every one sent to me for my friends.

Sincerely yours,
[Signature deleted by the editor]

In the spring of 1920 the Mississippi legislature passed "An act to make it a misdemeanor to print or publish or circulate printed or published appeals or presentations of arguments or suggestions favoring social equality or marriage between the white and Negro races."[1] The *Chicago Defender* and the *Crisis* doubtless were the publications at which this was aimed, in spite of the interpretations of social equality and disapproval of intermarriage as above given.[2] The following Associated Press dispatch speaks for Arkansas.

PINE BLUFF, ARK., Feb. 14.—Chancellor John M. Elliott today issued an injunction restraining John D. Young, Jr., Negro, and "any other parties" from circulating the *Chicago Defender*, a Negro publication, in Pine Bluff or Jefferson County.

The injunction was granted at the instance of Mayor Mack Hollis. It was sought following receipt here by Young of copies

---

[1] Printed in the *Crisis*, June, 1920.

[2] The *Chicago Defender* interprets "social equality" substantially as does the *Crisis* in the quotation used.

of the paper containing an account of the killing of George Vicks, Negro, here Thursday, February 5.

The *Defender's* account of the affair portrayed Vicks as defending his home, his liberty and his person, and was held to be false in its entirety by the court. . . . .[1]

The *Defender* itself prints the following (March 15, 1919):

YAZOO CITY, MISS., March 14.—Threatening her with death unless she stopped acting as agent for newspapers published by people of her Race, Miss Pauline Willis was compelled to leave town.

Letters to the *Crisis*[2] from agents in the South show that the hostility of the whites is no trivial thing. This came from Florida:

I would be glad to continue to serve you as agent and willing but you are aware of the fact that the crackers or the Ku Klux will beat a colored man for giving the *Crisis* away in some sections of this country. I wish to stop here a little longer as I make good wages in railroad service. . . . . As long as I can stay in peace I decided I would discontinue for reasons stated above. . . . .

From Mississippi:

I cannot make successful sale of the *Crisis* for the past three months. The people have been afraid to buy the books and have been trying to get me to stop handling them but I have not consented to do that. . . . . I am sacrificing to do this.

And Tennessee:

I am sending you a postal that I received from you last month. I have been to the post office every day since I received the postal card inquiring for the *Crisis*. On the 12th inst. I asked one of the clerks in the office stating to him that you had started the books to me on the 17th of last month and that I could almost walk to New York in that length of time. He went and looked for the first

[1] Taken from the *Montgomery* (Alabama) *Advertiser*, February 15.

[2] Copies of letters in the office of the *Crisis*. Names deleted.

time since I had been calling for them and told me that they had been in the office several days. . . . . You know I can't make these people give me my mail when it arrives. . . . .

The *Crisis* for June, 1920, states that a young colored minister, Rev. E. R. Franklin, having given away on the train a few copies of the *Crisis*, was mobbed on getting off at a little Mississippi station and took refuge in a swamp. After being hunted in a field at night and remaining there during a thunderstorm, he went into town and asked for protection by the justice of the peace, only to be thrown into jail. The justice of the peace refused to accept the bond offered by colored friends in Jackson and sentenced Franklin to the chain-gang. A lawyer coming to defend him was threatened with lynching, and the governor and lieutenant-governor of the state refused to intervene, saying that Franklin ought to be thankful for getting off so easily.

The *Crusader* (February, 1921) prints a letter from Texas and alongside of it the editor's comment. The original letter was smeared with large letters in black ink over the typewritten text so as to read, "TO HELL WITH NIGGERS! ! !"

"Nigger" Briggs:—

Your plan to organize an "African Brotherhood" to protect the gang of "black bellied" reptiles termed by you as an African and by a true Southerner a "black nigger" is amusing inasmuch as you state that your race "met and defeated the flower of the white race on the bloody fields of Flanders" which you know to be nothing but a damnable black lie! ! ! Being a soldier in the American Expeditionary Forces, I saw your gang of "niggers" serving in Labor Battalions *because* they couldn't stand the "gaff" of the big guns—the niggers got down on their knees and prayed for their lives whenever a German Gun would explode.

This is a notice to you to put the "soft pedal" on the organization of your society or *we will*. . . . .

Editor's Note.—The latter part of the letter was deleted because of indecent language. The letter bore no signature. In the place where a *brave man* would have signed his name were two badly scrawled initials. This is what comes out of Texas. The Negro's courage needs no defense. Texan can ask the Germans, who ran every time they faced our boys, or the French, who decorated a full Negro American regiment.

In carrying on their general fusillade of protest the Negro newspapers are careful to proclaim their patriotism. Their loyal attitude during the war has been remarked above. The *Buffalo American*, a paper which has given considerable space to news of the Garvey movement, keeps at the head of its editorial column the following:

OATH OF AFRO-AMERICAN YOUTH

I will never bring disgrace upon my race by any unworthy deed or dishonorable act; I will live a clean, decent, manly life, and will ever respect and defend the virtue and honor of womanhood; I will uphold and obey the just laws of my country and of the community in which I live, and will encourage others to do likewise; I will not allow prejudice, injustice, insult or outrage to cower my spirit or sour my soul, but will ever preserve the inner freedom of heart and conscience; I will not allow myself to be overcome of evil, but will strive to overcome evil with good; I will endeavor to develop and exert the best powers within me for my own personal improvement, and will strive unceasingly to quicken the sense of racial duty and responsibility; I will in all these ways aim to uplift my race so that, to everyone bound to it by ties of blood, it shall become a bond of ennoblement, and not a byword of reproach.

The essential Americanism of the Negro press is proved by the fact that its appeal is always to American constitutional rights. It wants its case handled by the United States. It does not desire to see the nation wrecked and rebuilt. "We are Americans always," says

the *Chicago Defender* (December 11, 1920). This is the
burden of the sentiment one finds in reading editorial
after editorial. Sometimes the expressions of frantic
protest become extreme, but there is always a line beyond
which denunciation must not pass. This is well exhibited
in the comments made by the *Guardian* of Boston and
the *Whip* of Chicago[1]—both rather "radical" champions
of rights—on the flag-burning incident in Chicago in
which the "Abyssinian movement" figured. The movement and the temporary wildness of that procession on
the June Sunday evening were not only repudiated by
the Negroes of Chicago, but were succeeded by the instant
vanishing of the "Abyssinians" from the map. Both of
these papers use extreme language in attempting to miti-
gate the offense on the ground of racial injustice, but
both state that the act of disgrace to the flag was wrong.
Bitter too as the comments have been on the Tulsa riot,
the press still represents Americanism. "God is not
dead, neither are all of the righteous people," admits the
Black Dispatch of Oklahoma City (June 3, 1921). And
the *New York Amsterdam News* for June 15 preaches
from the same text:

God is not dead in this Republic. Far from it. The Chris-
tians of the Republic, its rulers and those in authority, had better
come to their senses in dealing with the so-called relations of the
races, because the vengeance of the spirit of God's justice is after
the Nation, to rebuke and to punish it, for its violation of the law
of brotherhood and citizenship.

This is a far cry from revolutionary socialism or bolshevism. Kerlin finds "the attitude of the colored week-

[1] Editorial in the *Guardian*, July 1, 1920, quoting the *Whip*.

lies with not above three exceptions"[1] represented in an editorial from the *Denver Star* (September 27, 1919):

> We are face to face with anarchy and bolshevism which is applied socialism gone to seed and which is more likely to directly or indirectly affect the happiness, peace, and prosperity and even the life of our people. . . . . We cannot win by and through hate, loss of the church or Christianity, exchanging what we now have for a condition far worse than what we now have. . . . . Steady, Negroes, and pause, for you may have to save America from herself yet. Be wise.

That the Negro does not lack counselors who urge them toward bolshevism is witnessed by a dispatch widely carried[2] giving the news that John Reed had spoken of the desirability of enlisting Negroes in communism. This was at the Moscow meeting of the Internationale. The *Portland Times*,[3] however, thus interprets the Negro's response:

> John Reed, who died recently in Russia, and who lived in Portland a few years ago, gave the world his presumption, when he dreamed that American Negroes would be driven into the folds of radicals and embrace the doctrine of soviet government because of persecution and humiliation. . . . . John Reed showed how ignorant he was of Negro psychology.   Had he been versed in comparative psychology, or had recalled the historical error in judgment of John Brown at Harper's Ferry, he could not arrive at the conclusion that the Negro because of ostracism would revolt and embrace ideas of radical soviet government. . . . . At present John Reed's dream will find no American Negro who thinks seriously of it.

"When," asks the *Gary* (Indiana) *National Defender and Sun* (February 26, 1921)—"When did the colored man turn red?"

[1] *Op. cit.*, chap. viii.

[2] As by *Dallas Express*, December 2, 1920.

[3] Quoted in *Denver Star*, January 1, 1921.

He did not turn red for the sainted John Brown. He did not turn red when the slaveholder left him at home while he (the slaveholder) went to the front to fight for the perpetuation of slavery. He did not turn red in France, when that country was flooded with circulars attacking him and spreading the doctrines of Southern hate against him.

We never carry a chip on our shoulders. We do not like to fight. We are not brave, but we do claim to be courageous. If it is possible to fulfil our mission peacefully we welcome peace. If the enemies of the race force a fight on us, we will fight to the last ditch.

To the same effect is a full-page advertisement in the *New York News* (July 23, 1921) said to be paid for by subscriptions to the Afro-American Loyalty League, entitled "The Strong Black Arm of Loyalty."

There are those within your race who follow the false idols of Bolshevism and Socialism who urge you chase the delusive phantoms of hope that in "the revolution" and the destruction of law and order you would gain your equal rights. . . . .

Give neither mind nor time to those false prophets within, nor to your and the Nation's enemies without. Let us be forever loyal to the Stars and Stripes. Let us by word and deed continue to make it in fact as in name, "My Country 'tis of Thee, Sweet Land of Liberty."

Suspicions of Negro disloyalty have, however, been strong at times. In the fall of 1919 these suspicions led the federal Department of Justice to include Negro periodicals in the scope of its quest for bolshevism. The result, embodied in the concluding pages of the attorney-general's letter to the Senate,[1] will seem less conclusive to some minds than to that of the attorney-general of those days. The advocacy of the Russian system of

[1] *Investigation Activities of the Department of Justice*, Sixty-sixth Congress, First Session, Sen. Doc. 153, Washington, 1919, pp. 161 ff.

government, or bolshevism, along with theories of some form of socialism or radical labor organization, is evidently confined to a small group of New York magazines. Apart from their utterances, the undesirable matter seems to be mainly a rather intemperate use of terms in expressing Negro grievances and the summons to armed resistance. It should be noted that the Department took up the investigation of these papers at a time when a great many beside the Negroes felt that their grievances were by no means imaginary. At any rate the black man's feelings were raw and inflamed. Riots had occurred in Washington, Knoxville, Chicago, Omaha, and Arkansas. The soldiers of the Twenty-fourth Infantry punished at Houston were not forgotten. And after the experiences of war time, in which the troubles connected with segregation and discrimination were forced to the surface and the anomaly of Negro soldiers fighting for a country that refused them civil satisfactions tortured the Negro mind, extravagance of expression would certainly be expected. One who reads the Negro press today would feel its pulse beating more measuredly. This may explain the accusation made in the report referred to (p. 162).

Among the more salient points to be noted . . . . are first, the ill-governed reaction toward race rioting; second, the threat of retaliatory measures in connection with lynching; third, the more openly expressed demand for social equality, in which demand the sex problem is not infrequently included; fourth, the identification of the Negro with such radical organizations as the I.W.W. and an outspoken advocacy of the Bolsheviki or Soviet doctrines; fifth, the political stand assumed toward the present Federal administration, the South in general, and incidentally toward the peace treaty and the league of nations. Underlying these more salient viewpoints is the increasingly emphasized feeling of a race consciousness, in many of these publications always antagonistic to the white race and openly, defiantly assertive of its own equality and even superiority.

Whether this program is un-American or not and whether it is disloyal will be decided by each reader according to his own standard of Americanism. For the papers mentioned in the report to the Senate include only the few that seemed to be easily accessible to the investigators. Evidently no serious attempt was made to bring together representative Negro papers from the country at large.

An indication that confirms us in the view of the essential loyalty of the American Negro is the fact that he is now insisting more and more on the use of the constituted legal and political machinery to gain his ends. A speaker at the 1921 convention of the National Association for the Advancement of Colored People emphasized the fact that the grievances of his people are coming in increasing volume into the courts and spoke of this as a very good omen. Not only are the unceasing protests largely made up of demands for law enforcement under the Constitution, but there is heard an urgent call for political organization. The Republican administration now in charge of national affairs has been first looked up to with hope and then viewed with suspicion. Discussions as to the advisability of breaking into the white primary in the South, of preventing "lily-whitism" in the Republican organizations, of splitting the vote in the large city centers has been heard. "The forming of a permanent country-wide organization of Negro voters here begins an epoch," says the *Pittsburgh American*.[1]

[1] Quoted by the *Public Journal*, Philadelphia, June 18, 1921.

"Eight million Negro voters in this country if properly organized could swing any election," cries the *Bystander* of Des Moines (June 23, 1921). "We must show our strength in state party organizations from this time on," chimes in the *Kansas City Call* (June 18).[1] One of the most American editorials is this one in the *Raleigh* (North Carolina) *Independent*, October 9, 1920. Editor Ben Davis, of Atlanta, perhaps surpasses it in glowing enthusiasm, judging by the latter's hearty song of praise for Georgia;[2] but the Raleigh paper is perhaps more characteristic.

In a recent issue of a little weekly paper known as the "Express" published in Sanford, N.C., there appears an article entitled "Political Gab."

The writer seems to have been charged with much suspicion of the Negro entering politics. We are sorry that a few of our white people still hold to the idea of the "Red Shirts" and unfair means when they think of Negroes' political rights.

We, the proud citizens of North Carolina, feel ourselves capable of voting and when the times comes will show you that our votes will be cast for the good of the country.

The writer said that "Hell will break loose if the white man's power was at least suspected." I am sure that the writer could have expressed his mind in a better way than that.

We acknowledge that this is the white man's state. It is his because he founded it and now dictates affairs.

It is our state because we made it what it is today. We labored with ardent love and uncalculating devotion, for two hundred and fifty six years in this state. And we labored without honor and without pay. The constitution of the United States approves of our rights in the fourteenth and fifteenth amendment, which shall not be denied.

[1] For various state organizations for political action see the *Washington Bee*, October 1, 1921.

[2] *Atlanta Independent*, editorial, February 27, 1921.

With regard to national and international issues of all sorts, the opinions occasionally uttered by the Negro editor are colored by his "race problem." The League of Nations, immigration, the open shop, for instance, are three topics dealt with in the *Christian Recorder* (February 24, 1921) as "Some of the big national questions." The judgment of the editor is against the League, against immigration, and for the open shop. All Negroes would not agree with him on the last issue, but the agreement on the second would be virtually complete, and on the first fairly general. The Irish question is occasionally discussed only for the parallels it furnishes to the Negro question. There is a great interest in the matter of relations with Japan, sympathy for the yellow people being the general tone.[1] One paper hints mysteriously that the main thing to remember, while the nations are quarreling about Yap, is that the island is peopled by dark-skinned inhabitants and Negroes may have a stake in its disposal.[2] Recently there has been a strong interest in Haiti and general condemnation of its treatment by our government. The Associated Negro Press frequently reviews larger national issues in the light of racial demands.

So much for the policy of the Negro press on the race-problem, taking the press as exemplified by the great mass of newspapers throughout the country. They are contending for political and civil rights.

[1] Clippings from the *New York Dispatch*, *Detroit Contender*, *New Era* (Charleston, S.C.)—this last by W. H. A. Moore, of the Associated Negro Press—and the *Guardian* (head reads, "Negroes might take sides with the Japanese in event of war").

[2] *Chicago Whip*, April 30, 1921.

CHAPTER VII

OTHER SOLUTIONS OF THE RACE PROBLEM

There is a small group of Negro magazines in New York making an impression quite out of proportion to their number. Prominent among these is the *Crusader*, which looks from its safe distance on Russia with pleasure and even mentions socialism rather approvingly.[1] The *Challenge*, also of New York, makes fearlessness its selling-point: "It Fears Only God" is its motto. Garveyism is approved by this periodical, national loyalty is interpreted in a radical way, and violent statement is its rule.[2] The *Promoter*, a periodical which was recently issued, partakes somewhat of the tone of the *Crusader*. It is impossible to estimate the number of colored people who read these magazines. The *Crusader* varied in circulation between 23,000 and 37,000 copies during 1920 and went into "nearly every big town in the United States, and many rural communities." This magazine, like the others, and the *Negro World*, cultivates the field for racial propaganda in the West Indies. It prints a letter from Trinidad (January, 1921) telling of government agents who searched homes for the *Negro World*, the *Messenger*, and the *Crusader*, and who carried away the *Promoter* for examination. Apart from the *Messenger*, which must be examined separately, it is hard to distinguish a consistent policy in these publications. When the *Crusader*

[1] April, 1921, pp. 8 ff. [2] June, 1921.

began its work, the purpose was propaganda for "A Free Africa, A Strong Negro State (in Africa or elsewhere, e.g., South America, Haiti, etc.), Instruction in Negro History, etc." Cyril V. Briggs, the editor, is head of the African Blood Brotherhood. The April, 1921, number "invites discussion," but suggests as a basis for it the following program:

Combine the two most likely and feasible propositions, viz.: salvation for all Negroes through the establishment of a strong, stable, independent Negro State (along lines of our own race genius) in Africa or elsewhere; and salvation for all Negroes (as well as other oppressed peoples) through the establishment of a Universal Socialist Co-operative Commonwealth. To us it seems that one working for the first proposition would also be working for the second proposition.

All these magazines are intelligently and ably edited. They show interest in history, in the drama, in music, and in poetry. A vein of radical and undefined protest runs through them all. This is the attitude seen in the declaration of principles of the *Triangle* (March, 1920, Newport, Rhode Island), now defunct:

A Magazine that stands for a new Negro, a new day, a new order of society.

A Magazine that abhors the negative, effeminate stuff that passes for "conservatism."

A Magazine, exponent of neither Bolshevism nor Anarchism, but an advocate of that "Radicalism" which is the father of all true progress.

Similarly, after listening to a street harangue by a young colored man, a white man asked one of the group who seemed to admire the speaker, "What is he—Socialist, I.W.W., or what?" "He is just a radical," seemed to be the only answer. Another member of the crowd was giving his own version of the doctrine:

"Didn't we once have a fellow in that other war—not the Civil War, but the first war,—what was that war?"

"Revolutionary War," suggested another.

"Yes, that's it, the Revolutionary War. Well, in that war, didn't we have a fellow by the name of Chrismus Attucks? and he fought, but he fought the white man's battle.

"Then in the Civil War we fought, but it wasn't our battle; it was somebody else's battle.

"The same way in the Spanish War and the previous war. We always fought somebody else's battle, not our own.

"BY GOD! *Why can't we fight our own battle?*"

A corollary was then supplied by the additional suggestion that we may have arrived at a time when the oppressed of both white and black groups ought to get together.

The *Messenger* has a rather definite program. It is impossible not to know what the *Messenger* stands for. It is radical, its tone is emphatic, its challenge insistent. The editors, Chandler Owen and A. Philip Randolph, propound a socialistic solution for the great "problem" in the form of a reconstruction program, issued as a supplement and called, "The Negro and the New Social Order."[1]

The reconstruction program for the Negro must involve the introduction of the new social order—a democratic order in which human rights are recognized above property rights. We recognize, in sketching, in broad outline, this new order, that there can not be any separate and distinct principles for the social, political and economic emancipation of the Negro which are not applicable to all other people.

[1] Issued near the close of the war.

Suggestions are made under these heads:

Demobilization

Industrial Program—peonage, the company store, tenant farm-
    ing, socio-industrial psychiatry, industrial organization policy,
    child labor, woman labor, equal pay for equal work (white
    and black), equal opportunity, social insurance, co-operative
    movement

Political Program

Social Program—education, public education

Civil Rights—social equality, including intermarriage

Civil Liberties

Legislative and Administrative Invention—suggesting federal
    departments of education, prisons, recreation and amuse-
    ment, health, housing, fuel, munitions, transportation

The Negro and the Cabinet—a Negro representative in every
    department of the government

The New Negro

Peace Terms

The "Political Program," although elaborate, is, in
substance, that which we have already shown the weekly
press to demand. The suggestions for "legislative and
administrative invention" would be called state socialism. The "industrial organization policy" is this:

We recommend that Negro workers join the Union which con-
trols the industry in which they work, whether it be the American
Federation of Labor, the I.W.W. or independent labor organizations, such as, the Amalgamated Clothing Workers of America and
the International Federation of Hotel and Restaurant Workers.

We make this recommendation for this reason: We recognize
the fundamental difference in principle between the A.F. of L.,
the I.W.W. and the A.C.W. of A., I.F. of H. and R.W., yet we
realize that, with regard to the black workers, the issue is chiefly
getting them to understand the value of collective bargaining.
The relative merits of pure and simple unionism and industrial
unionism will assume their places of vantage in their class consciousness as their industrial education proceeds apace.

How thoroughgoing as well as consistent the *Messenger* has been in its underlying principle is seen in the fact that as far back as March, 1919, an article appears headed, "Lynching: Capitalism Its Cause; Socialism Its Cure." That this principle connects itself with what is popularly known as bolshevism is evident from page 8 of the May-June number, 1919: "Soviet government proceeds apace. It bids fair to sweep over the whole world. The sooner the better. On with the dance!" And this: "The time is come for a great mass movement among Negroes. It ought to assume four distinct forms, viz.: labor unions, farmers' protective unions, cooperative business, and socialism."

United with this advocacy of radical socialism is the bitter protest we are already familiar with, the cry for security and rights. A poem is printed (July, 1919) called "The Mob Victim," which describes in stark, hideous detail a lynching, the first lines being:

> And it was in a Christian land,
> With freedom's towers on every hand,
> Where shafts to civic pride arise
> To lift America to the skies.
> And it was on a Sabbath day,
> While men and women went to pray. . . . .

There is a cartoon above the poem with this legend across it,

A GLORIOUS DESECRATION

> Oh say can you see
> By the dawn's early light

and the figure of the victim hanging over a fire, with the flames, smoke, and embers wrought into the likeness of the American flag. Archibald H. Grimke's poem, "Her

Thirteen Black Soldiers," refused by the *Atlantic Monthly*, and even by the *Crisis*, found a welcome on the pages of the *Messenger* (October, 1919). This is a somber invective against the nation, which is held guilty for the fate of the Negro soldiers who rioted at Houston in the summer of 1917. In another issue the new Negro is cartooned as riding in an armored car and shooting down his white opponents in race riots (September, 1919). Nowhere is racial sentiment more strongly expressed. It is the *Messenger* that publishes Claude McKay's "If We Must Die" (September, 1919):

> If we must die, let it not be like hogs
>   Hunted and penned in an inglorious spot,
> While round us bark the mad and hungry dogs,
>   Making their mock at our accursed lot.
> If we must die, oh, let us nobly die,
>   So that our precious blood may not be shed
> In vain; then even the monsters we defy
>   Shall be constrained to honor us, though dead!
>
> Oh, kinsmen! We must meet the common foe;
>   Though far outnumbered let us still be brave,
> And for their thousand blows deal one death-blow!
>   What though before us lies the open grave?
> Like men we'll face the murderous, cowardly pack,
>   Pressed to the wall, dying, but—fighting back!

The *Messenger* attacks all Negroes who are less radical than itself, including Kelly Miller, Emmett J. Scott, Robert R. Moton, Roscoe C. Simmons, even the editor of the *Crisis*, Dr. Du Bois. Because Simmons said in a speech, "I am an American, proud of it and jealous of both the power and reputation of my country and countrymen," the *Messenger* retorts, "Think of a

Negro being proud to be an American!"[1] The editors insist on taking as a compliment and printing as an advertisement the evaluation placed upon the paper by the Department of Justice: "The *Messenger*, the monthly magazine published in New York, is by long odds the most able and most dangerous of all the Negro publications."

The paper was first sold from street corners at the time when Owen and Randolph were conducting Morris Hillquit's mayoralty campaign among the Negroes. A letter says:

On August 4th, 1918, the *Messenger* editors were speaking in Cleveland, Ohio. One of the copies of the *Messenger* had an article entitled—"Pro-Germanism Among Negroes." With the characteristic stupidity of the Department of Justice, they did not understand that the article was satirical and sarcastic, but arrested us, confiscated about 100 copies which we had with us, put us in jail for $2\frac{1}{2}$ days. Within the next two weeks the associate editor, Chandler Owen, was drafted. Second class mailing privileges were, and still are, being denied. . . . .

With respect to circulation, we may say that upon coming from camp, January, 1919, we immediately published 10,000 copies which went very rapidly; then 12,000, increasing to 15,000 . . . . and 26,000, which is the highest circulation . . . . its readers are about $\frac{1}{3}$ white and $\frac{2}{3}$ colored. . . . .[2]

Those, both white and black, who are interested in radical labor are probably the ones who buy this publication. What success the periodical has in promoting Negro labor organization can be set over against the fact that the large majority of Negro workers are still unorganized and very few are found in the ranks of the I.W.W.

[1] P. 25, December, 1919.   [2] Letter bears date of March 19, 1921.

There are other papers that show some interest in the labor problem. The *New York Dispatch* speaks out thus (May 27, 1921):

The problems for our leaders to solve are, first, how to insure to every colored person, able and willing to work, an opportunity to earn an honest livelihood. Second, to effect a better or larger distribution of the wealth of the nation created in the sweat of colored men's faces. All other problems pale into insignificance.

Two news weeklies, the (Birmingham) *Times-Plain Dealer* and the (Memphis) *Western World Reporter*, are representatives of the active Railway Men's International Benevolent Industrial Association. A few other organization papers exist. Others here and there realize that labor conditions enter into the race problem. Labor unionism is discussed, some articles advocate membership, some still stand for the open shop, some endeavor to suit their advice to time and circumstance, while others again point out the difficulties that organized white laborers present to the further organization of Negroes. The American Federation of Labor declared in 1910[1] for inviting colored men into unions; but Negroes resent the fact that the local and international bodies affiliated with the general Federation have not freely followed this policy. The *New York Age* says (July 2, 1917), quoting Samuel Gompers at Denver, "The American Federation of Labor has previously declared that it is the duty of all workers to organize regardless of sex, nationality, race, political belief or color. The Federation, however, cannot force this view upon individual or affiliated unions without their consent."

[1] *Negro Year Book*, p. 341.

One of the most striking attempts to solve the problem of the Negro by economic organization was the Progressive Farmers' and Household Union, which was made to bear the blame for the riots near Elaine, Arkansas, late in 1919. The *Arkansas Gazette* (white) published at Little Rock, is authority for the following description and quotations (October 10, 1919). This Union circulated considerable pamphlet literature among the colored farmers and tenants. In particular the words of a song, to be sung to the tune of "Maryland, My Maryland," came to the notice of the *Gazette:*

> Ye farmers of this mighty land,
>   Organize, oh, organize!
> Its bulwark evermore to stand—
>   Organize, oh, organize!
> For with the flag of right unfurled,
> In spite of darts against you hurled,
> You still must free this hungry world—
>   Organize, oh, organize!
>
> If you would come into your own,
>   Organize, oh, organize!
> Or be forever overthrown,
>   Organize, oh, organize!
> Yes, everywhere throughout this land
> The tillers of the soil must stand
> And be a firm united band—
>   Organize, oh, organize!
>
> To firmly stand against each wrong,
>   Organize, oh, organize!
> Your only hope is union strong—
>   Organize, oh, organize!
> To break the bonds of slavery
> That bind you now from sea to sea
> And from oppression to be free,
> Organize, oh, organize!

> Your calling was the first on earth—
>   Organize, oh, organize!
> And ever since has proved its worth—
>   Organize, oh, organize!
> Then come, ye farmers, good and true;
> The die is cast—it's up to you—
>   [line omitted?]
>   Organize, oh, organize!

Among the circulars one has sentences like these:

The time is at hand that all men, all nations and tongues must receive a just reward!

This union wants to know why it is that the laborers cannot control their just earnings which they work for. Some of the leading business merchants and authorities are saying we are pleading the right cause and due consideration.

There are many of our families suffering because our men are forced to act as children. . . . .

Remember the Holy Word, when the Almighty took John upon the mountain and commanded him to look, and asked John what he saw, and John said, "I see all nations and tongues coming up before God."

Now, we are a nation and a tongue. Why should we be cut off from fair play? Hear us, O God, hear us!

We only ask every negro man for $1.50 for joining fees, women, 50c.

Write Box 31, Winchester, Ark.

And we will come down and set up a lodge among you. Get 15 men and 12 women. We will set you up together.

In the application blank for membership an affirmative answer seems to be expected to the following questions:

Did you register for war?

Do you obey the laws at all times?

Do you believe in court?

Will you defend this government and the constitution at all times?

This prayer follows: "God grant that all men will be equal in Thy sight and the sight of men."

To many leading Negroes "the economic way out" would suggest things quite different from the foregoing. The term generally means: Invest in property, get into business, accumulate wealth, and thus attain a standing that will be independent of your racial status. This would not be considered a satisfactory entire program by most editors. The radicals criticize Booker T. Washington on this point: the Negroes that have gained wealth and ability have not escaped but only intensified racial prejudice, and hence this by itself still leaves a "race problem." The "radical" editor now urges the economic advance but would supplement this by agitation for rights. One of the more conservative editors, Dr. R. R. Wright, in the *Christian Recorder* (April 28, 1921) states his view of "the economic way out":

While we did not get a civil rights bill in the State of Pennsylvania, there is no cause for discouragement. One of the reasons given for not giving the colored man civil rights was that it would invade the social life of the white people. Many, even good white people, seem to think that the Negro wants what they call "social equality." The other side of the question is that we must build up our own institutions, we must build the basis of a firm and respectable society among us. We must build up our people in education, in business and in all the fine things of life. We must provide our own hotels and club houses, and other places of entertainment, labor and amusement, in order that as far as possible we may take care of our own group. The more this is done the more people will see that it is not so-called social equality that we want, but that we are able more and more to take care of ourselves. We will get more respect in all hotels, in moving picture houses, etc., when it is known that we have our own. We will get more accommodations in white banks and trust companies when we are known to have our own. So that the real big work to be done is not to work so much in getting a law upon the statute books of the state as it is getting hold of the social, political and economical resources of our community in order that we may build firmly and solidly the kind of manhood and womanhood that will make the finest kind of American citizenship. At best, a civil rights bill would have protected us legally in the things we are able to maintain economically. The civil rights bill, as equitable and just as it was, would have solved nothing. If we should put half as much energy in developing our economic resources as we have in agitating for a civil rights bill, we would carry ourselves far ahead. But we have not yet learned to organize economically. Hence we are the playthings of the politicians.

The nationalist movement is represented almost entirely by the United Negro Improvement Association and African Communities League, of which the moving spirit is Marcus Garvey and the official organ, the *Negro World*. As has been noted there are other voices calling for a Negro state, such as that heard in the *Crusader*, and there are occasional articles in newspapers indicating possibilities for Negroes in Africa and other parts of the world. But in the *Negro World*[1] we have the real propaganda for a "free Africa."[2] Yet with all the writing and

[1] The *Voice*, at Buffalo, New York, is a weekly organ of the local organization of the U.N.I.A.

[2] Representatives of the movement acknowledge the articles published in the *World's Work* (December, 1920, and January, 1921) as authentic history, while Du Bois in the *Crisis* (same dates) has written a critical account from the viewpoint of one who disapproves. *Current Opinion* (March, 1921) and the *Independent* (February 26, 1921) also have something to say about the movement. This and the "Pan-African Congress" fostered by W. E. B. Du Bois are not only distinct from each other but mutually hostile. The Congress "has nothing to do with any 'Africa for the Africans' movement," says Du Bois (*New York Age*, June 25, 1921).

talking it is difficult to find in the literature on the subject any clear statement of its aims. The following points seem to stand out:

Protest against the wrongs of the Negro both in America, including the West Indies, and Africa.

Summons to all Negroes of the world (counted as 400,000,000) to unite, pooling their grievances and their energies, so as to become, in some sense at least, a nation.

Project of making Africa free from the white man's dominion and open to all blacks as a home and refuge. This does not mean to get all the blacks of the world into Africa: that is not thought of as immediately practicable.

In the meantime to stimulate economic independence on the part of Negroes wherever they are, and to link their economic advance with the fortunes of Africa. Hence the Black Star Line, the Negro Factories Corporation, the Ethiopian Engineering Association and so on.

Perhaps the last of these points is the main objective. The general betterment of the Negro lot in localities where he now dwells may be the attractive force for some. Doubtless others are drawn to the organization because of its value in stimulating racial solidarity. In Du Bois' words in the *Crisis:*

What he is trying to say and do is this: American Negroes can, by accumulating and ministering their own capital, organize industry, join the black centers of the south Atlantic by commercial enterprise and in this way ultimately redeem Africa as a fit and free home for black men.

While the first steps in this program may be said to date from 1914, when the Negro Improvement Society was launched in Jamaica, it is only in the last two or three years that it has attracted attention in the United

States. Even today the *Negro World*, judging from the letters from readers, gets a large part of its support in the West Indies. We know, too, that the Negro population of New York, where the movement is at home, has been largely augmented by arrivals from the West Indies since the days of the war. Northern cities in the United States certainly have heard of the organization, as their press reflects the activities of Garvey followers, sometimes favorably, sometimes adversely.

It is difficult to give an adequate idea of the enthusiasm and rainbow-tinted outlook that any casual reader must discern in the *Negro World*. The fifty-four articles in which the policy sketched above is outlined[1] are called the "Declaration of Independence of the Negro Race." There are reports of gorgeous processions, solemn Easter services, powerful sermons, flowing robes and a flag of red, green, and black. Accounts of new branches organized are constantly coming in. A large part of the news in the official organ is made up of speeches. Of these Garvey's are the most striking. Here are some of his sentences:[2]

We are going to build up in Africa a government of our own, big enough and strong enough to protect Africa and Negroes anywhere.

Here you have three men, one white, one black, one yellow, all came into the world at one and the same time. The white man has guns and swords, daggers and other implements and keeps them with him; the yellow man does the same, and this

[1] *Negro World*, September 11, 1920, reporting a convention in Liberty Hall, in August of that year. The convention lasted the entire month, and called itself "the first international convention of the Negro people of the world." There were conventions also in 1921 and 1922.

[2] Speech in Chicago: see *Negro World*, February 12, 1921.

foolish black man stands up in the middle—between these two men—with two bare hands. You must realize that you are flirting with your own future, your destiny, and your race. . . . . What is the idea of Japan having a big navy? The idea is to protect the rights of the yellow man in Asia. The nations of Europe have navies to protect the rights of the white man in Europe. Negroes, the time has come for you to make and create a nation of Africa and have the greatest army and navy in the world.

Africa must be redeemed. There is no doubt about it, it is no camouflage. The Universal Negro Improvement Association is organizing now, and there is going to be some dying later on. We are not organizing to fight against or disrespect the government of America, I say this plainly and for everybody to hear—we are organizing to drive every pale-face out of Africa. [Applause.] Do you know why? Because Africa is mine; Africa is the land of my fathers; and what my fathers never gave to anybody else, since they did not will it to anybody, must have been for me. . . . . Some of you turn up your noses against the Africa of Africans. Africa was the land from whence our fore-parents were brought three hundred years ago into this Western Hemisphere. They did not probably know what the consequences would be. But that God who rules, that God who sees and knows, he had his plan when he inspired the Psalmist to write: "Princes shall come out of Egypt, and Ethiopia shall stretch forth her hand unto God."

If anybody should be a radical it should be the Negro. We are not radicals, even though some men think that we are. The I.W.W. are radicals, and so are some Socialists; but they are white people, so let them "raise Cain" and do what they please. We have no time with them; we have all the time with four hundred million Negroes. . . . . So, please understand that Marcus Garvey is no I.W.W.; he doesn't even know what it means; he is no anarchist, as far as Western civilization is concerned; but if anarchism means that you have to drive out somebody and sometimes kill somebody, to get that which belongs to you, then when I get to Africa I am going to be an anarchist.

If it is right for the white man and the yellow man to rule in their respective domains, it is right for the black man to rule in his own domain. Remaining here you will never have a black man as president of the United States; you will never have a black Premier of Great Britain; you need not waste time over it. I am going to use all my time to establish a great republic in Africa for four hundred million Negroes, so that one day if I desire to be president, I can throw my hat in the ring and run as a candidate for the presidency.

The United Negro Improvement Association and African Communities League are not to be looked upon as having great political or international significance on account of the absence of ways and means to political power as well as the lack of recognition by political units now in Africa.[1] The organization is rather a nationalistic movement bearing the characteristics of a religious revival and including an effort toward economic independence. Sometimes one of these aspects is stressed and sometimes another. It is the economic phase for example that appears in this advertisement (February 26, 1921):

If Negroes during the time of prosperity had subscribed the $10,000,000 capital of the Black Star Line we would today have at least twenty large ocean going ships, and we would be able to ship at least 5,000 unemployed Negroes from America and other parts every week during these hard times.

The emphasis on nationality seems generally to be uppermost.

The following are illustrative expressions used by Garvey himself in various speeches reported in the *Negro World* (July 30, 1921).

[1] A disclaimer by the Liberian Secretary of State is printed in the *New York Age*, July 16, 1921.

You will understand that the U.N.I.A.'s programme is nowhere different from that of George Washington when he attempted, about 140 years ago, to form his own government and throw off the British yoke. He laid the foundation for a Republic which has become the greatest in the world today. I am determined that with the help of God I will lay a foundation for the Negro race.

Touch the Englishman anywhere about the spirit of his race and he will stand up and die in defense of his empire. Touch the Frenchman and the American and they will all die in defense of their countries. Touch the Negro and there will be no responsive chord. He dies for no flag or country that is his own. But soon 400,000,000 Negroes of the world will demand what is theirs by God's help.

Africa can only be won through sacrifice, through blood. All of us will not die. Whether I die here tonight, or in the West Indies, or any part of the world, I will die for the aims and objects of the U.N.I.A. and A.C.L., and in the cause of Africa; whether I die in jail, on the gallows, or by the guillotine, in whatsoever way I die, I will die for the freedom of Africa.

I appeal to you men to give your support to the U.N.I.A.; the propaganda that we teach is not mere sentiment; death may be the price of leadership. Look at the long line of martyrs. Let us take the history of Ireland; for the last seven hundred years Ireland has been bleeding for her freedom. I repeat again the words of Patrick Henry, the patriot, "I care not what others may say, give me liberty or give me death."

They talk about the New York 15th; that was only an experiment in warfare. [Cheers.] They talk about the Illinois 8th; that was only a pastime for the boys. They talk about the prowess of the West Indian regiments; those fellows were only having a picnic; it was a gala day. No man has ever yet seen the Negro fighting at his best, because the Negro has never yet fought for himself. [Loud and prolonged cheers.]

Here stands a Negro who is black, and who would never care to change it. God made me for a purpose. . . . . We can't all go to Africa; we will leave the black-white man, the brown-white man, the yellow-white man, and the aristocrat Negro when we go to Africa. I would rather be in Africa with my Prince Albert coat—no, by that time we will have another name for the coat [laughter], my gold-headed cane, my bell top, walking down the African boulevards than anywhere else in the world.

Let us not lose hope; have courage, there is great work in store for us. Let me ask you to do the best you can for the Black Star Line; buy bonds in the Liberian Construction Loan. When we go to Africa we will need doctors, lawyers, preachers and teachers also. By that time we will also have a language of our own.

A large amount of space in the *Negro World* is taken up with huge advertisements of the subsidiary corporations. The absence of statements of financial condition and of banking references does not seem to hinder the success of this appeal, although there have been occasional financial reports. There are also advertisements of a "Catechism for instruction to our people in new Religious Knowledge, Racial History, the U.N.I.A. and the Declaration of Rights," the price being thirty cents. Along with this a "Universal Negro Ritual" is spoken of. The religious note is stressed in the motto, "One God, One Aim, One Destiny," and the place for the meetings of the order is often a church. One finds also, in the advertising, notices to beware of "fakers" ostensibly collectors for the U.N.I.A. Another advertisement offers for sale flags and banners of the red, black, and green, "an assortment of photo post-cards of each of the executive officials," and

Photo Medallions beautifully finished of the Hon. Marcus Garvey, the Potentate; Dr. J. D. Gordon, Miss Henrietta Vinton Davis, Rev. Dr. McGuire, and Dr. W. H. Eason, in Pontifical

Robes, as he appeared at the International Convention. Medallions emblazoned in the Red, Black and Green, unbreakable work by our colored artist, at $2 each for double and $1.75 for single portraits.

Much space is given to letters received. These are generally full of enthusiasm for the movement. One from Brunswick, Georgia, runs like this:

Please permit us a place in the *Negro World* to exclaim and proclaim to the world the good done us. Oh! for the wonderful work wrought in the city of Brunswick, Ga., in the shortest month of the year, the month of February, 1921, by our Hon. Dr. Eason and Sec. Prof. Prendergast. When these marvelous and powerful men came to us they found us because of the want of race consciousness, race pride and true religion, because of the want of stronger faith, stronger hope, and charity in God and in ourselves, to do something real, something necessary and wonderful, they found us practically dead, but with stern personality, strong determination, and Christ-like spirit to conquer though they die, they are, we are proud to say, living, and we, the members of the Sixty-seventh Division, Brunswick, Ga., are proud to be able to say that these men have wrought into us new life, new inspiration, and new aspiration. . . . .[1]

Adulation of Garvey goes to great lengths, for "Bruce Grit" can liken him to Jesus.[2] W. H. Ferris, the editor, likens him to St. Patrick. The use of the term "Jesus," in a bit of contributed poetry (July 30, 1921) is peculiarly enlightening, indicating as it does the strong religious sentiment involved in the use of Garvey's name. The verse comes from a reader in Cuba.

[1] Issue for March 26, 1921.

[2] Rather than "Negro Moses" a better name would be "Negro Messiah," as a sobriquet for Garvey. There are parallels with Jewish Messianism here. The appellations mentioned in the text are from the *Negro World*, March 26 and April 2, 1921.

While Garvey's spirit bid you come,
Sinner do not longer wait,
'Less you seal your hopeless doom,
    Be in time.

Time is gliding swiftly by,
Death and judgment draweth nigh,
To the arms of Jesus fly,
    Be in time.

Oh, I pray you count the cost,
Ere the fatal line is crossed,
And your soul in hell be lost,
    Be in time.

Sinners, heed the warning voice of Garvey,
Make Garvey your final choice on earth,
Then all African sons and daughters will rejoice,
    Be in time.

Come from darkness into light,
Come let Garvey make you right,
Come and start for Africa tonight,
    Be in time.

Indeed one of the most arresting features of the *Negro World* is the poetry contributed by the readers.   Lucian B. Watkins is the author of several such poems; but most of the "poetry" is of little literary value.   The writers seem to have experienced a new birth in dedicating themselves to the great cause.   Here we might find grounds for the assertion that there was already a great sentiment existing in Negro minds which needed only to be touched into flame by the man, Marcus Garvey. Ethel Drew Dunlap, of Chicago, who sometimes, after an uplifting meeting of the local U.N.I.A., would go home and put her emotions into verse, is a very frequent contributor. This catches the attention (*Negro World*, April 30, 1921):

> Come out from behind the flag
>   And show us you're for the free,
> We know by the way you treat
>   The captive from over the sea.
>
> . . . .
>
> Come out from behind the flag,
>   If you hate men that are black,
> Don't cover wrath with the stripes
>   In order to hide your lack.
>
> . . . .
>
> Come out from behind the flag,
>   Garvey is waiting for you,
> He's black, and if you're not right
>   You certainly will be blue.

O. M. Skinner contributes the following (April 23, 1921):

> O Africa, sweet Africa!
>   The land so rich and fair,
> I want to see thy sunny shores
>   And feel thy acrid air.
> I want to place my feet
>   Upon thy golden soil,
> To enjoy the warmth of tropics sweet
>   And share in all thy spoil.
>
> O Africa, sweet Africa!
>   I am in love with thee
> And all my soul's desire's
>   To see thy liberty,
> To see thy sons and daughters
>   Enjoy their bounteous store,
> And all that are thy fathers'
>   Be theirs for evermore.

O Africa, sweet Africa!
How can my soul be free
When thou art fooled and robbed by those
Who stung thee like a bee?
My spirit sinks within,
My feeble body shakes
To know the grossful sin
Of what they give and take.

O Africa, sweet Africa!
All Negroes turn to thee,
All thoughts are centered on thy cares,
And how long can it be
Before thy thrones and places,
Kidnapped by thievish men,
Be given thy princes and princesses,
So innocent and clean?

O Africa, sweet Africa!
The time will come some day,
And all the world shall hail thee
In spite of all they say,
Thy sons shall lift their heads
Above the present tide,
Shall see just why the Savior shed
His precious blood and died.

For Ethiopia's calling,
She's stretching forth her hand,
While Pharaoh's hosts still ruling
Are scattered through the land.
But God has raised a Moses
Who takes the word of cheer,
Hurrah! The time approaches,
Redemption day is near.

The triumph of the "chosen people" seems to be identified here with the triumph of Christianity. If taken as
a symbol or collective representation of group spirit,

"Africa" seems to have been a word in season. Sometimes instead of Africa as a whole, the apostrophe is to Abyssinia, or some other division of the continent.

> My heart is over the sea
>   In Abyssinia's land.
> And, when my fancy is free,
>   I sail for its beautiful strand.

Thus begins another poem (in the *Citizens Advocate*, Los Angeles, February 26, 1921). And Nathaniel Charles Miller of "Savannah, Ga., R.F.D. No. 2, Box 45," thrills to the theme of "The Black Star Line" (*Negro World*, April 2, 1921).

> Sail on, O glorious ships,
>   O'er rough and tempest seas!
> O brave and gallant men
>   That man these ships with ease!
> . . . .
>
> Sail on, staunch ships,
>   Over the seven seas!
> May your flags unfurled aloft
>   Never cease to weave!
> May we some day on Africa's soil
>   Garner in our sheaves.

The *Negro World* has contributions in one issue (March 12, 1921) bearing the following headings: "The Ethiopian as Viewed by the Bible," "The Pyramids of Egypt," "Negro Nationalism." The writer of the last feels that his experience has been a conversion and writes, "As a Negro born anew in spirit, I say, let us forget our grievances and petty jealousies toward one another and work unitedly for the dawn of a brighter day." The same experience in different form has evidently been the lot of the other two writers. The first of these, who signs his name as usual, but says in his first sentence, "I truly hope that this will not be considered anonymous," argues against the use of medallions and pictures by the U.N.I.A. The other letter, that on the pyramids, says,

It has been my good fortune, dear sir, to have discovered the real purpose of the erection of the great Pyramid and Sphinx of Egypt, and the disclosure is a noble indication of the genius of the Negro race.

These monuments constitute the earliest reliable records of the doctrine of the atonement and the advent of a redeemer. Not merely this, but in the astrological calculations . . . . are recorded the exact time and place of the birth of the redeemer. The time is yet to come, and the redeemer in question is of the Negro race. . . . .

In the interest of truth, therefore, dear Mr. Ferris, I offer to submit for publication in your paper a special article upon this most interesting subject. I seek no compensation. . . . .

No doubt the strong group sentiment aroused by this movement, and the evident awakening of race-consciousness, make it possible for editors who disagree with Garvey to congratulate the race upon his organization. The newspapers are not all friends of the movement, but neither are they all as curt as the *Charlottesville Messenger* (March 19, 1921):

The back of [*sic*] Africa advocates never seem to take into consideration the fact that this country is ours, and that nothing can be done which will result in our wholesale removal to Africa or any other country. We are here to stay.

Du Bois, in the *Crisis*, points out the dangers of the U.N.I.A. Several papers print news of the movement ("Garvey Movement Spreading in Spite of Severe

Criticism," *Dallas Express*, March 26, 1921). A curious comment is made in the *Michigan State News*,[1] which refers to the *Chicago Whip* as having called Garvey the race's first "great man," although not itself indorsing his movement. This the *State News* calls "the groping masses' growing desire for a great flag and country of their own"; but goes on to say, "Garveyism may be a menace or a mania—it possibly and probably is both." The failure of the Negro press to adopt a tone of consistent hostility to the Universal Negro Improvement Association may suggest that possibly a large number of its readers are well disposed toward that organization.

Side-eddies in this current exist. The interest in Liberia may grow independently of Garvey though nourished by his efforts. "A society of engineers plans to develop Liberia," announces the *Brooklyn and Long Island Informer* (April 9, 1921). "The Independent Industrial League of North America, South America and Mexico held a meeting recently at Wewoka, Oklahoma, to encourage colored people to locate in Mexico," reads the *Beaumont* (Texas) *Monitor* (February 19, 1921). "Garvey's Assistant Endorses Lower California Movement," says the *New Age* (Los Angeles, March 25, 1921)—the object being "a liberation settlement in Lower California." The Associated Negro Press sent out a note originating in Rio Janeiro, Brazil, and containing the sentence: "This historical fact is pointed out as good and sufficient reason why Negroes from the States should settle in this part of Brazil." Brazil is often mentioned in the Negro press. A long article in the *Denver Star*, April 23, 1921, headed "The American

[1] Date of clipping lost.

Negro in the Far East," sets forth the inducements of the Philippines.

In the preceding chapter four solutions of the race problem were mentioned as indicating the types of policy generally represented by Negro periodicals. Three of these have now been considered. The fourth, however, cannot be so clearly stated. It is intended to give merely a glimpse of other thoughts that prevail among colored writers, thoughts that are as various almost as the individuals, and yet in general look toward the lessening of struggle. There is the "too-proud-to-fight" attitude, the advice to other Negroes to get their minds off the race struggle and upon some practical advancement, and even a movement that calls for forgiveness and friendly reconciliation. Most important, however, may be a movement that belongs in this class because it seeks in immediate, pragmatic ways to lessen the race conflict. This is the organization of inter-racial committees for practical local co-operation.

These inter-racial committees are being formed throughout several states and countries of the South. As a rule the Negro press favors the plan. There is suspicion in certain quarters, some saying with the *Crisis* (May, 1921) that the Negroes must not name any "pussy-footers" on committees. The *New York Dispatch* does not believe in these organizations, judging by the following:

The public is growing impatient with that class of Colored men and women who attend joint conferences, take off the hat, coats, wraps and rubbers for white members of committees, and then come to us and pose as great. Co-operation? Yes, any time, anywhere, with anybody, or any movement which tends for a development of our full manhood rights—but to walk between the huge legs of inordinate wealth and exchange honorable opportunity and manhood for positions—N-o, a thousand N-o-e-s.

There does not seem to be any southern paper that actively opposes the plan. The *Black Dispatch* (Oklahoma City) is an ardent supporter of it, as also the *East Tennessee News* (Knoxville), the Birmingham papers, and the *Houston Informer* which is as aggressive as any. The *Charleston New Era* (July 23, 1921) presents a cartoon in which an arm called "Inter-racial Commission," is watering a plant called, "Friendly Race Relations," by means of a watering-pot that bears the legend, "Mutual Interest, Frank Discussion of Conditions." The *New Age* of Los Angeles (April 15, 1921) prints Mrs. Drusilla Dunjee Houston's words on the subject.

The appointment of these commissions over the South, to study the relations between the races and to help bring them to equitable adjustment, is the most hopeful sign in fifty years of reaching a true solution of the Negro problem. Fifty-five years ago the SOUTH BY FORCE, was compelled to give up her slaves. Had the powerful logic of Clay, Webster, and Calhoun been used upon the crying subject of human slavery, this nation today need not be reaping the whirlwind of hate, because we forced the South to do what she might have been *won* to do. The day has passed for compromise.

The work that Clay, Webster, and Calhoun failed to do lies before us. We need pass no more laws compelling the South to justice, that is not the wisest way. *Sentiment is stronger than law.* The Inter-Racial Commissions must change this sentiment. Today, the heart of not only the South but of the average American is turned from the Negro by *calumny*. A spirit of justice can only be won for him by the *truth*. The sword of truth is the only weapon given us by the Master.

This movement is young, however, and its youth explains why it has not yet won a more hearty response from many influential members of the press. A pronouncement by the Federal Council of Churches looking in somewhat the same direction as this movement is commented on by James Weldon Johnson in the *New York Age* (July 23, 1921) in such a way as to suggest that success will come "*if*"—that is, if the organization will work honestly for justice.[1] Judging by an editorial in the number for May 21 of the same year, the *Chicago Defender* is cautious on the subject, not being willing to believe that southern white men are in earnest when it comes to the real grievances of the Negro.

Occasionally one comes upon a Negro paper that has made it a policy to stay out of the race conflict and minimize the problem. Perhaps this is one way to lessen the tension of struggle. The *Phoenix* (Arizona) *Tribune*, for instance (June 4, 1921), says:

Again we wish to express our thanks to the white as well as to the colored people, for the loyal support they are giving the *Tribune* in the form of subscriptions and advertising. We are a firm believer in the divine injunction: "Whatsoever A Man Soweth, That Shall He Also Reap," and accordingly we have tried to keep the columns of this paper free from those articles that would antagonize one group or the other. Our policy is to be fair and impartial and, in consequence, we number today among our subscribers and patrons as many people of the white race as among our own people. Every day brings requests from some member of the white race to be placed on our mailing list. And, too, our own people seem to appreciate the *Tribune* now more than ever. We had no idea that conservatism in journalism would pay such big dividends, notwithstanding, we adopted it as our policy and have no regrets.

[1] The *St. Luke Herald* (Richmond, Virginia) in its issue of June 4, 1921, evinces a similar attitude.

It is not strange that a paper will adopt a careful policy in some parts of the South. Letters from publishers to this writer tell of the difficulty in getting papers delivered to subscribers in case the surrounding white population thinks the paper radical.

A unique publication is the *Cotton Farmer*, published ostensibly by the "tenants of the Delta Pine Land Company," a concern that operates eighteen plantations in Mississippi. There is a committee of reporters on each plantation to keep in touch with the editor. The syndicate under which the tenants work is praised in this periodical, and white people are mentioned with gratitude. The motto is: "Labor overcomes all things—everybody work." "School teachers or preachers not willing to work and who think themselves above working in the field, are a positive injury to the race" (July 9, 1921). There is news from the welfare activities of the syndicate, "Base Ball Games" vying for space with "Better Babies." Someone writes, "The Syndicate certainly looks out for the welfare of each and every tenant regardless of circumstances. . . . . It is a real *father and mother to the tenantry*." Apparently this organ is also interested in lessening the race conflict.

A remarkable attitude toward the racial difficulties remains to be noticed. It is summed up in the word "reconciliation," and found in Fenton Johnson's *Favorite Magazine* (Chicago). Johnson has given us his autobiography through a letter to the *New York Tribune*.

What is the remedy when one has spent all he had in the world, $10,000, in trying to solve the race problem through the doctrine of co-operation of the races, and finds himself with only

$30 in the bank, a wife whom he loves above everything else, and the magazine that he edits, that has never brought a cent? Does it pay to work for humanity?

And in literature I have published three volumes of verse, two of prose, contributed to *Poetry* and other magazines, have been in nearly all anthologies and have honorable mention from *Poetry* for 1918—but no income from literature.[1]

In his magazine, he has been seeking to establish this "Reconciliation Movement."

[It] aims to enlist on its side the best social settlement workers of both races whose hearts will be in the work for no mercenary gain but for the sole purpose of building up a greater America and a more happy and contented people. . . . .

It is the aim of the movement for "the reconciliation of the races" to institute Sunday afternoon clubs which are to be operated through a social settlement and a vigorous system of propaganda. At these meetings the ablest white and colored speakers are to lecture on the subject of "reconciliation." . . . .[2]

The editor of the *Richmond* (Indiana) *Blade*, another poet, thinks that the colored race must be one of great promise because even after Tulsa it forgives (*Blade*, July 1, 1921). Fenton Johnson speaks[3] for this quality (whether indeed it be a racial gift or not) in his poem, "A Prayer for Our Enemies."

ALMIGHTY FATHER I am praying for my enemies!

Almighty Father lift up my enemies.

Almighty Father be as honeycomb to my enemies.

Almighty Father be to my enemies as the moon to the young
    lovers in the June of life.

Almighty Father be to my enemies as the voice of Gabriel laughing
    in the Heavens.

Almighty Father be to my enemies as the smiling face of God.

[1] Quoted by the *Brooklyn and Long Island Informer*, May 14, 1921.

[2] Issue for autumn, 1920.   [3] *Ibid.*

ALMIGHTY FATHER be to my enemies as the Song of Israel when the hosts assembled for the evening.

Almighty Father be to my enemies as the breath of the Holy One.

Almighty Father be to my enemies as the Day is to the soul of the wayward child.

Almighty Father be to my enemies as the Light is in the night of despair.

Almighty Father be to my enemies as the love of a Christian for the Church of God.

Almighty Father deal with the white South as I would have you deal with those who hate me for they know not what they do.

Amen.

It must be evident, now, that these variant voices may produce discord within the group. How do the leaders of the race harmonize? How does the whole group get itself integrated?

Discord does exist. The voices jangle. Race leaders appear in the press as disputants of each others' abilities, motives, and policies. The *Hopkinsville* (Kentucky) *New Age* (February 5, 1921) defends the honor of the orator, Roscoe Conkling Simmons, one who stands for as much co-operation with the whites as possible. But Simmons attacks Marcus Garvey. So for that matter do many others: Garvey has more enemies than friends among the race leaders. The *Crusader* (July, 1920), the *Crisis*, and various newspapers[1] have disputed his attempt to represent all the Negroes of the nation and of the world, his apparent commercialism, his back-to-Africa program. But the *Negro World* is an able defender. Choice literary invective, giving hints of having been written by the scholarly W. H. Ferris,

[1] Instances: *Kansas City Sun* (J. Dallas Bowser) of March 19, 1921, and *St. Luke Herald*, May 28, 1921.

appears as, for example, under the caption, "Roscoe Conkling Simmons Brays Again" (November 27, 1921). An outstanding opponent of Garvey is Du Bois, whose Pan-African Congress has itself been discounted by other leaders.[1]   One newspaper attacks Du Bois because he does not recognize that Garvey is doing a great thing for group consciousness, although this paper disagrees with Garvey.[2]   Fenton Johnson in his magazine (January, 1921) points out further failings of Du Bois, in that the latter has attacked not only Moton—as was to be expected—but even Emmett J. Scott, "blaming him," says Johnson, "for everything that happened in the army." The newspaper just referred to prints, with evident approval, Du Bois' criticism of the Chicago Commission on Race Relations appointed by Governor Lowden after the 1919 riots. This Commission had colored members who were suspected of not standing up strongly for their group. While the newspapers carry a great deal of the propaganda issued by the National Association for the Advancement of Colored People, it is interesting to see that this organization too is sometimes spoken of disparagingly.[3]   On the other hand one is likely to happen next upon a letter in the *New York Age* "Readers' Forum" (April 16, 1921) defending that body and decrying the National Race Congress.   Finally, the *Messenger* (March, 1921), speaking of the refusal of "white capitalists" to support the Y.W.C.A., because of its industrial program, characterizes wholesale a goodly number of leaders:

[1] *New York Age*, June 18, July 23, 1921.

[2] *Chicago Whip*, January 15, 1921.

[3] *East Tennessee News*, March 17, 1921.

The ignoramuses who edit most of the Negro papers, the pedagogical poltroons who teach history in most Negro colleges, the pigmy-minded preachers who infest many of the Negro churches, the political prostitutes who ply their trade for petty gain, the social work yeggmen who fatten off the bodies of human derelicts, the vast army of me-too-boss Negro leaders who bask in the beams of white financial bosses—may well give attention to this attitude toward chiefly white girls by the so-called best and richest white people. . . . . But how can leaders learn who are enthralled by financial latch-strings!

That this situation as a whole is decidedly unsatisfactory to the people is evident, and one often reads an article calling on the leaders and organizations to get together. Yet acute differences serve the purpose of making the whole matter of a race policy an interesting one. They keep the great cause alive and the whole people alert. It is possibly a logical and necessary part of the process a group must go through in integrating its ideas or "making up its mind."

Meanwhile there is a fair amount of concord on a few things. Already some sentiments and ideals may be discerned disengaging themselves from the welter of the discussion and coming gradually into wider and wider acceptance. The group-idea itself is one of these. Looking through the window of the Negro press we see the growth of solidarity. If an individual Negro makes a success in the world it is credited not only to him but to the group. This is the constant newspaper policy and it is what the individual expects. If a Negro experiences some distress at the hands of the white man he at once gets it into the papers, if possible, and the race makes the matter its own. Successful business men cause business advancement to become a definite ideal: the whole group unites on this. Successful students raise the banner of education. So in art, in music, in drama, in literature. And the process is one that is accelerated, if not partly made possible, by the existence of the press, the common looking-glass before which all strive to see and be seen.

Not only for this reason, but also because the colored people take an interest in their papers as literature and the papers often contain Negro poetry, some attention should be given to the more significant poems recently current. Kerlin says in his *Contemporary Poetry of the Negro:*

A people's poetry affords the most serious subject of study to those who would understand that people—that people's soul, that people's status, that people's potentialities. A people that is producing poetry is not perishing, but is astir with life, with vital impulses, with life-giving visions. . . . . Poetry, I say, is perhaps the most potent and significant expression of the reborn soul of the Negro in this our day.[1]

Where indeed is there a better statement of the things agreed on by this greatly striving people than the poem standing at the head of this chapter? It is the voice of "the new Negro." On the other hand if one wants an expression of the bitter, fighting-back spirit, the spirit fanned into flame by the post-war riots, one must take not simply the more careful line of Georgia Douglass Johnson—

> Spurn the handicap that binds you, taking what the
> world denies,[2]

but the two poems that have been printed again and again on newspaper pages. I refer to Claude McKay's

[1] *Hampton Bulletin*, February, 1921.

[2] In "The Question," *Crisis*, August, 1919.

"If We Must Die," quoted above, and Carita Owens Collins' "This Must Not Be."[1]

> This must not be!
> The time is past when black men,
> Laggard sons of Ham,
> Shall tamely bow and weakly cringe
> In servile manner, full of shame.
>
> Lift up your heads!
> Be proud! Be brave!
> Though black, the same red blood
> Flows through your paler brothers.
>
> And that same blood,
> So freely spent on Flanders fields,
> Shall yet redeem your Race.
> Be men, not cowards,
> And demand your rights.
>
> Your toil enriched the Southern lands;
> Your anguish has made sweet the sugar cane;
> Your sweat has moistened the growing corn,
> And drops of blood from the cruel master's whip
> Have caused the white cotton to burst forth in mute protest.
>
> Demand, come not mock suppliant!
> Demand, and if not given—take!
> An eye for an eye;
> A soul for soul;
> Strike, black man, strike!
> This shall not be!

Representative of another aspect of Negro feeling is the poem of Roscoe C. Jamison, "Negro Soldiers."[2]

[1] *Chicago Defender*, April 30, 1921.

[2] *Crisis*, September, 1917; quoted from Mr. Braithwaite's article in the same periodical, April, 1919.

Its burden is the inevitable sacrifice and inevitable patriotism of the Negro of today. William Stanley Braithwaite says it is the "finest contribution in verse to the Negro's participation in the war." It is more than that indeed when thought of as echoing the larger situation and the Negro attitude even in peace time.

> These truly are the Brave,
> These men who cast aside
> Old memories, to walk the blood-stained pave
> Of Sacrifice, joining the solemn tide
> That moves away, to suffer and to die
> For Freedom—when their own is yet denied!
> O Pride! O Prejudice! When they pass by,
> Hail then, the Brave, for you now crucified!
>
> These truly are the Free,
> These souls that grandly rise
> Above base dreams of vengeance for their wrongs,
> Who march to war with visions in their eyes
> Of Peace through Brotherhood, lifting glad songs
> Aforetime, while they front the firing-line.
> Stand and behold! They take the field today,
> Shedding their blood like him now held divine,
> That those who mock might find a better way!

Perhaps, however, no one lets us see the mind of the present-day Negro in its deeper and more religious moods so well as James Weldon Johnson in his "Fifty Years and After." Here we find the consciousness of race history and the vision of a race future. The poem is too long to be quoted entire. Brander Matthews has said: "In it he speaks the voice of his race; and the race is fortunate in its spokesman. . . . . In it we are made to see something of the soul of the people who are

our fellow-citizens now and forever—even if we do not
always so regard them."[1]

> O brothers mine, today we stand
>   Where half a century sweeps our ken,
> Since God, through Lincoln's ready hand.
>   Struck off our bonds and made us men.
> . . . .
>
> Far, far the way that we have trod,
>   From heathen kraals and jungle dens,
> To freedmen, freemen, sons of God,
>   Americans and citizens.
> . . . .
>
> This land is ours by right of birth,
>   This land is ours by right of toil;
> We helped to turn its virgin earth,
>   Our sweat is in its fruitful soil.
> . . . .
>
> That banner which is now the type
>   Of victory on field and flood—
> Remember, its first crimson stripe
>   Was dyed by Attucks' willing blood.
>
> And never yet, O haughty Land—
>   Let us, at least, for this be praised—
> Has one black, treason-guided hand
>   Ever against that flag been raised.
>
> Then should we speak but servile words.
>   Or shall we hang our heads in shame?
> Stand back of new-come foreign hordes,
>   And fear our heritage to claim?

---

[1] Quoted by Braithwaite in article just cited, *Crisis*, April, 1919.
The poem itself may be found in the *Dunbar Speaker and Entertainer*,
etc., pp. 270 ff., or the author's volume, *Fifty Years and Other Poems*, New
York, 1917.

No!   Stand erect and without fear,
   And for our foes let this suffice—
We've bought a rightful sonship here;
   And we have more than paid the price.

. . . .

Courage!   Look out, beyond, and see
   The far horizon's beckoning span!
Faith in your God-known destiny!
   We are a part of some great plan.

CHAPTER VIII

NEGRO LIFE

The deepest interest in the Negro press will spring from a desire to see as clearly and as intimately as possible the life there mirrored. While it is true that possible anxiety over the racial problem ought to send students to Negro newspapers to discover what Negroes are think-ing, a still more satisfactory impulse is the wish simply to become acquainted with these new reaches of human experience.

It must not be forgotten, of course, that no white man will be as greatly interested in journalistic glimpses of Negro life as the colored man himself will be. In the first place the life of his own group was never so exciting as now, and it is daily growing more so. Group conscious-ness is growing, various individuals are opening up new doors of racial activity, new adjustments with the white group are being demanded. The economic movements in both South and North—largely those involved in increased industrialism on the one hand and better farm-ing on the other—and the shifting of population both from South to North and from the country to the city, added to the teasing uncertainty of present political tendencies, democratic agitations, international realign-ments and all—these bring fresh zest every day to the Negro's appetite for news and discussion. Pictures, de-scriptions, and reports of others like himself are in demand. In addition, the colored man wants publicity. It is isolation which has always been his *bête noir*. His passionate evaluation of his own press is due to this urge for recognition. To be sure, we all like to see our names in print and sometimes the pleasure of having a party is blighted if we do not find a report of it in the social column the next day. But in the Negro's case the instrument of publicity is still new and hence more fascinating. Still another appeal of the newspapers lies in this being a means through which intra-group discussion can go on. Arguments can be heard pro and con, and the group can thus make up its mind. It is not surprising if the Negro turns with more than ordinary devotion to the printed page. To him it is an institution peculiarly embodying his group life, something like his church or his lodge, but even more like some public work of art symbolizing his aspiration.

In what follows there has been an endeavor to bring together a representative selection of newspaper and magazine sidelights on the Negro. It can scarcely be claimed that these cover with accurate proportion the representative areas of all Negro life. The effort has been made indeed. But it may be that the press gives more space to some areas of life than to others; it may be that the city community is over-represented; it may be that more emphasis is placed on the rising, learning, upward-struggling, contingent of the race.

It might be hard to find anything different from this in the publications of any people that is similarly awakening into self-consciousness. As a people effects larger contacts with its own units through increasing industrialism and business organization, as it begins to swarm into the city hive and build its cellular tissue there, it develops new interests in communal life, language comes to be important, it seeks art-expression, and so it develops a press. In the country one can get along without reading, or at the most need read but a little. There, reading of papers is a luxury, something to relieve the tedium of twilight hours. In city life one's very existence depends on being able to read signs, advertisements, news. The social contact is of a secondary kind and the newspaper becomes its common carrier. Rural Europe might be kept in social and political impotence with more or less difficulty; but an urbanized Europe means compact political organisms, thriving nationalistic movements. And of course the city and the newspaper go together. It is so among the Negroes of the United States.

One must immediately add, however, that the country tends to copy the city. The rural life is not unrepresented. It is consciously endeavoring to keep going some form of publicity commensurate with a growing sense of importance. For the emphasis on farm life, while a consequence to some extent of the cityward drift, is very real. Certain educational centers, like Tuskegee and Hampton, are consistently standing for this.

I. THE CITY

It is a long way from the corn and cotton fields of the sunny South to the commercial enterprises of big, beautiful Harlem, but we are here, one hundred and fifty thousand of us, forming perhaps the largest Colored community in the entire United States. Here, where money will say more in *one moment* than the most *eloquent lover* can in years, a happy, thrifty people are working out a greater destiny for the Race, by solving their economic and political problems day by day. Fifteen years ago, Colored Harlem was confined to one or two city blocks. Today, Harlem's Colored People proudly claim almost the entire area north of 128th to 148th streets, from Park to Eighth avenues, a city, "as it were," within the city. About two miles long by two miles wide, having more people than the entire combined population, whites and blacks, of Richmond and Lynchburg, Va., together. Here thrive many enterprises, such as light manufacture, commercial and professional life affords, with a large number of Colored people doing excellent business.

Large public schools, library, Y.M.C.A. and Y.W.C.A. buildings; casinos, theatres, political, social and music club houses; fraternal homes, and 60 per cent of property in this area is owned by Colored people. There are two Colored representatives on the Board of Aldermen, and one in the State Legislature, all from *big, beautiful Harlem*, to represent her interests. Our Churches are palatial. Our professional and business men are among the best in the country; here, too, the Colored artisans have commenced to grow strong. Our women, God bless them, are the prettiest and best dressed in the world.

Unity within the Race, *here as elsewhere*, is the Colored People's greatest concern; and when Harlem finds it, the so-called "Race Problem" will crumble before an intelligent, determined group, and Colored Harlem will not only be *big* and *beautiful*, but will become *great* and *powerful.—New York Dispatch*, January 7, 1921.

THE LOVERS

A youth moulded of the night and a young girl dipped in the sunset. The moon peeps from behind a gigantic building and smiles. Such is love in Harlem.

—WILL SEXTON in *Favorite Magazine*, Autumn, 1920.

The editor asked Capt. Abram Simpson, who has just returned from Memphis, to tell the readers of the *News* what he saw there.

In response to our request for an article, he sat down at the typewriter and "knocked off" the following: . . . .

To understand and enjoy Memphis of today one must have seen other cities, scattered throughout the country where Colored people are assembled in large numbers, with their laissez-faire attitude and the absence of the pioneer spirit. Then he can appreciate this busy, prosperous, and promising city. . . . .

Go there today and you will find—

Four hospitals, one having recently been purchased at an initial cost of thirty thousand dollars;

Twelve or more drugstores, furnished with the most modern of equipment;

Eighty-nine doctors, dentists, and pharmacists who have graduated from the leading medical colleges of the country;

The courts of the city,

Twelve lawyers practicing in all; undertaking establishments, restaurants, haberdashery stores, grocery stores and other forms of business which give to it the commercial spirit of New York. But thanks to its heritage, it has not lost the social spirit of the South.

Behind the movement for advancement and individual expression in financial circles stand the two Colored banks of Memphis with their combined resources of over a million and a half dollars. They are the Solvent Savings Bank and Trust Co. and the Fraternal Bank.

One of the most outstanding features of the business life of Memphis is the Roddy Co-Operative Grocery Concern. This organization has a chain of fifteen groceries scattered throughout the city and the towns surrounding Memphis. In some cases they have established and in others acquired groceries. Mr. B. M. Roddy, the cashier of the Solvent Savings Bank and Trust Co., is at the head of this organization. It is operated under the same general plan as the Piggly-Wiggly or the Quaker Maid chain of stores. Their business outlay represents an expenditure of thousands of dollars and their turnover yearly is in the hundreds of thousands.

Recently the Mississippi Beneficial Life Insurance Co. with a capitalization of one hundred thousand dollars, moved their home office to Memphis. This concern operates in four states and employs in the home office over sixty persons. Dr. Walker is the President. Its city branch with an agency of twenty-five or more is under the management of Mr. G. W. Lee, a young politician of national repute.

During the present week the Negro Coffin Manufacturing Concern, of which Mr. Hayes, Vice President of the Solvent Bank and

Trust Co. is the President, opened its factory for the manufacturing of coffins and accessories. It is a hundred thousand dollar concern with most of the capital paid in. Its field of activity is unlimited, having all of Southern States from which to draw.

The American Home Investment Corporation, realtors, is trying to solve housing conditions in Memphis by opening additions and securing desirable property for resale on easy payment plans.

This in brief is Negro business in Memphis. Thousands of people together. And behind them all stand two *Negro banks* ever ready to give financial aid and backing to help build up the Negro business.—*Louisville News*, January 1, 1921.

Greenville, Miss., is my home town and Nelson is the main street in the city for colored business enterprises, of which all the colored people of the town are justly proud.

Nelson street is the home of the Y.M.C.A., the Pythian Castle, Delta Hall, Mt. Horeb missionary Baptist Church, St. Matthew A.M.E. Church, ten grocery stores and three first-class cafés; three ice cream parlors, the high school and the grammar school, in the East end of the street while the West end contains the beautiful homes of some of our most prominent men of the race, viz., Dr. Miller, physician and surgeon; Dr. Overton, surgeon dentist; Rev. W. T. Strong, preacher and writer, Dr. A. A. Wedington, pulpit orator and leader. There is not a single white resident in this street, and only four small grocery stores.

I think a street with so much, representing the prosperity and prospects of the race as this one does should be named from one of the men of the race. I suggest the names: Dunbarton avenue, in honor of the Poet Paul Laurence Dunbar.—*Afro-American*, February 25, 1921.

At present in the city of New Orleans our people are doing nicely along certain lines. In many instances the enterprises are very new and yet others are quite old. Along society lines they have enough organizations to care for all of the people. . . . . Many barber shops ought to be combined and thereby secure larger and more modern and up-to-date accommodations. Restaurant business is all right and yet room for improvement.

There is plenty of room for launching other enterprises. We need first grocery stores, clothing, shoe and hat stores. If we could see more of these enterprises going along, employing the girls and boys who come out from our schools will encourage one to live and hope for better and higher things. . . . .

Carpenters, bricklayers and building tradesmen ought to perfect a strong real estate company in the city and encourage our people to secure homes and how they can pay for them. Our people must be saved by those who are able; by those who have such visions. . . . .

The Negro population is said to be 90,000 or 100,000 strong in the city of New Orleans. This is about a third or more of the entire population of the city; nine times the size of Alexandria, La., Shreveport and almost as large as the population of the city of Nashville, Tenn. In fact the Negro population here represents to a large degree a city within a city.—*New Orleans Searchlight*, November 26, 1920.

GREAT GET-TOGETHER MEETING

Representing Texarkana and adjacent towns will march to the Mt. Zion Baptist Church, Friday, March 4th—

PROGRESSIVE CITIZEN DAY

The 12 Baptist Churches, led by their pastors, will be the guests. The inter-denominational alliance and their Churches will be on hand.

The lodges and business men will be there, and every effort will be made to put the *Citizen* in every home in Texarkana.

The day will open with a Sunrise Prayer Meeting, in which Divine aid for victory will be sought.

At 11 A.M. all ministers will assemble to hear a special message dealing with some vital questions of race development.
Symposium
How can our preachers promote a healthy growth in business among our people? (6 minutes each)
Business men's league
At 3 P.M. the women and men of the race who are engaged in any sort of business will assemble in Mt. Zion Church to hear a special address on some topic vital to the business life of the race.

Symposium

The brass band of A.W. will give an open air Musical Concert from 7 to 8 o'clock

Oratorical Contest

The six colored schools of this city will be represented in an Oratorical Contest at 8 o'clock P.M. using as a subject: "The Value of a Colored Newspaper."

Charming Music

Will be rendered by the Sunset, College Hill, Polly Chapel, Canaan, Oak St., and Mt. Pisgah Choirs.

Barbecue, ice cream and soft drinks of all sorts will be served on the grounds all day. We want you to be one of the 10,000 colored people who will meet at Mt. Zion determined to make our own paper, The Progressive Citizen, the South's greatest weekly.

All day meeting, March 4th, Mt. Zion Church

Progressive Citizen Day

—*Progressive Citizen*, February 26, 1921

II. THE COUNTRY

For approximately half a million people to have accumulated 4,460,457 acres of land valued at $227,757,850 in a half century is remarkable and inspiring. And no less startling is the fact, as shown by a recent census release, that in the past ten year period, the increase in improved farm land owned by Negroes was more than 1 million acres valued at approximately 13 million dollars.

These figures represent the holdings and increases of the Negroes of Texas. These facts should be gratifying. They denote progress.

Men who own farms and homes contribute largely to the welfare of the communities in which they live. They enter largely into the scheme of production. They are doing their share of the work of the world.

Farm ownership is worth while.

But with this ownership there comes an increased duty to become efficient.

A few days ago a government extension worker spoke of the fact that Negro farmers and producers did well as individuals, but as a group they failed of that intelligent co-operation which made possible the marketing of their products under more favorable conditions.

While it is not definitely known that marketing organizations seek the membership of Negro producers, it is reasonable to suppose that Negro communities could employ their more modern methods of production and marketing to great advantage.

What is true of Texas is true of Negroes in all Southern states.

The aggregate of farms owned by the Negroes of 16 Southern states totals 41,346,943 acres valued at $2,239,062,790.

There is no doubt but that the products of these farms total a staggering yearly sum.

Producers with a common aim and idea become factors worthy of recognition in the great business of determining price and labor cost.

The speculation in terms of what the efficient control of that vast amount of land could accomplish is interesting.

And we do not consider it a waste of time to engage in them.

The lemon, citrus and orange growers of California have become a national institution controlling the price of their products all over the field of their distribution. This was made possible by co-operation and specialization.

The application of this same spirit among the Negro owners of these millions of acres can result in good to them and those whom they serve.

We all take pleasure and derive profit from the possession of these farm lands. But it is no less the duty of the owners to specialize and improve marketing methods to the end that these acres may become productive of more good to them.—*Dallas Express*, June 18, 1921.

UTICA, MISS., Feb. 24.—This has been a great day for the farmers of Mississippi, it being their annual gathering at the Utica Normal and Industrial Institute, Utica, Mississippi, for the purpose of discussing their problems and trying to find a way out. The number and character of the men, alone, present would have been sufficient to guarantee the success of the gathering; but the fervor with which these people discussed their problems and the earnestness with which they sought to find solutions, will long be remembered by those present.

In regard to the progress of the Negroes, reports showed that in the community surrounding the Utica Normal and Industrial Institute, Negroes have been steadily gaining in land ownership for the past eighteen years; so that at the present time about 30,000 acres of land are owned by them, and although this is small by comparison, it still shows that commendable progress has been made.

William H. Holtzclaw, Principal of the Utica Normal and Industrial Institute and re-elected for the fifteenth time President of the Utica (Mississippi) Negro Farmers' Conference, delivered an address to the farmers.—*Dallas Express*, February, 1921.

The Negro has found that the white race is expecting something of him and he don't mean to disappoint them. The white man has had his fair, his races, showed blooded cows, hogs, fowls and everything; now he has stepped back, and said to the Negro, here is our fair ground, race track, grand stand and all, now use it to your own pleasure for a fair.

Now in August at the West End Fair Ground, at Paducah, Ky., we will all be there with our race horses, breed mares, cows, fine hogs, sheep, carpenters, mechanics, plumbers, teamsters and the best line of cooks that can be produced by our race.

Now this talent has not been given us in the last few years; the Negro has had them all the time, but the time has just come for him to put them in use. Now as this is our first attempt to show the public what we are doing I hope the farmers of Ballard County will not let her fall behind. This will be a great fair if we make it one. The men who have planned this fair deserve credit for their undertaking.

Everybody should take a part in this and stick to them and say with an earnest heart, if they fall, we fall with them. If they stand, it is because we have upheld them.—*Paducah* (Kentucky) *Light*, July 7, 1921.

HAMPTON, VA., Feb. 10.—"Some Suggestions for Improving Rural Life through the Church, the School, and Recreation" was the topic for the recent "Workers' Day" program of the thirtieth annual Tuskegee Negro Conference. This topic, dealing with rural life needs and methods of improving rural life, attracted several hundred school officials and teachers, county and home demonstration and other community workers who are interested in rural organization and the making of good and happy citizens.

A large number of intelligent and thrifty Negro farmers came to Tuskegee institute specially to attend the well known workers' conference, which has today as much vitality as it had thirty years ago and a great deal more definiteness in program.—*Dallas Express*, February 12, 1921.

The Seaboard Air Line from Savannah to Montgomery, Ala., the Central Railroad of Georgia, from Savannah to Macon and Birmingham, and the Southern Railroad along its route, may testify to the fact that the automobile has helped rather than hurt their business, for thousands of colored people are to be found at every station and at almost every cross-road waiting to take the trains or to meet their friends who use them.

With the advent of the motor cars and the increase in revenue in the form of real money in the South, during the war, thousands of colored people who seldom left their houses, remote from the highways, have taken to traveling up and down the lines to all kinds of meetings and to visit their friends.

Saturdays and Sundays the trains are crowded, and it is in line with the American "Week end," that the people in this distant section have taken to using the automobile and the road in such proportions as to make a profit for the roads there while the people in other sections have decreased their traffic because of the high rates.—*Washington Colored American*, April 13, 1921.

Mrs. Carrie Watkins, of North Main Street, saw an opossum going across the field and she ran after him, and finally she caught him after much running and it was a nice size one and she cooked him with sweet potatoes around him.—*Hopkinsville* (Kentucky) *New Age*, April 2, 1921.

III. THE CHURCH

Last Sunday saw the old church in her pristine glory from the time Sunday school began at 9:15 until the doors were shut at

10:15 in the evening. The work in the Sunday school was as intense and steady as the work in a bee-hive, and Mrs. A. L. Somerville, the superintendent, was as happy as she could be, Mrs. Brinkly from Prentis Park was present and being introduced made a very pleasant address.

At eleven o'clock Rev. Joel King of North Carolina was introduced by the pastor and preached a very interesting sermon that seemed to please the congregation very much indeed. Two persons came forward and offered themselves for membership bringing their church letters. At Night the Children's Day program was carried out without a hitch. The music furnished by Mrs. Lillian Jones.

The Church is alive and much interest is manifested in the forthcoming anniversary of the pastor and the church which begins on the first of July running through for two weeks. The matter of remodeling will also hold the attention of the congregation in the near future since the motion has been adopted to remodel.—
Vigil (Portsmouth, Virginia), June 16, 1921.

CLYDE, GA., Feb. 15.—Israel Waters owes his life to the deep religious nature of the colored people of this section. On Monday night he was captured by posses of white and colored men for an alleged outrage upon a colored school girl.

The whites turned him over to the colored men to deal with him, and when arrangements had been made for a necktie party with gun shot decorations, Waters asked the mob to pray for and with him.

The effect was such that they deliberated and finally decided to send him to jail and adjourned the lynching party.

Today, Waters, like many others, believes in the efficacy of prayer.—*Richmond Colored American*, February 27, 1921.

The Ministerial Alliance through Rev. J. H. Smith has invited the business men of Dallas to co-operate with it in observing Business Men's Day, Sunday, June 19th; at some service during the day a special sermon to business men will be preached, short talks on the need of the development of business and its relation to racial and community life will be delivered.

We consider this step by our pastors highly worthy of commendation. We feel that it will be productive of much good. It will help the business man, pastor and pew member, by making more clear to each his part in the development of that which may prove of unlimited benefit to all concerned.

It is to be hoped that the response to this invitation of the pastors may be heartily complied with and that this Business Men's Day may mark the beginning of a series of such meetings which, if carried to their fullest development, will help all members of our racial group in this community.—*Dallas Express*, June 18, 1921.

RED ROCK, MISS., April 15.—A local Colored preacher startled his auditors last Sunday morning with the following somewhat remarkable prayer:

"Oh, Lawd, give Thy servant this mornin' de eye of de eagle and de wisdom of de owl; connect his soul with de gospel telephone in de central skies; luminate his brow with de sun of heaben; pizen his mind with love for the people; turpentine his imagination; grease his lips with 'possum oil; loosen his tongue with de sledge hammer of Thy power; 'lectrify his brain with de lightnin' of de word; put 'petual motion in his ahms; fill him plum full of the dynamite of Thy glory; 'noint him all over with de Kerosene oil of Thy salvation, and sot him on fire.—Amen!"—*Associated Negro Press*.

On July the 8th of 1920, there appeared upon the streets of Houston, a colored man, who seemingly was a stranger in a strange land; shabbily attired, unattractive but above all polite to an extreme which caused him to be tolerated if not appreciated. This individual we are now speaking of secured a permit from the city officials that same day, July 8th, 1920, and began a bitter tirade against Satan and his host which he has kept up incessantly ever since up to this writing, but he is no longer a stranger in a strange land; far from it. He is more widely discussed than any other one man in the city of Houston for he is known and reverenced as Rev. E. L. Jeremiah, the Peer of Divinities and the friend of the down-trodden. From the streets of the city, he repaired to an open lot at the corner of Meyer and Robin St., and demonstrated to the world his power to gather more men, women and children together in a short space of time than any other man in the confines of the city.

His fame as a healer of divers diseases pronounced incurable by some of the best medical doctors, is gaining as the days roll by.

Only a few short months ago, Rev. Jeremiah moved from his stronghold under the Tree, to a church edifice at No. 1702 Andrews St., known as the Union Tabernacle Church, which is a credit to any denomination, and was built and paid for in fourteen weeks at a cost of nearly $41,000.

Not being satisfied, he immediately began the erection of a swell little bungalow adjoining the church as his home and office. The exterior is very unique in design but the interior is a dream. All modern appliances and elaborate furnishings are there.

He seems to accomplish one given thing only to find himself wanting and planning other things greater and grander.

He is now constructing one of the most commodious buildings belonging to our race in the city. It measures 100 x 50 with seven distinct business apartments. Consisting of a Grocery Store, Café and Cold Drinks, Newspaper and Shoe-shining, Dress-making, Beauty Parlor, Tailor Shop and Barber shop. Most of the furnishings for the Cold Drinks Stand are installed and will be as soon as the carpenters are out of the way. The Fountain alone cost $5,100.

The upper story will be the home of The Faith Hospital, chartered by the State of Texas, with fourteen large and spacious rooms.

It also contains a large hall, well lighted and ventilated. There will be long or short distance telephone service, two cold water baths, two hot and cold shower baths with lead floors and Laboratories for both men and women on each floor. It is entirely modern and all lumber and material including paints, paper, canvas, hardware and electrical supplies are being furnished by the contractor, Mr. Lincoln R. Jones.

These are a few of the accomplished objectives of Rev. Jeremiah but many surprises are in store for those who watch his movements.

Easter Sunday will find the new pews for the church installed at a cost of $6,657.68. Union Tabernacle enjoys a membership of 4,329 and as the church only seats 2,000 a new church or an addition is in order.

To show his deep appreciation of all he has accomplished in these few short months, he will baptize Easter Sunday on the banks of Buffalo Bayou below Sabine St. bridge. Services will begin at 9 o'clock sharp, preaching at 9:30; all are invited.—*Houston Observer*, March 19, 1921.

IV. THE LODGE

Colored Masons in Chicago have purchased a site upon which a Masonic Temple is to be erected at a cost of $600,000. The president of the Prince Hall Masonic Temple Association is Samuel Matthews.

The Pullman Porters' Beneficial Association, organized in Chicago during February of this year, has a membership of 3,904 and a bank account of $25,000. Thomas R. Webb is head of the organization.

In New York City Negro Masons have bought property for a $300,000 Masonic Temple. David W. Parker is president.

Negro Knights of Pythias at Boston have purchased the Ruggles Building, a 4-story structure in the business section.

Royal Arch Masons of Texas have held a 3-day meeting at Fort Worth, as its 35th annual session. A. W. Edwards, grand high priest, of Cleburne, presided. The report of the grand secretary showed a large increase in the number of companions over the previous year.—*Crisis*, August, 1921.

Why do Masons speak of those outside the Order as profane? Such is the question of a young Mason who does not like to have it implied that he is sacred and his father "profane," as this manner of speech seems to say.

The answer is, that a Mason, by his initiation, is set apart, symbolically, to a dedicated life, devoted to moral truth, spiritual faith and human service. If he is a Mason in spirit—in fact—he is committed to a life that is sacred in its purpose and ideal, and while he should not regard others as "profane" in the ordinary use of that word, he must regard himself as obligated to a life of chastity and good will.

The word has also a further allusion. Why do we regard the street as profane and the lodge room as sacred? Because anything may go on the street—a cat, a dog, a cow may litter the street; fight in it; defile it. Not so in a lodge room. There such things are excluded, and the place is set apart to high and beautiful uses. Just so, a man who is really a Mason will regard his mind as a sanctuary from which unclean thoughts, dirty motives, unjust suspicions, unworthy ambitions are excluded. Some thoughts cannot gain admission, no matter how many knocks they give at the door. The filthy jest; the irreverent oath; the slimy slander against his fellow, will be regarded as a Cowan; an Eavesdropper [*sic*] and will be treated accordingly.

Truly, this matter of being a Mason is something more than ritual and the wearing of a big square and compasses.—*Square* (St. Louis), February, 1921.

More about the Royal Circle of Friends of the World and other things:

Now Dear Friends of the Royal Circle:—This is my second article on the benefits of the Order. Now remember your policy is $350 face value and a $60.00 Burial, and a $30.00 monument which amounts to $440.00. Now listen if you live in the Royal Circle of Friends for ten years straight and keep absolutely financial, and at the end of ten years you become disabled to support yourself by the loss of hands, feet, eyes, dropsy or anything that totally disables you, the Order will pay you One Hundred Dollars while you are in this fix, and remember the One Hundred Dollars paid you for this disability has nothing to do with the face value of your policy.

Now again, there is in or will be in the course of erection just in a short time, a Hospital for the sick Friends of the Royal Circle, where they will receive medical and surgical treatment free of charge, board and train-nurse service all absolutely free of cost to the member. Now what other secret order has such a feature as that? So it is enough for us to be encouraged to go forward in the Royal Circle of Friends of the World and see to it that we speak out for the Order, and when you speak, speak the truth, for the truth will stand.

Now let everybody subscribe for the *Royal Messenger*, you should read it because it gives fresh and interesting news. Subscribe for it.

Let all the members of the Royal Circle stand fast for the time is coming when all Negroes will have to belong to a Negro secret society. Of course those who are at the head of other orders that are not originated by Negroes will tell you the above statement is untrue, but you can see why he differs. He is at the head. —*Royal Messenger*, December 18, 1920.

A feeling of warmth and good cheer enhanced by the soft red draperies, rugs and other embellishments of the home-like hall pervaded the atmosphere of Auditorium hall Tuesday evening, when about two hundred guests came in response to invitations sent out by Excelsior Lodge of Masons, to meet and mingle with their Grand Master and high churchman, Rev. J. H. Wilson, of Los Angeles, Cal.

The Program for the evening was delightful and as follows: Piano solo, Mrs. Charles H. Downing; invocation, Rev. A. R. Fox, pastor of Bethel Church; welcome address, George W. Kinney on behalf of the local order; O'Hara's "Deep River," sung very sweetly by Mrs. L. E. Johnson, and was enthusiastically received by the audience; Tosti's "Good-Bye" was delightfully and artistically sung by Miss Clifford Freeman, who was forced to respond to an encore. John Guy was the Master of Ceremonies and presided in a most efficient manner. The speaker and guest of the evening, Rev. J. H. Wilson, after expressing his hearty appreciation for the warm welcome extended to him on behalf of the lodge and the people, through George Kinney, talked at length to his audience upon practical, sensible things, the theme of which was "Organization."—*Portland* (Oregon) *Advocate*, February 4, 1920.

V. THE SCHOOL

Mr. Brownlow, the new City Manager of Petersburg, is asking for suggestions from the citizens of Petersburg for civic betterment generally. It is but natural to presume that Mr. Brownlow will weigh carefully the recommendations submitted and make an effort to remedy them in the order of their importance. We have diligently sought to ascertain whether or not any suggestion had been made pertaining to the needs of the colored people here, but were unable to learn of any. Therefore, we shall take the initiative in the matter and respectfully submit for the consideration of the Honorable Mr. Brownlow, what, in our estimation, is the most important and acute problem of the colored citizens of Petersburg —the Public School situation.—*Weekly Review* (Petersburg, Virginia), March 12, 1921.

The *Sun* has refrained for many months from discussing the deplorable conditions existing in the Negro Schools of this city but it is an indisputed fact that there never was a time in the history of this city that the schools devoted to Negro youth were in a more dilapidated, unkempt and unsanitary condition than they are today.

The pleas of parents and teachers have apparently fallen upon deaf ears and no one seems less concerned about the existing conditions than does *the present school board*.

It is cowardly to cringe and whimper and beg for what properly, fairly belongs to you, and as taxpayers and citizens who pay their proportionate share of the taxation of this community according to their holdings, we have a right to *demand equal facilities* that are accorded under the damning and humiliating segregational laws of this State to the white youth of this city.—*Kansas City Sun*, February 5, 1921.

An event of the past week was the closing exercises of Mt. Nebo school, of which Mrs. Leila R. Williams is the efficient teacher. In spite of the torrents of rain an appreciative audience enjoyed the excellent program. The spacious auditorium was beautifully decorated with smilax, vines, roses in profusion and lovely dogwood blossoms; an improvised canvas decorated with ferns and smilax formed a lovely background while a mound of roses adorned the front of the stage. At the appointed hour a march was played and the student body marched in to the seats reserved for them. All of the girls wearing pure white.—*Samaritan Herald*, April 22, 1921.

Allow me to let the many readers know that by the invitation of Miss Nettie Williamson, teacher of the Oldfield Public School, I made the closing address to the parents and friends of the said school, Friday March 11th, 1921. I wended my way to the Oldfield Baptist Church arriving there at 1 o'clock. There were a few children at the church, and the way those children were romping in the church I thought they had a big dance going on. The teacher wasn't present, she came in at 1:30 and the exercises began at 2 o'clock. After a song the teacher read the Scripture lesson and called upon the manager of the News Club School to lead in prayer. After the song was sung, the manager was asked to address the school and the parents.

I commenced my address by asking the teacher to call out one of the pupils of the fifth grade. I told the little girl, who was 14 years old, to come up on the stage and to read an article in the newspaper. She did so and read it very nicely. I asked the students if the word schoolmaster was in the Bible. This little girl quickly answered yes; I asked her what chapter it was found in and she said she did not know. I told them all that I was going to put 25 cents on the table and the boy or girl that finds it in the Bible I will give them the 25 cents. None of them could find it.

Now the Bible is the chief text book I teach in the News Club School. I am a daily reader of the Bible. I will now call your attention to the chapter in Galatians, 3rd chapter and 25th verse. We are no longer under a schoolmaster, boys and girls. I want you all to continue your studies in your books until your school opens next November and study the third chapter of Paul's letter to the Galatians. If you will obey the law I am sure grace will save you.—*Charlottesville Messenger*, March 19, 1921.

Among the prominent senior co-eds on the campus of the University of Chicago deserving particular mention for her scholastic attainments, is Miss Mary E. Link. Miss Link hails from Kansas City, Kan., where she graduated from Sumner High School in 1917. A notable record in this institution prefaced her entrance and subsequent achievements in the University of Chicago. She began her collegiate career on the Midway in the fall of 1917, holding an honor entrance scholarship, and so high has been the standard of her class work that she has been awarded the scholarship each succeeding year. She has specialized in English and French. Miss Link has the unusual distinction of winning the Phi Beta Kappa key in three years. This is the more remarkable because the honor is rarely conferred even in four years. She has been the secretary of the local chapter of Alpha Kappa Alpha sorority for the past three years. . . . . —*Chicago Defender*, May 17, 1921.

VI. POLITICS

In order more perfectly and completely to form and establish a state-wide organization among our people for the better promotion of our civic and political interests throughout the Commonwealth, a call is hereby issued to every loyal and interested race man and woman of the state to meet in session assembled at Harrisburg, at high noon on June 8, 1921, when and where a constitution and suitable by-laws will be adopted, and the purpose and scope of the organization determined by the people. Every district in the state is requested to send representation.—ROBERT L. VANN, State Chairman,

Public Journal (Philadelphia) May 7, 1921

RICHMOND, July 26.—Acclaiming their candidate for chief executive as the next Governor of Virginia, Negroes from every part of the State in a convention held in True Reformers Hall tonight nominated tentatively a full State Ticket for State Officers at the general election to be held in November.

Barred from the Republican convention in Norfolk, Negroes of Virginia led by Joseph R. Pollard, a Richmond attorney who was a candidate for United States Senator at the last senatorial election, met in the first convention of its kind here since "carpetbagger" days and put up their slate independent of the white Republicans.

John Mitchell, editor of the Richmond *Planet*, president of the Mechanics Savings Bank of Richmond and a committee chairman of the American Bankers' Association, was nominated for Governor of the tentative slate.

A full and final State convention will be held at Richmond September 5. A preliminary convention will be held at Buckroe

Beach, August 6, to formulate a plan of organization designed to reach every precinct in the State.

P. B. Young, of Norfolk, was nominated for Lieutenant Governor. Young is president of the Tidewater Bank and Trust Company and editor of the *Journal and Guide*. J. Thomas Newsome of Newport News and Joseph R. Pollard of Richmond were nominated for Attorney-General.

Mrs. Maggie L. Walker, president of St. Luke's Savings Bank of Richmond and president of the Independent Order of St. Luke, said to represent 200,000 Negroes in the United States, was nominated for superintendent of public instruction.

It was unanimously decided to nominate full State, city and county tickets. It is expected that the September convention will make the tentative nominations permanent. City and county conventions will be held to nominate members of the House of delegates, sheriffs, city sergeants, commonwealth attorneys and others, after the September convention. Sixty-eight delegates were present representing all parts of the State. Norfolk, Richmond, Petersburg, Roanoke, Lynchburg, Newport News, Staunton, Hampton, Bristol, Fredericksburg, Charlottesville and a few of the counties were represented. Eight delegates from Tidewater, Virginia were present.—*Washington Colored American*, July 28, 1921.

The game of politics now being played in Philadelphia took a sharp turn during the past week. The result of the ups and downs proved a gain of one point for the colored brother.

It all came about in the following manner. First, the forces of the Mayor sent a chill down the backs of colored citizens by discharging Patterson Carter, a most efficient colored inspector in the Highway Bureau. Mr. Patterson leaves a splendid record behind and people interested in safeguarding worthy members of the race will undoubtedly rally to his support.

After sending Carter out in the world to get a new start, the administration came back strong to win favor with colored voters by appointing a colored carpenter and a colored bricklayer to positions in City Hall.

In the little game of politics this week, the colored politicians are ahead by one.—*Philadelphia Tribune*, July 23, 1921.

The largest and most important political organization in the city is the Citizens' Republican Club, which has its own home. The President of the Club is Edward W. Henry, a business man and lawyer. But he is more, he is a natural born leader, with a fine personality, and the confidence of the people. Mr. Henry is even more, he is frank and independent, a good mixer and he sticks to his friends. Edward W. Henry is one real big reason for the Philadelphia awakening. His friends are urging him to be a candidate for Magistrate, which he will probably consent to do.— *Associated Negro Press*, July 21, 1921.

VII. SOCIETY

NEW YORK, July 22.—Probably the most unique social function the Liberian dignitaries now visiting in this country have ever attended was the reception held in their honor by Mrs. Lela Walker Wilson, wealthy daughter of the late Mrs. C. J. Walker, and one of the East's leading society matrons, in Villa Le Waro at Irvington-on-the-Hudson.

Here in the greatest of all mansions of celebrities the country over are resting the president of Liberia, his staff and other dignitaries and prominent personages of the Race, 40 or more in number, the guests of a woman whose wealth, composure and refinement make it easy for her to play the hostess to such a distinguished and large assemblage.

The prolonged stay in this country of President C. D. B. King of Liberia has given him and the members of his cabinet an opportunity to see many of the natural beauties of America and some of its magnificent homes and public buildings. All of these sights have been pleasing and instructive to President King and his staff and they so expressed themselves.

To this magnificent Italian villa, the "home of homes," located right in the midst of America's most wealthy and exclusive social group of the other race, President King and his attaches were whirled by the most luxurious cars of the Wilson garage. The approaches to Villa Le Waro, so named by Enrico Caruso, the famous Italian tenor, on his visit to this beautiful palace, are on all sides so picturesque and commanding that President King gave audible expression to his admiration for all that he saw. As his car drew up to the wonderful palace, where he was to be the guest of honor, and where 40 of America's most representative citizens were along with himself to be the house guests for a whole week of the country's wealthiest and one of the most refined and cultured women of the Race, the president realized that he was confronting a condition he little dreamed existed anywhere under the possession of any member of his Race.

During his visit the president's joy enhanced as it was by a relaxation from his arduous duties, knew no bounds. He loved to walk with members of the household or the special guests, or to roam along through the beautiful groves, or to angle in the well stocked fish pond on the estate, or to accompany his hostess on delightful trips around the wonderful country surrounding the beautiful villa and sloping banks of the Hudson river.

A special feature of the Wilson estate which called forth appreciative comment from the president and others of the party was the splendid conduct of the well groomed servant body found everywhere on the estate and always courteous in their desire to attend to the every want of the guests of their employer.—*Chicago Defender*, July 23, 1921.

The marriage Monday night at St. Stephen's Episcopal church of Miss Jenette Eloise Branham to Hazel Lee Skipper was a beautiful affair and was witnessed by a large crowd.

Just prior to the entrance of the wedding party to the church the choir with Miss Alice M. Ellis at the organ sang "To Thee, O Father" and then the doors of the church were swung open and the ushers, Earl A. Ashton and Nathaniel B. Branham, the latter a brother of the bride, entered, the choir rendering softly "The Voice that Breathes O'er Eden." Following the ushers came the little flower girls, Talulah King and Louise Butler. Next came the little ring bearer, Richard Des Verney, who was followed by the matron of honor, Mrs. Charles P. McClane, of Charleston, S.C. The bride, leaning on the arm of her father, came next. She was met at the altar by the groom and his best man, Benjamin Boozer, of Columbia, S.C., his cousin.

Beneath an arch formed by beautiful palms, the ceremony was performed in a most impressive manner by Archdeacon J. Henry Brown.

The party filed down the aisle of the church to the strains of Mendelssohn's Wedding March, played by Miss Ellis.

The bride wore a gown of white charmeuse with a waist made of silk lace with an overblouse of the material. The skirt, with double puffs on the side from which hung panels of the silk lace, was also paneled in front with the same. The train from the shoulder, looped at the waist, fell to the floor about one and a half yards. The front panel and train were hand-embroidered. Her veil was of tulle with a wreath of orange blossoms, and she wore a corsage bouquet of bridal roses. She carried a white prayer-book used by her mother at her wedding.

Mrs. McClane, matron of honor, wore a jade green pussy willow taffeta, touched with pink. She carried a shower bouquet of pink roses.

The little flower girls wore dresses of green organdy with sashes of pink tulle and carried baskets of sweet peas which they strew in the pathway of the bride as she left the altar.

The little ring bearer wore a white suit and carried an Easter lily, to the piston of which was tied the wedding ring.

The bride's mother, Mrs. Mack B. Branham, wore black lace over black.—*Savannah Tribune*, April 23, 1921.

VIII. MUSIC

PARIS, May 14.—In a special to the *World*, it is said that all Paris is turning out to hear the Negro American Southern Syncopated Orchestra which has just opened at the Theatre Champs Elysees.

Serious critics declare that the concerts strike a new note in the music world. Crowds stand for hours in the lines for seats which sell at 30 francs each.—*Washington Colored American*, May 17, 1921.

LONDON, ENGLAND, May 12.—Roland W. Hayes, the celebrated Negro tenor, has had fine recognition during his visit to London where he has been giving a series of recitals in the best concert halls. His accompanist, Mr. Brown, has been equally praised for his fine playing. Last November he was selected from among a group of American artists in London to sing the "Star

Spangled Banner" at the Thanksgiving Celebration by Americans in London.

Mr. Hayes left New York for Europe last year. The remarkable success he has enjoyed since coming to England culminated in an invitation from King George to sing before the Royal family at Buckingham Palace. Mr. Hayes sang some beautiful numbers, among them some Negro Spirituals to the delight of the Royal family. The King took occasion to compliment him on the excellence of his voice, its range and firmness and the skill displayed in the rendition of his songs. The King observed how different the Negro Spirituals were from what the English people have been taught to believe were the characteristic Negro melodies. Mr. Hayes was presented with a diamond pin by King George.— *Houston Observer*, May 14, 1921.

Last Sunday at the Bethel Baptist Church here the colored people held what will go down in history as perhaps the greatest public meeting in the history of Troy. Surrounded by hundreds of white people from this and adjoining counties, their singing was the best ever heard here, and possibly in any part of the State. At 2:10 the meeting was opened with the following program: . . . .

In response to the many requests from white people and with due regard to two choirs who were unable to obtain entrance to the church on account of the crowd, another contest will be held on the fifth Sunday in May, under more auspicious weather conditions and at a larger church, the First Baptist (colored) with more and bigger prizes.

There will be some difference in the manner of distribution of the prizes.

In the next contest prizes will be given for the following:

First and second prizes for best of seven shape singing.

First and second prizes for best of Sacred Harp singing.

First and second prizes for best negro melodies.

First and second prizes for best solos.

No musical accompaniment will be allowed in this contest.

The contest will be given under the auspices of the *Pike County News* and the proceeds will be for the benefit of the colored school building fund.

Both contests are given in the interests of the advertisers in the *Pike County News*. . . . .

The following letter was received from Mr. Clarence L. Mc-Cartha:

TROY, ALA., April 10, 1921.

Dr. S. B. Innis.

Troy, Alabama.

Doctor:

I have just returned from the great singing contest at Bethel Church in this city and as I am leaving town and didn't want to leave without thanking you for the invitation, I do so in this way. In sincerity I say that I have never enjoyed a program more, nor have I heard better singing. The singing was typical and characteristic, harmonious and inspiring, and the program makes me feel like a better man. Please invite me again. I had my entire family out, and we were all delighted. I forgot to tell that fine audience what I had in my mind—that there are no better singers in the South than we had this afternoon.—*Pike County News and Troy Record* (Alabama), April 21, 1921.

It has been learned through Prof. H. B. Johnson of Nashville, Tenn., the chairman of the local committee of arrangements, that all things are now in readiness for the coming of the National Association of Negro Musicians which is to meet in the city of Nashville, July 26 to 28. The first day's session will be held in the spacious auditorium of the Mount Olive Baptist Church. Other meetings will be held on the campus of Fisk University, the insitution which has done so much for the musical development of the race.—*Washington Tribune*, July 9, 1921.

NEW YORK, N.Y., Jan. 9.—Announcement has just been made of a new departure in music and business on the part of the race. A corporation with a capital of $100,000 has just been formed for the purpose of making phonograph records using exclusively the voices and talent of colored people. It has long been a subject of comment that although colored people are very large buyers of phonograph records, our best voices and high class musicians have had no recognition from the large white companies who furnish all the records that are supplied.

While not deprecating the commercial values of comic songs, "blues," and ragtime songs, the new corporation proposes to furnish every type of race music, including sacred and spiritual songs, the popular music of the day, and the high class ballads and operatic selections. It proposes to use some of the most famous quartetts, concert artists, church and school choirs and glee clubs, together with many colored vaudeville acts, for which contracts are being prepared and sent out.

The organization of the company is in charge of Mr. Harry H. Pace, who has been identified with the establishment of some of the largest and most successful business ventures of the race, including the Million Dollar Solvent Savings Bank and Trust Company, of Memphis, Tenn., the Standard Life Insurance Company of Atlanta, Georgia, and the Pace and Handy Music Company of New York, N.Y. Mr. Pace is desirous of getting in touch with singers and musicians of the race who have talent along this line and with race merchants and dealers who are interested in handling such records.—*Baltimore Herald and Commonwealth*, January 21, 1921.

Our folks have started a music roll company in New York, and they will make their first releases on June 1. These will be word rolls and will fit any player piano. Luckeyth Roberts will be one of the players making these records. It is understood that all the Mamie Smith songs will be recorded. The Black Swan Music Co., 1547 Broadway, is the name of the firm.—*Chicago Defender*, May 7, 1921.

IX. THEATER

The *Billboard*, commenting on its appointment of J. A. Jackson on its editorial staff, prints the following: "When the publisher of the *Billboard* inaugurated Jackson's page in the interest of the Colored artist and his employer, many regarded the move as being visionary, as entering the field devoid of possibilities."

This seemed true, because few even in the amusement business were aware of the tremendous artistic and financial strides that had been made in this particular field in the last decade.

The first six months of cultivation in this phase of theatrical enterprises has disclosed the following interesting facts. Already there is listed on the desk of the Editor: 87 picture houses, nine of which are equipped for shows, 112 theaters, playing vaudeville, road shows and pictures.

112 are owned by white persons, five of these managed by Negro managers.

74 are owned by Negroes. In 14 the race of the management has not been ascertained.

Of a total of 200, 81 are connected with organized circuits.

In addition to these interests there has come to the attention of the *Billboard:*

14 film companies, producing pictures with Negro casts. Seven of these are owned by Negroes.

9 parks in five different states have communicated with the editor of the page, as have four fair associations.

47 theatrical companies and 12 companies with carnivals are listed on the desk.

39 bands and orchestras, 12 booking agencies and 3 professional clubs are listed in the files; so are 5 circus groups. Medicine men, scene painters, composers, authors, modistes, advance agents and singers are among these folks.

170 vaudeville and burlesque actors have approved the page by letter or personal calls. These represented more than 500 partners or associations in their respective acts.

On a recent trip across seven states, going as far south as Chattanooga and as far west as Chicago, 377 Colored performers and 857 musicians of the race were encountered. . . . . —*Wichita Star*, May 27, 1921 (by the Associated Negro Press).

For six years the Lafayette Players, the only legitimate Negro dramatic organization, have been interpreting plays. . . . . For six years, the Lafayette Players have been attending the university of dramatic art—stock. For six years the Lafayette Players have been developing that dramatic talent so long lying dormant, developing a dramatic standard for the future generations. . . . .

Now is the time for every Negro to be up and doing! Not tomorrow, for "Tomorrow is but the yesterday of today!"

The church must take its sermons from life as it is. . . . . A beautiful and glorious life after death is a cherished hope of every one, but life as it is is an undenying [*sic*] reality!

The press, with flowing words and blazing head lines, must carry this message into every Negro home, "Now is the time for every Negro to get right with himself!"

The Negro stage must cast aside the frayed and tattered cloak of imitation and garb itself in the new and spotless robe of origination. We want a real Negro drama now! We want to give vent to our smothered emotions that have been stifled these 300 years! We want the whole world to know our aspirations, our achievements, our grievances!

O stage, awaken from your lethargy! Tear from your sightless eyes the hood of imitation that is binding you! Create a standard truly your own! Give our Tolstoys and Ibsens an opportunity to send their messages unto the world so that the entire universe might hear, and hearing, listen to our distressful plea! With your aid, O stage, we will depict our lives as we have been forced to live them! And how patient we have been! Who knows, O stage, but that humanity, viewing the hideous, though truthful pictures we so vividly and artistically paint, might not take compassion upon us as it did upon our Jewish brethren, when you, O stage, brought to the world the true conditions existing in Russia through the medium of that great dramatic masterpiece, "The Resurrection!" Amen!—*Public Journal* (Philadelphia), February 26, 1921.

Frank Montgomery, Blondi Robinson, Henry Jines, Frank "Chinese" Walker and graceful Florence McClain, surrounded by a strong company including a real beauty chorus, are offering what Montgomery calls a "Hodgepodge of Nonsense" at the Booker Washington Theatre this week. The ingredients are song, dance and fun, compounded purely to amuse in a quick succession of big doses. Frequent changes of scenery are required and at times the limited stage space allotted is not sufficient to fully display the artistry of certain song and dance numbers.

There are a number of good features, the most laughable being a cafe scene in which the patrons are kept so constantly rising in response to patriotic orchestral selections that they miss all the courses served at their table.

Montgomery and Robinson pull off a safe blowing burlesque, followed by Montgomery singing "That's All I Remember"; Vigel and the girls in "Good Bye Broadway"; and the comely Miss McClain in a reflector song, "Sweet Daddy." After the cafe scene the show closes with a novel "Shimmie and Jazz" done before the curtain. It is a big show by a big company and is making a big hit.—*St. Louis Argus*, February 25, 1921.

The remarkable growth and development of moving pictures, and their hold upon the public is attested by two announcements that have come directly from New York within a week. Through Lester Walton, now the general manager of the Quality Amusement Corporation, ... announcement has been made that the Lafayette theatre in New York will henceforth show first run pictures, instead of having drama, which has made that house famous.

At the same time, Robert Levy, former president of the Quality Corporation, has issued an announcement of "Regular monthly release of super-features," with Colored artists. There are now more than 500 theatres throughout the country catering almost exclusively to Colored patrons in pictures. Only a small percentage of them are owned and controlled by Negro capital. . . . . —*Detroit Leader*, February 11, 1921.

J. Williams Clifford, president of the Monumental Picture Corporation, recently made the announcement that his organization was now releasing each month a Negro News Reel, picturizing the achievements of the American Negro in this country and the progress of the darker races of the world.

"The educational and inspirational news that this News Reel will give to the masses of colored people in this country is beyond estimation. Each month you will have an opportunity to see on the screen members of our own race that have achieved success along all lines of endeavor, and there will be an opportunity for propaganda in the interest of my people," Lieutenant Clifford said. . . . . —*Progressive Citizen* (Texarkana) March 26, 1921.

X.   SPORT

Another Colored athlete has come forward to follow in the footsteps of men like Jackson, the hurdler; Cable, the hammer thrower; Matthews, the crack baseball player, and Lewis, the

greatest center of his day, in the person of Ned Gourdin, the star
sprinter and broad jumper. . . . .

Harvard has now taken part in two dual meets, and in each
one, Gourdin was her bright star and highest individual point
scorer.   Penn State was her first opponent on April 16th, and Gourdin won both the 100 yard dash and the running broad jump.   He
was clocked in 9⅘ seconds for the hundred, a remarkable performance, that stamps him as one of the greatest of present day
sprinters.   Last Saturday, the 23rd, Harvard met the University
of Pennsylvania, and here again the great Colored athlete won
the 100-yard dash, got second in the 220 yard dash, and won the
running broad jump.—*Brooklyn and Long Island Informer*, April
30, 1921.

It appears that Dempsey wants to fight Willard on Labor Day,
and Tex Rickard is reported as already making arrangements for
another championship bout on that date.   Several writers have
again voiced the sentiment that Harry Wills should be given a
chance for the title.   In reply to this sentiment Dempsey states
that he will give Wills a chance for the title if the public wants the
fight.   Whether he means that part of the public that is interested
in boxing or the public in general, he does not say.   But if he
means the boxing fans, there will be no question about a fight
between Dempsey and Wills, for they have on numerous occasions
expressed a desire to see those fighters meet.

Although the newspaper men as a whole do not like Dempsey,
and would like to see him defeated, many of them take the stand
that a mixed bout for the championship would be against public
policy, as it would tend to increase race prejudice.   For this
reason few of them are advocating a Dempsey-Wills fight.   Hugh
Fullerton, a noted authority on sports who opposed the Carpentier-
Dempsey fight on the grounds that it was an uneven match, has
stated on several occasions that Wills was a logical contender for
the championship, and should be given a chance.

The best opinion available now is that Dempsey can defeat all
of the white contenders, and although they may not get first
chance for the title, the public will eventually turn to Wills as the
most formidable opponent of Dempsey, which will bring on this

fight.   How soon this will be remains to be seen.—*New York Age*, July 9, 1921.

> Hail to the Continental League,
>   The Champions of a nobler plan,
> Whose motto is "Democracy"
>   Whose aims are true American.
> For they would save the nation's game
>   And free it from a selfish few;
> Who have dishonored it for gain
>   And barred the men of darker hue.
>
> The Baseball Park is soon to be
>   A place where players, white and tan,
> Shall demonstrate pure sportsmanship
>   And man will love his fellow man.
> Where grandstand, box and bleacher crowds
>   Will feel a new and greater thrill;
> When pale and dusky Ruths and Cobbs
>   Will match their fleetness, nerve and skill.
>
> Proclaim the news from coast to coast,
>   Let every true, red-blooded fan;
> Support the worthy enterprise
>   Of Andy Lawson and his clan!
> —ANDREA RAZAFKERIEFO in *New York News*, April 21, 1921.

CHAPTER IX

NEGRO CRITICISM OF NEGRO LIFE

Negroes are greatly interested in appraising their own social life. The old and the new are coming into juxtaposition and frequent conflicts of standards result. Just when the church is in a position to assert and exemplify the Puritanism of nineteenth-century Christianity, the pleasures and vices of the city come in with their allurements. Rural recklessness of personal appearance confronts the city clothes and manners now coming into fashion. Then, too, there are as many different sorts of people included within the Negro group as among white people; and, with the increasing intra-group contacts, the process of criticism is bound to be more and more in evidence.

Besides this there is a tendency to ask whether Negroes may not have some things that are just as good as what white people have or even better. It may once have been orthodox to consider the white man's complexion and culture as superior and to approximate this as far as possible. But the present-day criticism is setting these values over against a new pride in Negro art, literature, sport, and even skin color.

The process of appraising his own life will lead the Negro also to take particular interest in outstanding individuals, who come thus to represent certain desirable or undesirable types. A few of these "interesting people" are described in this chapter.

But whatever the inquiries are that colored people make into their own condition, they can never get away from the underlying feeling of tension or friction arising out of relations with the other race. The friction may exhibit itself in comparatively trivial incidents. And again it may be so interpreted as to add a pathetic and romantic glamor to life—such, at any rate, is the burden of the closing quotation.

I. MORAL AND AESTHETIC ATTITUDES

Our hope as a race cannot be found in characters like "Alabama Joe." It is a sad commentary on the press leaders in racial progress and moulders of public thought to find some local contemporaries devoting columns of space to and even extolling the virtues of this unfortunate man, rather than those of the brave officer who, in performance of his duty as a sworn officer of the law, entered the building where this notorious character had barricaded himself, and while his white brother officers found a safe refuge from a hail of bullets, entered the house and after a two-hour wait killed him and thus rid the community of a character destined, if permitted to go his way, to bring reproach upon a whole race of people.

It is claimed by man that our race is in its infancy; that it is a child race. The danger, therefore, in overlooking the bravery of our colored policeman, who was, after all, the real hero, to ferret out whatever virtues the victim may have had lay in the fact that the maudlin sentimentality of the illiterate and uneducated among us might be led from a false sense of proportion to unduly exalt and make a hero out of a villain.—*Public Journal* (Philadelphia), February 26, 1921.

It was a great relief to the colored residents of this place when the trial of one of their race, George Washington Knight, for the murder of the pretty white organist in Perth Amboy March 12, came to a close last week. The crime had aroused so much feeling against colored persons by the whites that a race riot seemed immediate almost any moment.

Knight, 22, was found guilty of first degree murder in connection with the death of Mrs. Edith Wilson, a church organist, near her home at Perth Amboy, March 12, and was sentenced to die during the week of May 2.

The jury was out only fifteen minutes.

When the verdict was announced Knight showed no emotion. . . . .

The colored citizens of this part of the state are rejoiced to be rid of Knight and his degraded pals. An investigation of the blind tigers where Knight got his maddening liquor has begun.— *New York News*, March 31, 1921.

The city of Charleston . . . . has a popular club called the "Blue Goose," which the police visit with regularity and from which they take seldom less than 15 members caught indulging in dominoes with cubical pieces and mystic moans and words or "skin."

Last Saturday was the occasion for one of these visits.

"The American" sees in so many of these illegal and foolishly expensive luxuries, the expenditure of energy which lacks an outlet. The curse of segregation is that it throws men and women back upon their limited avenues of expression. Who will find a way?— *Washington Colored American*, May 23, 1921.

New Orleans is noted for its hospitality, cheerfulness, and the friendly feeling exhibited by the inhabitants therein to home folks as well as to strangers. Carnival in New Orleans is an institution and no one in these parts hopes for its discontinuance. However, the carnival spirit among the colored population is very much stretched. Our city has been mockingly, through abuse, often referred to as the Carnival City, the city in which the people indulge in revelry to the exclusion of other things. This is not true—but the Sunday parades given by numerous social clubs, among which are the "Joy Givers," "Merry Makers," "Swells," "Money Wasters," etc., some truly significant titles, besides a lot of others representative of the animal kingdom, will force the above impression among visitors. There are, however, a few clubs that parade annually usually celebrating a holiday at that time. The parade is inaugurated for the purpose of securing new members.   These clubs have comfortable quarters for the recreation of their members, and they are not organized for pleasure only, while the Sunday Serenaders seem to be organized for pleasure only.   The Serenaders, with gorgeous uniforms, silk shirts, vari-colored caps and ties, tinsel decorated automobiles and a truck full of Jazz, speed through the city every Sunday with clock-like regularity and offer the tired public a free entertainment on the street corners.

These Sunday parades have grown so monotonous that everybody speaks of them in the most derisive terms.   Aside from the desecration of the Sabbath Day, these clubs, from an economic point of view, are engaged in a dangerous practice.   Prices of food, clothing, etc., are falling—with them the reduction in wages is inevitable.   Are the members of these clubs making too much money?   Will the reaction from this abnormal state find us prepared?   In other words, what will be done when the bottom falls out?   The capitalists are watching.   The practice of those clubs that parade on Sunday under the guise of advertising a forthcoming ball serves no good purpose and it should be discontinued.—*New Orleans Searchlight*, December 11, 1920.

Two Washington Streets

Ralph W. Tyler

I.   S Street

Out along a tree-lined boulevard
  I have wandered often.
She my Heloise and I her Abelard—
  Naught our love could coffin.
And again on Sunday morn
  Solemnly to church,
Wond'ring how so fine a world
  Could a soul besmirch.
    Your homes I've wondered at—
    Their domes, their colors flat,
    Their blinds that never looked a bit forlorn,
    Like gay, bright banners in procession borne.

II.   SEVENTH STREET

Street of divers things, e'en "Uncles"
  And his motley pawn-shop crew—
The festering carbuncles
  Of a town that healthy grew.
    Past your eat-shops, with their smells,
    Past your pool-shops, gambling hells,
  I have hurried many a time—
    You the mingling of two races,
  You the jangled bells o' chime,
    Street of white, black, yellow faces.
                          —*Washington Bee*

Not long since, I saw a statement made by a large employer of laborers of color: that daily, ninety per cent of his employees were from ten minutes to one hour late.   There are those in our race who without investigating will rashly denounce this as a falsehood whether absolutely true or not; it at least indicates a possible tendency and lamentable tendency it is.

To any person who has observed our race it is all too apparent that we are not as prompt, punctual, regular, systematic and methodical as we should be. . . . .

The lack of these essential qualities means disaster for the race, both for the present and the future.   The workers of today are not only deciding their own fate, but they are shaping the outlook of the man of tomorrow: for no man lives to himself alone.

The man who habitually drags to his work late, not only hurts himself, he hurts his brother in black, who labors by his side.   He is laying the foundation for dissatisfaction.   He is opening the door for his own discharge.   He is joining himself to the great idle class, who can and will be no more merciful to him than they were to the Prodigal son.—*Unmarked clipping.*

People we can do without:
The fellow, who, for reasons known only to himself, thinks he is too good to work.
The cabaret hounds who think of nothing but bright lights, jazz bands and the merry tinkle of wine glasses.

The slouchy fellow who, through lack of pride, makes himself a nuisance with his unkempt appearance in public places.

Women who haven't self-respect enough to put on proper clothing before going to market.

Those who think an open window facing on the street is the proper place for airing one's feet.

Scantily attired women who lean out windows and engage in idle gossip.—

(Cartoon) *Chicago Defender*, July 9, 1921

Many concerns whose stock is being peddled in Harlem have never paid a dividend and the chances are they never will. Quotations as to the value of their stock are hard to obtain and at best unreliable. Others that have paid dividends have only been able to do so by using money obtained from sales of stock, in order to boost further sales. Their balance sheets, when they are honest enough and frank enough to submit any, often show but a slim margin of surplus, arrived at by the transparent expedient of padding the values of office furniture and buildings.

If the intending investor would recognize these risks before putting up his cash, well and good. He would be taking a gamble, even if the enterprise was conducted on a legitimate business basis. But too often he puts his money into a game, which is stacked against him from the start. In such a case it would be far better to keep his money in the savings bank or buy some more Liberty bonds at the low market price prevailing.

Blowing stock bubbles is an expensive game.—*New York Age*, May 28, 1921.

In entering into business it was intimated recently through the columns of this newspaper to those who have had no previous experience, that nerve and a few dollars are not the only requisites. The unappealing names that describe so many of the new undertakings prove that the advice of expert advertisers is sadly needed. We observe the "Easter Lily Barber Shop," the "Tin Can Grocery Store," the "One for All Co-operative Society," the "Arctic School of Beauty Culture." These crude names repel rather than attract customers and the idea of window decoration is absolutely foreign. In some windows a gay-colored bottle will be seen resting upon a strip of common calico and for a background will be seen a multi-colored circus poster. It is hoped that those entering into business pursuits will consult those who know how to make their trade names appealing and their places of business attractive.—*Chicago Whip*.

I am afraid that there is not much wonder that so many beautiful homes of the Race are being bombed. Let us not fail by any means to give it a good trial through your greatest Race paper of the world in keeping all sorts of dirty paper and cans from the front way and sweep daily from the pavement through to the alley to see if it will stop this unmerciful bombing. It might be that the other race are bombing us to get us out of the way of turning their magnificent boulevards and broad avenues into slums. Once Wabash avenue was like the Lake Shore drive. Now, it is getting to be one of the filthiest streets in the city of Chicago. We don't want to be judged by filth and dirt. Let us make a better showing in neighborhood pride. It might stop all kinds of ill feelings toward the race. I am ashamed to be seen in some of our districts, so you may know the other race of pride is bound to be. Cleanliness goes a long way and it is neither impossible or too late to cooperate to make the once beautiful streets and neighborhoods beautiful and sanitary again. My sole object in this is to see if it will stop this bombing. If not, the color of our skin will solve the mystery, but we must not let this discourage us in race pride. Letter to the editor, *Chicago Defender*, April 16, 1921.

At the Sacrament the pastor and officers had prepared two large beautiful cut glass bowls full of clean water and towels, where each minister that was to assist in administering the holy and consecrated elements of the Lord's Supper, would publicly clean their hands before approaching the table or handling the elements. This is a good example worthy of all emulation. It is such a desecration for any minister or person to handle the bread and wine with unclean hands and some preachers do persist in handling the small pieces of bread after broken for each communicant. Some even want to put it in the mouth and lips of each person. This is unsanitary, unclean—it is so much better to pass the plate with the bits of consecrated bread and let the communicant take from the plate the bread and here is where we see the delight in the individual communion set. Every church ought to strive to get and use the individual communion set.—*Dallas Express*, April 16, 1921.

For many years we have observed with painful regret the (unintentional) disposition of certain of our fraternity leaders to develop their societies at the expense of grief stricken relatives while their hearts are still bleeding and their souls are yet crushed under the heavy load of indescribable grief.

We have seen the poor widow gowned in deep black urged, in spite of her weakness, and her indisposition to parade her sorrow before the vulgar world, to "come to hall and get your check." To a deeply sensitive nature this is nothing less than revolting. And the only purpose such a proceeding can accomplish is to incite some witness to join the order, by harrowing the already broken spirit of the beneficiary.

But lately this advertisement, emboldened by the success of the past, has moved us up several notches. In fact this last move has capped the climax. We recently witnessed two rival orders at the ceremony over the dead vieing with each other as to the priority of paying the claim. They seem to have anticipated each other, for they both were there with the goods. After a most impressive service the representatives of these orders obtained permission to, and proceeded then and there to speak in favor of their respective orders, and to hand over the checks to the sorrowing widow in the presence of the hundreds assembled. One of the speakers averred, "The deceased has been in our order five months, and in this other order five years. We pay him three hundred and fifty dollars for five months; they pay him five hundred dollars for five years." This was using the sacredness of the hour for speculation with a vengeance. It was naught else but the commercialization of the dead.

How much more impressive it would have been for the proper authorities to have gone to the widow in a quiet manner, either before or after the funeral services, and as men in deep sympathy for a woman bereft of her all to have offered words of genuine sympathy, and in the execution of their official duty, to have reverently and tenderly put into her hands the pledge of the fraternity.—*Progressive Citizen*, November 27, 1920.

Parents should go to school at least two or three times a month and see about their children.   Both in the grammar and the high school the parents should see the teachers about their children. See that your child obeys the teacher, is not saucy and does not talk back when the teacher tries to correct it for its wrongdoings.

The trouble with the colored parents, they do not take an interest in their children, paying no attention to them when they are "in bad" while at school.   The children should be made to do the right thing whether in or out of the school.   See that they are not rowdy and rough in the streets and all public places.

Do not allow your girls to run the streets with boys hanging onto their clothes.

It is a disgrace to see some of the children in the black belt. Their actions are really their parents' fault, as they do not take the proper interest in their children.   Always see that your children's report cards are brought home, see that no one but yourself signs the card, and that the card is not signed by the child herself.

Stop the rough boys from carrying knives and rocks in their pockets, as in some cases the teachers are almost afraid of the half grown boys who carry these things around in their pockets.

Above all things, send your children to school clean.   We know you cannot dress them in fine clothes, but you can keep them clean, as soap and water are plentiful.   Keep their clothing in repair.   Do not wrap her hair with strings, but comb it out, or else your child will be made a laughing stock for the whole school.

Here's Hoping You Parents Will Take More Interest in Your Children.—Chicago Advocate, February 26, 1921.

II.   ATTITUDES TOWARD RACIAL VALUES[1]

It was . . . . at Southern Brum that, calling on Reverend Williams, I happened upon this singular conversation:

"Now, isn't it absurd for us to have white angels?"

[1] Under this heading are set down indications of interest in the race itself and racial possessions, including even the matter of skin color as something that is able to evoke interest.   What the Negro may think of

"You surely would not like them black?"

"We give Sunday School cards to our children with white angels on them. It's wrong."

"Black angels would be ugly."

"No more ugly than white."

I thought the whiteness of the angels was as the whiteness of white light which contained all color. That, however, was lost on the reverend, who happened to be a realist.

"Christ himself was not white. He would have had to travel in a Jim Crow car," said he. "But put it to yourself: isn't it absurd for us to be taught that the good are all white, and that sin itself is black?"

"It does seem to leave you in the shade," said I.

"Expressions such as 'black as sin' ought to be deleted from the language. One might as well say, 'white as sin.'"

I ransacked my brain rapidly. . . . .

"Then Adam and Eve in the Garden," he went on, "are always shown as beautifully white creatures, whereas, considering the climate, they may well have been as dark-skinned as any Negro couple in Alabama. Babylon was built by Negroes." . . . .

This struck me as rather diverting, but it was quite serious. Later, in New York one night at Liberty Hall . . . . I heard an orator say: "Why, I ask you, is God always shown as white?

---

his own racial heritage Robert R. Moton shows in his autobiography called, *Finding a Way Out*, Garden City, New York, 1920, pp. 57–61.

"A few Sunday evenings later, when General Armstrong returned to the Institute, he spoke in his own forceful manner to the students about respecting themselves, their race, their history, their traditions, their songs, and folk lore in general. He referred them to the Negro songs as 'a priceless legacy,' which he hoped every Negro student would always cherish. I was impressed with him and with his address, but I was not entirely convinced. However, I was led to think along a little different line regarding my race. The truth is it was the first time I had ever given any serious thought to anything distinctively Negro. This also was the first time in my life that I had begun to think that there was anything that the Negro had that was deserving of particular consideration. This meant a readjustment of values that was not particularly easy for a raw country lad."

It is because he is the white man's God. It is the God of our masters—(Yes, brothers, that's it). It's the God of those who persecute and despise the colored people. Brothers, we've got to knock that white God down and put up a black God. . . . ."— *Afro-American*, February 25, 1921, quoting Stephen Graham, *The Soul of John Brown*.

This past Christmas I noticed, with delight and satisfaction, that many of our children had been presented with dolls having colored faces, some black, some brown, some yellow. At last we have come to recognize merit in things typical and representative of our own race. Other races teach their children to admire and adore their own. Why should we not do likewise? We have many beautiful specimens in our race, worthy of as much admiration as those of any other race. No longer do we need to hang up on the walls in our homes pictures of the white race, or even works of art created by them, when we can use pictures of our own people and art works produced by their hands. This spirit of race pride it is well to instill and cultivate, not only in the hearts and minds of the young, but in the hearts and minds of us all, old and young alike.—Letter to *New York Dispatch*, January 7, 1921.

Negro Pictures for Negro Homes

Now on sale, just off the press, "Contentment"—a beautiful lithograph picture, size 10 by 12 inches. Reproduced from photograph of young Negro mother with a nursing babe in her arms as she sits by the window with every expression of comfort and contentment. A picture that should be in every Negro home. By mail, post paid, 40 cents each, 3 copies $1.10, $4.00 per dozen. . . . . —*New York Age*, April 23, 1921.

Dear Aunt Pat:

I hear so much about using face powder, some say our women should never straighten their hair nor powder their faces. It denotes a lack of race pride and aping after other people.

Yours,

CARRIE

My dear Carrie:

It is an inherent part of woman to wish to be charming and the condition of her complexion, hair and costume have each an important role and [sic] in the accomplishment of her wish.

We should study our complexion and try to use those shades of powder which harmonize with our national color. I heartily endorse the use of any cosmetic which will give the face a smooth, clear surface. The market offers powders in the brunette and pink shades which blend beautifully with our brown complexions.

If one uses a cosmetic with the express purpose of "getting white" I feel that she shows a serious lack of self respect and race pride. I believe very few women guilty of this offense.

Now, as to the care of the hair, this has been the greatest blessing that women have received since Freedom—"Hair Culture." How much better she looks with clean, smooth hair, how easily it can be arranged. It is really shocking to meet a woman who does not care for her hair.

If to these we will add the care of our teeth and keep them white and shining we will be truly charming and "Brown" will continue to be the leading shade, "African Brown," "Velvet Brown," et cetera.—From "Aunt Pat's Forum," *Dallas Express*, March 26, 1921.

The Annual Intercollegiate concert proposition—or whatever it is, we do not know—is a striking illustration of the failure of education and religion to develop in the Negro manhood, self-respect and racial consciousness. These people could have pulled off their concert in the Odd Fellows' Auditorium, Big Bethel A.M.E. Church, or in other racial houses, for either of these places will hold the crowds they always have. But they cannot get away from that racial weakness that a thing belonging to or used by white men is better than an article belonging to or used by Negroes.

Then these misguided creatures flock to these white places with a view of exhibiting their talent to white people instead of catering to their own race, with a view of building a place large enough to accommodate their entertainments in the event that the Negro places are too small.

Another example of jim-crowing self is the great crowds of educated and cultured Negroes who crowd the "peanut" galleries in the white theatres trying to see a good picture when in fact the same pictures are seen on the screen in Odd Fellows' Theatre.

Still another example is the dances given in Taft Hall instead of on the Odd Fellows' Roof Garden, as a rule, by cultured Negroes. These Negroes are so intelligent that they actually believe that it is reverence and service to God to dance in Taft Hall, but a sin and a curse to dance on the Odd Fellows' Roof Garden. They are just that ignorant and blind.

Still another example of acknowledged inferiority on the part of cultured Negroes is the position of the Atlanta University students and athletic authorities take, insisting upon white officials in intercollegiate football, basketball and baseball games. They insist that no Negro is competent, but any white man will do. The motto of this school seems to be that any white man is able, which we regard as a disgrace to the lamented founders of this old institution—Presidents Ware, Bumstead, Francis and Chase.

But the race, like the boy who cannot rise above his home, will never rise in the estimation of the white man any higher than the force of his race pride and racial consciousness lifts it in the estimation of the people who control our community and national life.—*Atlanta Independent*, March 31, 1921.

TWO WHITES AT THE SHOW

(During the Act)

Those actors are not colored,
    Look for yourself and see—
Here, take my opera glasses;
    They're just as white as me.
You say that they're mulattoes?
    Go on! You've lost your sight!!
Why any fool can look at them
    And see that they are white!

(On the Street)

What man? Those are the players
    We've just been looking at?

Why these are colored people—
     Say you're talking through your hat!
By Jove! You're right—the joke's on me—
     But what a funny race!
If I were doing such great work
     I'd never hide my face!

—A. RAZAFKERIEFO, *Crusader*, April, 1921

The *Philadelphia Protector* is a newsy race organ of that city whose managing editor is Mr. W. H. Wright. The *Protector* is a weekly organ devoted to the interest of colored citizens, and takes a strong stand for a larger democracy, for which our boys fought. In its issue of the 20th of last month the *Protector* carries an editorial headed, "Colored Theaters Draw Color Line." Among other things said, this editorial wants to know why the black face is used to portray the servant and the fool and why this type is always used to humiliate the race.—*Florida Sentinel*, December 4, 1920.

THE MULATTO TO HIS CRITICS

Ashamed of my race?
And of what race am I?
I am many in one.
Of Red Man, Black Man, Briton, Celt, and Scot.
Through my veins there flows the blood
In warring clash and tumultuous riot.
I welcome all,
But love the blood of the kindly race
That swarths my skin, crinkles my hair,
And puts sweet music into my soul.

—JOSEPH S. COTTER, Jr., from *Hampton Bulletin*, February, 1921 (Kerlin).

THE OCTOROON

One drop of midnight in the dawn of life's pulsating stream
Marks her an alien from her kind, a shade amid its gleam.
Forevermore her step she bends, insular, strange, apart—
And none can read the riddle of her strangely warring heart.

The stormy current of her blood beats like a mighty sea.
Against the man-wrought iron bars of her captivity.
For refuge, succor, peace and rest, she seeks that humble fold
Whose every breath is kindliness, whose hearts are purest gold!

—GEORGIA DOUGLASS JOHNSON in Kerlin, *The Voice of the Negro*,
pp. 186 f.

We all do it.   The writer of this article is black, and he has
passed for white a thousand times.   When we "Call up over the
phone" to make a reservation from Baltimore to Richmond instead
of going in person to the ticket office, we are "passing"; because
we know by experience that white people are more polite and just to
the colorless phone than they are to our colored faces.   The Negro
may get "lower six" over the phone, whereas he usually gets
"upper one" at the window.   Once upon a time the writer wanted
to charter a freight car to carry his goods from Alabama to Texas
and he went down in person to ask the price.   The agent looked
up at him and said with a hiss: "One hundred and twenty-five
dollars!"   But something looked wrong and crooked in that
agent's eyes.   We therefore went back home and let the matter
rest for a few days until memories should pass away, and then we
sat down to our Remington and wrote a letter requesting full
information about the chartering of a car from Talladega to Mar-
shall, and there came an immediate, courteous and honest reply,
which began, "My dear Mr.——", and concluded "Respectfully
yours,"—and mentioned in between that the cost of such service
would be eighty-five dollars!   We passed for white and saved forty
dollars.   In other words, our typewriter and letter were colorless
in fact, but were white in the consciousness of the freight agent.
We allowed his own conceit to cheat him to keep him from cheating
us.   Every colored adult in the United States has done the same
thing in numberless different ways: they have gotten better service
by keeping their color out of the consciousness of the color-maniac
with whom they had to deal.   Pullman reservations, seats in the
middle of the car, staterooms not located over the throbbing
engines, theatre tickets in the first five rows, first-class goods by
mail order, guns and ammunition by express, and patience and
courtesy over the telephone.

That is, the black Negro passes for white in his personal absence, while the white Negro may pass in his personal presence—but both of them for the same purpose and usually in the same spirit. We are not talking about those people who "pass for white" for the mere sake of being white and because unnatural conditions in America have builded into their morbid minds an idea that there is some virtue in whiteness as whiteness. There are very few such abnormal people. But there are some, just as there are some idiots, maniacs and deaf-mutes. And we are not talking about those who may prefer whiteness, not as something better, but just as a mere matter of taste in color, without any thought of virtue in his choice. One may prefer a black coat or a white coat without any idea that the other color is "inferior." Other people may not admire his taste, they must allow it, or they themselves become color-maniacs. But we are talking about the great All-of-Us who pass every day for mere conveniences.

We know colored people who are thus passing, in person, all the way from office clerks and salesgirls to professors and deans in great universities in America. And I agree with them. They are entirely within their human rights. They are doing only what they should be permitted to do even if they were coal-black and had the fitness which they have. The littlest human I can think of is another colored person who would betray one of these. If I had any contempt for them, I should have still more contempt for those whose irrational prejudice makes it necessary for these white Negroes to "pass." And I could not betray those for whom I had less contempt to those for whom I had more. But there is nothing essentially contemptuous about the position of these people who cheat unreason—or better stated, who allow unreason to cheat itself. By stratagems and decoys man leads the wild beast to cheat itself out of its undeserved prey—and the beast of race prejudice is no better. . . . .

White-colored people are in high places in almost every large city of the Union especially in the North and West. Many have gone from the South to the Pacific Coast and engaged in various enterprises. Sometimes when the Negro who can not pass on his face, is visiting the Coast, he is greatly surprised at the number of his friends in exile, who may come to see him by night, as Nicodemus came to Christ. There are many divided families, some individuals having gone over to the white race and others remaining colored. They often write each other but seldom visit. What would the poor maniac do if he knew that his sister-in-law with whom his wife corresponds in the far South, is colored and married to an unmistakably colored man? Some of these girls have been wise enough to tell the man and his family before marriage that they are colored, so as to avoid giving him the advantage which is often taken in American courts, to plead deception, when it may be for other reasons that he wants to get a divorce. . . . . Many colored men are in prominent places in business and education, filling positions which they could not possibly have the "ability" or "capacity" to fill if they were only known to be colored. One is among the highest officers in one of the most prominent state universities and has been repeatedly honored above all his associates.

These people naturally have a genuine contempt for the idea of "racial superiority," for they know what a humbug it is. They are intimately acquainted with both white people and black people, and they are a competent authority. They testify in general that white people are not to be discredited intellectually as a group, but that many of them counterfeit their individual insignificance with the stamp of "race" superiority. They are sure that the variegated colored American group is the more interesting and likable. There is one testimony that is absolutely uniform from all these sources: that white people have no moral superiority.

These people have really lived in two worlds, and they may ultimately destroy many illusions and expose many lies.—WILLIAM PICKENS, in *Houston Observer*, June 18, 1921.

The faculty of the Julia Richmond High School, West 13th street, has been arranging in accordance with a city-wide program, for the presentation of a pageant, symbolizing "America's Making," in which the various peoples making up this country's population shall be represented, through the pupils attending the school, in some distinctive rendition which will show the race contribution to America's development. Each pupil to be assigned a place on the program will be called upon to contribute a number that would typify some element of progress made by the pupil's race. This pageant is to be presented in October, and in the meantime, as a preliminary presentment, a May Party was arranged for in which the pupils would be given a try-out.

One of the pupils attending this school is Miss Lucille Handy, of 232 West 139th street, eldest daughter of W. C. Handy, the originator in modern music of what is known as the "Blues" type of composition. Mr. Handy is head of the firm of Handy Bros., music publishers, at 232 West 46th street. When her teachers spoke of the character of the program to be arranged for the May Party and the "America's Making" pageant, Miss Handy informed her instructors of the work of her father along musical lines, and they quickly agreed that such a distinctive development deserved recognition. The composer's daughter was asked to prepare for rendition such of her father's compositions as would best show the character and style of his work.

Other colored girls attending Julia Richmond High heard of this arrangement and did not approve of it. One of them spoke to Miss Handy in person. . . . . Miss Handy received through the U.S. mail a letter from an alleged *"Colored Girls' Circle,"* . . . .

"Dear Miss Handy:

As members of the colored girls circle we have investigated and found out that you are making a *fool* out of yourself in school. It is not appropriate for you to sing and dance the blues (*jazz*) at the May Party. If you do, it will be under the peril of death and great danger to yourself. Therefore we warn you to watch your step. In case you do dance (which we doubt very much) pin your curls? in tight and beware of rotten eggs.

Beware. The Colored Girls Circle. . . . ."

Of course, this note is as ridiculous as it reads, and Miss Handy's mother was written to by instructors in the Julia Richmond High, who told of the high regard which is entertained for her daughter, and who characterized the writing of the letter as ignorant, stupid and maliciously devoid of intelligent comprehension. So far as I am able to learn, the program will be arranged as intended and Miss Handy will exemplify the compositions of her father in accordance with the original plans.

This leads up to a discussion of the "Blues" type of music in its relation to other forms. . . . .

It will not be surprising if the "Blues" music is eventually placed in the same category as the Spiritual. I mean the real thing, not the perverted and distorted product of the vaudevillian who seeks through low comedy to gain plaudits of the amusement-seeking public, and who does not hesitate to change words and phrases or make additions of his own which carry a *double entendre* or innuendoes which appeal to a vitiated taste. The composer nor the music should be blamed for the performer's vulgarity. . . . . One who has heard the workers of the Southern states in the fields and on the roads, with a singing leader whose clear musical voice rings out in a strain, always melodious but usually in a minor key, which is taken up and harmonized by his fellow workers, recognizes in Mr. Handy's "Blues" many of the same melodic themes, amplified, of course. This comment does not apply to the words, which are usually much more modern than the musical idiom.— *New York Age*, April 23, 1921.

Have you seen the new year books of the East Side Culture Club, under the caption of *Who's Who in the Negro Race?* The club will study the life and works of the following Negro leaders during the coming year: Henry O. Tanner, artist; Edmonia Lewis, sculptress; Chas. W. Chesnut, author; Kelly Miller, educator; Stanley G. Braithwaite, poet; W. S. Scarborough, educator; Lucy Laney and Mary McLeod Bethune, educators; Robert Moton and Emmett Jay Scott, educators; R. R. Wright and John Hope, educators; Drs. Dan Williams and C. V. Roman, physicians; Harry T. Burleigh and Marion Cook, musicians; Anita Patti Brown, Prima Donna; Mrs. Joseph St. Pierre-Ruffin, club worker; Major Chas. Young, U.S. Army; T. Thos. Fortune, Bishop Hurst, and Bishop R. E. Jones, churchmen; Granville F. Woods, inventor; William A. Sinclair, historian; Mrs. Maggie L. Walker, Negro woman banker, and Mrs. Aaron E. Malone, millionaire business woman.—*Black Dispatch*, February 25, 1921.

The history and literature of any race are the credentials on which that race is admitted to the family of civilized man and are the indications of its future possibilities.   Through all ages and in all nations civilized man has justified his existence by pointing to his history and literature not only as his proofs of development, but as evidence of his contribution to the total sum of human betterment and of the torch he has lent to light the path of man's onward march.   The Jew, the Greek, the Roman, the Hindu, the peoples of China and the people of Western Europe are known and esteemed for what history and literature reveal of them and for the contribution they have made to man's knowledge and welfare. The descendants of these races may well study with pride and profit the history of their fathers and justly look with confidence towards the future.

The ancient history and literature of Negroes in Africa have not been emphasized by other races which have dominated the world with their language and civilization, and therefore the modern Negroes, enjoying the civilization of other nations and races, know little of the ancient civilization and customs which still find expression in native tribes of the mother land.   It is entirely possible that the destruction of the great Alexandrian library deprived the world of much of the history and literature of ancient Africa.

The campaign for the study of Negro history and literature conducted by the Omega Psi Phi Fraternity during the week of April 24 should meet the approval and secure the co-operation of all Negro men and women who are interested in the intellectual growth of the race and its future achievements.—*Negro World*, April 30, 1921.

Saturday, May 7, marks the opening of the Negro National League for the season of 1921 in Detroit.   Behind this opening should be the concentrated support of every race man in Detroit. In this support should be good-will, finance, influence and presence of every race-loving man.   The league should be considered your personal league; if it succeeds you should feel that you have succeeded; if it fails, you should consider it a personal failure.   Your heart should vibrate sympathetically with the heart of the league.

If the league succeeds, the race succeeds; if the league fails, the race fails.

You should realize that this is one of the largest organized movements ever advanced by our group, and that our ability to put over large projects will be measured largely by the way we handle this one.

Last season's baseball was prosperous because of abnormal conditions, but this season it will be given the acid test. If you are reluctant in giving of your support, you are lending aid to its failure. Now, attention, fans! Forward march! Eyes right! While we pass in review the opening of the Negro National League. —*Detroit Contender*, May 7, 1921.

III.   INTERESTING PEOPLE

We first stop and weep with the family and friends of Mr. Rube Johnston, who lived in this world 103 years and eight months, born a slave, but with no mind of a slave and given a chance, bought his own freedom and married his 13 year old bride 88 years ago.   Separate only three years during the war and as soon as the chance presented itself returned to his wife.   They were blessed with 6 boys and 4 girls, all full of pep and determination to do business.   He was born in Virginia and picked his changes through Tennessee, Mississippi and Arkansas to Kansas where he spent a busy life until death, never in bed sick a half day in his life until an injury by his frightened horse some weeks ago.   He was faithful to his vow to Nancy until death, leaving her a home at 1010 N. Washington Ave.   They were proud of the success of 16 grandchildren and 4 great grandchildren.

He was a proud and ambitious old man until death, not the character by any means that the *Wichita Eagle* wishes you to see in their write-up.

This faithful life demanded that they say something, but there was enough prejudice in the write-up to show that he was a long liver, but a southern type of something funny with a bad appearance.   We stop here to wonder if there is a white man in America who could go through what he went through and live and make a living at the age of 103.   Then we wonder again, could he have bought himself and then served in the war for another man (a coward) then have sense enough to make his way from one disgraceful state to another, looking for safety for himself and his family, using diplomacy that would suit the condition, though ambition ran high, not be in direct support of the State. We wonder again how can our people read the *Eagle*, which has such desire to picture the dark side of the Negro race, which could not have been of any asset to a citizen who has lived a pure life in their midst since 1893.

His funeral was attended last Thursday from the St. Paul A.M.E. Church by pastor J. R. Ransom, with Mrs. J. E. Lewis, James R. Johnston, George Johnston, W. E. Johnston, A. F. Johnston and Rev. Reuben Johnston of Philadelphia. We bow in humble submission to the will of God and especially with Mrs. Nancy Johnston, who has been so faithful for so long with this noble husband, father and Christian.—*Negro Star* (Wichita, Kansas), April 15, 1921.

WASHINGTON, D.C., April 15.—Taking with him to the grave the secret of the whereabouts of the great seal of the Confederacy, which he hid when Jefferson Davis was captured, James Jones, the colored bodyguard of the president of the Confederacy, died here.

Jones was born in North Carolina, and his body will be taken to Raleigh for burial. The man had been failing for some time, but even as death approached he kept silent about the Confederate seal.

Throughout his long life, with his latter years spent in the government service in Washington, James Jones would never reveal what became of the Confederate seal. "Marse Jeff" had bidden that he never tell—and he never did. Veterans of the Union and Confederate armies, newspaper writers, curiosity seekers and curio hunters from time to time urged Jones to reveal where he buried the great seal. They argued that the Civil War was far in the past and the seal should be produced for the inspection of the younger generation of today and the generations that are to follow in a reunited country. Always James Jones shook his head, and to the end he maintained his silence.—*Pittsburgh American*, April 15, 1921.

In last Sunday's *Times-Dispatch* Doctor C. A. Bryce has an interesting article on "Dusky Fiddlers" a part of which follows:

"The name Scott was a prominent one in colored musical circles, nor was it monopolized by the Charlottesville Scotts previously mentioned, for there lived in Richmond, more than a half-century ago, a noted violinist by the name of Joseph C. Scott, who played for the wealthiest and most aristocratic people of Richmond, and at many of the watering places during the summer seasons. He was bright-skinned, dignified, middle-aged, and gentlemanly in his address.

"He showed in every way that he had been thrown with the cultured people of Virginia, was used to the best and knew how to accept nice treatment without embarrassing his white friends by forgetting his color. He was an educated musician, as far as it went in those days, which meant that he could play a piece 'at sight.' He had seen service in the Mexican war, and, if I mistake not, was bugler for some command from Richmond."

In all probability the writer meant no insult to the colored audience of the *Times-Dispatch*. That is the pity of the whole affair. He felt that he was saying things that his white and colored readers would be pleased to read. Yet how galling it is to read these lines: "*He knew how to accept nice treatment without embarrassing his white friends by forgetting his color.*" Ye gods, when will the day come when the colored man may deal with the peoples of the World without ever remembering the color of his face! A Negro artist even, to this day, must necessarily embarrass his white friends if he forgets his color. How unspeakably damnable!—*St. Luke Herald*, May 28, 1921.

GALVESTON, TEX., Feb. 19.—Inspired by a desire to bring about a bettering of the conditions of the negroes of Liberia, Africa, William Gales, a well-to-do negro farmer of Florida, sold out his holdings in that State eight years ago and migrated thither with his son and family. A few days ago, forlorn and penniless, he and his son and eight grandchildren arrived here on the steamship Cushnet, from Barcelona, Spain. He now has a different view of the people of his race in Africa than that which caused him to undertake the work of their uplift eight years ago. He said that his main purpose in going to Liberia was to demonstrate to the natives modern American methods of farming.

He found that they were indolent and not at all concerned about their material condition. The negroes there, he declared, manage to get enough to eat without working, and when he sought to show them how they could produce abundant crops by manual labor and modern farm implements, they looked upon him as an interloper, and he and the other members of his family were ostracized by the natives.

Things went from bad to worse, and finally, with what little money he and his son had left, they set out toward the United States. They made their way to the northern part of Africa, where they found a small steamship that would take them as far as Barcelona on their way home. When they arrived at Barcelona they were in tatters and without money. They appealed to the American Consul there and he arranged for their passage to Galveston. On the way over the members of the party worked about the ship as a means of helping to meet the cost of the voyage.

The first thing the old negro did when the Cushnet was docked was to kneel upon the deck and offer a fervent prayer of thanksgiving that he and his progeny had been permitted to return to the land of liberty. From here they were sent to the farm of a relative in Oklahoma.—*Louisville News*, February 26, 1921.

RED OAK, GA., March 31—Farmers and others in College Park and Red Park and vicinity are expressing great interest in a boll weevil preparation invented by Jasper Arnold, a Negro farming tenant of W. W. Sigman of College Park, who has "the papers" to show he raised eight bales of cotton on twelve acres last year, in a "boll weevil year," with not a trace of the pest to be seen on the plants or at the gin.

"I made it myself," says Jasper, "and I spray it on the plants with a machine I made myself. I was a blacksmith for a long time, and I can make almost anything."

"This preparation is remarkable," stated B. E. Dewberry of Red Oak, a prosperous planter. "I tested it out first to see if it injured vegetation. It did not, so I had it used on my place. I am frank to say I wouldn't have got my rent if it hand't been for this preparation and its effective stopping of the boll weevil. I have seen it stop army worms in corn overnight." J. W. Tumlin and J. F. Lamber of College Park, the latter a minister, signed testimonials of their own observation that Arnold's preparation was surprisingly effective. Homer Thanes of Red Oak, who ginned most of Arnold's cotton, also signed a statement that he saw no evidences of the weevil in it. "I buy the stuff at the store," says Jasper, with a grin, "and make it up at my own house, and shoot the weevil with a gun I made myself—and he sure does die."— *Buffalo American*, March 31, 1921.

ATTLEBORO, Dec. 10.—Mrs. Annie J. Evans, colored, who has the distinction of being the first woman in this city to receive a police appointment, was 60 last August, looks about 40, and says the pay does not interest her as much as the chance offered for her to do good. Like Mrs. Eliza G. Daggett, who is a candidate for mayor, Mrs. Evans severely criticizes dancing as carried on these days and is for reform. "My ideas on this subject are based on what I have observed in this city and elsewhere. The dances of today are the most vulgar things I ever saw. I thought there ought to be something done here, talked the matter over with Mayor Brady and he appointed me. I expect to be sent out to clean up the halls."

Mrs. Evans desired it made plain that her appointment did not come because of complaints of the organizations of colored people in the city. There are over 2,500 women registered as voters in the city, and she feels highly honored that from among this number she should be selected to be the first woman to be vested with the authority of a police officer. She says she is in no way afraid of the size of the job, and, having been given the right to carry a revolver, will carry one—also a billy.

As she resides only a short distance from the police station, she will probably be called to attend to women prisoners. This city is without a police matron, and the fact that female prisoners have been kept at the station without a woman being present has been the cause of much adverse comment.—*St. Luke Herald*, February 5, 1921.

Mamie Smith, the famous singer of "Crazy Blues" and other popular hits, who will appear in Beaumont at the Community Center Hall, Saturday night, March 27, is said to be one of the most gorgeously dressed stars of the musical comedy world. With the enormous royalties which Mamie received from her phonograph recordings (and her income from this source is said to rival Caruso's) and from the profits of her concert tours, the popular young colored star is enabled to indulge her fancy in the latest creations both from Paris and New York, and in each city in which she has appeared a gasp of astonishment has greeted her appearance, for her gowns are described as riots of color and beauty. Each gown has been specially designed by Mme. Hammer herself for Mamie, with a view to fitting the individuality of the star and the various songs which she sings on her program.

Beside her high powered car which the new star skillfully drives herself, there is nothing in which Mamie takes more pride and interest than her stage gowns, her favorite one being a creation of white silver trimmed with American Beauty rose, with head dress and huge ostrich feather fan to match. This gown Mamie has promised to wear at her concert here, as well as several other of her latest creations.—*Beaumont Industrial Era*, March 19, 1921.

Pretty soon Jack Johnson, the grand old man of many fights, will leave Leavenworth where he has served a sentence imposed by the courts of the land. Whatever the crime the ex-champion may have committed, he has paid with full interest the price of his folly. He will be turned back pretty soon to the world from whence he fled, to start all over again to make good if he can.

He will come back to us with a clean slate, for Johnson owes no man. He paid in Spain, France, and Mexico compound interest for a simple investment in sin. While in exile he lost his mother, wealth, and all that earth holds of cheer. But lest some enemy should think that he is yet a debtor, he crossed the ocean, walked into the prison doors, and offered this government the pound of flesh nearest the heart. . . . . He has paid; so let him come back to us untaunted. If we can not breathe a word of praise then let us close the book on the conqueror of Jim Jeffries.

Prize fighters are not supposed to be moralists.   If they were they would perhaps be following another trade.   Johnson was a fighter with the common faults and virtues of his profession. . . .

But he will soon be back, back to the old haunts and friends we suppose are true.   Back on State Street, and perhaps in the ring again.   Give him every encouragement for Johnson is staging a "Come Back" which has not its counterpart in history.

We know not what the impression of the world may be but here is hoping that his last days be his best days, and when the little slip with its attendant horror is forgotten, may he yet be remembered for his golden smile at Reno.—*Detroit Contender*, May 14, 1921.

LAKE CHARLES, LA.—Joseph Barry, a Negro, who is to be hanged here on May 6 for murder, has requested that the scaffold in the jail yard for his execution be painted snow white in keeping with the white suit, shoes, tie and socks he is to wear the day of the hanging.   He also asked that the executioner and attending deputies be clothed in white.—*Detroit Leader*, May 7, 1921.

BALTIMORE, MD., April 8.—Doctors are examining with the greatest interest a horn, five inches long, which was removed from the head of Lee Wilson, Negro.

Doctors Kelly and Culverhouse, who performed the operation, call the horn a "cornucornutum," its medical name.

The horn looked like a large round fingernail and grew from the scalp, not the skull.

It's a rare disease, say the doctors. . . . .

Lee Wilson, prior to the operation, had followers who believed he had voodoo powers.—*Detroit Leader*, April 22, 1921.

AUGUSTA, GA.—The Rev. Charles T. Walker, D.D., LL.D., founder of Tabernacle Baptist Institutional Church, and its pastor for more than forty years, died here at his home, 1011 Gwinette street, on Friday morning, July 29th, at 2 A.M., after having been indisposed during a period of about two years.   He was 63 years old.

Dr. Walker's reputation was international and his eloquence in the pulpit had caused him to be designated as "The Black Spurgeon."   This title was given to him in England during a visit to that country when he preached in the church pastored by that famous English Baptist divine, the Rev. Dr. Charles Haddon Spurgeon.

About twenty years ago Dr. Walker was called to the pastorate of Mount Olivet Baptist Church, New York City, and he served that congregation for five years. . . . . He made frequent trips from New York to Augusta during these years to serve Tabernacle's people under a mutually satisfactory agreement with the New York congregation. He finally gave up the New York church and returned permanently to his Augusta home and church.

While in New York City he established the Young Men's Christian Association branch for colored men, located at that time on West 53rd street, but now occupying a costly modern building of its own in the Harlem section, where the bulk of the race is located. . . . . Recognized as the ablest Negro pulpit orator in America, he attracted to his audiences and congregations men and women of all ranks of life. During the winter season, when the resorts in and near Augusta were thronged with notables from all sections of the world, Tabernacle Church congregations were made up largely of the tourist visitors. Supreme Justice William Howard Taft, ... was a frequent visitor . . . . and he spoke to Tabernacle's congregations more than once. Other notables included John D. Rockefeller, who was almost an every Sunday worshipper, Lyman B. Goff of Providence, Augustus D. Heinz of Cincinnati and F. T. Stanton. . . . .

Dr. Walker made three trips to Europe, lecturing and preaching in the most famous churches and halls of England and the Continent, and he has been heard by thousands in practically every city in the United States.

Tributes have been paid to the dead minister by the entire city and county, and the suggestion was made by several leading white citizens that official Augusta show respect in some way. The county officials and county police united in sending a handsome floral tribute to the home, and gave verbal expression at the same time to the esteem and respect which was felt for the colored leader who had fallen. . . . . *New York Age,* August 6, 1921.

His father and mother were both slaves in a backwoods county in Georgia, and he himself was too young to comprehend when

Lincoln's famous edict removed the shackles from their shoulders and proclaimed him a "free" child.

At 12 he had "hired out" and was working 14 hours a day for a crust and a mattress.

The only money he saved was by surreptitiously selling burnt pine tar for grease, making baskets for cotton pickers, gathering black walnuts, which he held over until Winter and sold at 10 cents a hundred; burning charcoal at night and carrying it five miles to sell at five cents a bushel, cultivating and marketing the tiny crop of his Lilliputian cotton patch. . . . .

His first job was the last chair in a barber shop, where his smiling willingness, courtesy, industry and general bearing soon won him a foremanship. Later he was made manager. And still later he had laid by enough to buy a barber shop of his own.

Today Alonzo Herndon owns and operates chain tonsorial shops on many of Atlanta's most fashionable streets. His biggest establishment is worth $30,000. Some of his others are worth $15,000 each. He himself is rated at $500,000; and he is one of the richest members of his race in the South.

Herndon's career was brought to light by his recent purchase and equipment of a magnificent house to be used as a day nursery and kindergarten for Negro children. Some years ago he founded the Herndon Community Center, a group of orphanages and hospitals. He has given large sums to the Y.M.C.A., and to Atlanta University. His endowments, benefactions and charities are statewide, and the character of many of them is such that they do not get into print—paying the rent for old, poor people; sending sick children to the country and seashore; supplying medical aid and food to those who are in need.—*Birmingham Times-Plain Dealer*, February 21, 1921.

IV.   RACE FRICTION

G. Tom Taylor, long a big factor with the Negro vote in the Republican party in Tennessee and who has been considered a friendly Southerner by many of the Race, has been sued by a Colored tenant, Pleasant H. Brown, due to the operation of one of the Taylor plantations near Crenshaw, Miss. Brown charges that his store account in the general store which Taylor owned, for the crop of 1919 was $499.19, that he raised 10 bales of cotton; that Mr. Taylor got that and the seed, but that he has never been able to get a settlement out of Mr. Taylor. He sues also for damages for being intimidated and for $1,000 as the value of his household goods which were taken. This is a typical Southern case but usually they do not get into court.—*Charleston New Era*, May 7, 1921.

The reading public has not so soon forgotten the big scare headlines which appeared in the local daily papers a week or so ago describing an alleged assault by a "burly Negro" on a "pretty white woman" in one of The Dalles, Ore., hotels. One paper ran the cut of the alleged "beautiful" victim and another paper said editorially: "It's good for the Negro who attacked the white woman of The Dalles that he was not in the South, or he would have been lynched or burned at stake." The object of these papers was to start a race riot or to have a "necktie" party; but the law-abiding people of The Dalles were not swayed by such inflammatory utterances of the newspapers and as a result the colored man was arrested, placed in jail and a grand jury was called in to investigate, and their finding was that the whole business was a "frame-up" on the colored man in order to have him mobbed or sent to the penitentiary. The colored man has been set free. Now, what about this "pretty" white woman who helped to frame up on this burly colored man and her coterie of conspirators? Why didn't the daily papers give as much publicity to the vindication of this colored man as they did in trying to have him murdered by fastening the crime of rape upon him? And what about this "pretty" woman, who is a perjurer and a would-be murderer? Thousands of innocent colored men are lying in their graves today through just such dirty frame-ups as the one in this case.—*Atlanta Independent*, December 9, 1920.

We had occasion on Sunday . . . . to be returning home from one of our near-by points. When we got on the coach was crowded by a number of women and children going to Charleston from the near-by country . . . . to witness the . . . . parade. A seat was vacant in the smoker; and though we do not smoke we cheerfully took the vacant seat.

At the next and succeeding station they kept crowding in bent on the same mission. A man was stationed in the door of the Negro coach, with his arm across the door and the surplus passengers, after the aisles were crowded, were bidden go into the baggage car, where our women had to either stand up during the ride or else sit on the few trunks in the car.

In the mean time the "Brethren," who has no right on the car except as a renter to sell his wares at twice the original price, and whose place is in the baggage car, according to law, had his wares spread over two seats which, ordinarily is supposed to seat two passengers, but in a pinch three, a price thereby taken away from at least four persons the seats they paid first class fare to occupy. Some will ask why not report the matter to the proper authority. So we did upon one occasion reporting to the state Rail R. Commission, stating place, day and state of some indignity which was practiced at the time, and is being practiced now, after at least seven years. Did we even get an answer from the commission elected by the white people to see that the white people get what they pay for, but pass the treatment of the Negroes by with silent contempt? We got no more answer than if we had addressed a letter to the bronze statue of Wade Hampton on the grounds of the State Capitol.—*Columbia* (South Carolina) *Standard*, January 7, 1921.

NEWPORT NEWS, VA., Jan. 7.—What is expected to be a forerunner of similar movements throughout the South was taken here recently in a protest of Colored citizens at the presence in their section of houses of ill repute, voiced at a meeting of the Inter-Racial Committee. The strenuous protests started the committee delegates to work at once with the city authorities in their anti-vice crusade of the city authorities.

Colored people of Newport News last night registered protest of the presence of houses of ill repute in their section of the city. . . . . Most of the houses, it was charged at the meeting, are patronized by white men despite the fact that they are maintained by Colored women. Colored people with the exception of the inmates, are barred in most instances, the committee's informants declared.

. . . . They further declared that nothing is quite so disgusting to respectable Colored people as the sight of white men skulking through the darkness to be in the company of Colored women who often are social outcasts of their own race.—*New Era* (Charleston, South Carolina), January 8, 1921.

Commenting on the familiar form of address employed by Atlanta store clerks in accosting colored customers, the editor of the Texarkana *Progressive Citizen* said:

"We have no objection to those white folks who are of blood-kin with us calling us according to the blood relationship we sustain to them. But to be indiscriminately called 'Uncle George,' 'Auntie,' 'Boy,' is regarded by all Negroes as an insult. If it will tend to lessen one's manhood by calling us by our own proper names, then leave off all names, and merely say, 'What will you have?'"

Well put. This one-sided relationship has been overworked, without rhyme or reason.—*New York Age*, April 16, 1921.

It is from the spiritual nostalgia that the American Negro suffers most. He has been away so long from that mysterious fatherland of his that like all the other descendants of voluntary and involuntary immigrants of the seventeenth century,—Puritan, pioneer, adventurer, indentured servant,—he feels himself American. The past is too far past for him to have memories. Very, very rarely does he have a backward reaching bond, be it never so tenuous.

Mr. Du Bois, indeed, in his "Darkwater" tells in a striking passage in that striking book of a Bantu ancestress who hugged her knees and swayed and sang:

> "*Do bana coba—gene me, gene me!*
> *Ben d'nuli, ben d'le . . . .*"

Who knows what scene of Afric sands and Afric freedom those words may have conjured up? How the bleakness of New England and the harshness of captivity must have fostered her homesickness!

In the main, the American Negro is without ties and the traditions that throw back. Instead, he has built unconsciously from his childhood a dream-country, and yet surely no dream-country since it is founded on that document which most realizes and sets forth the primal and unchanging needs of man—the Constitution of the United States.

Where the Greek dreams of his statues, he dreams of Justice; where the Italian yearns for his opera, he yearns for Opportunity; and where the Jewish visionary longs for freedom of sect, he cries out for an escape from Peonage.

As a child in his readers, he learns of great principles in the Declaration of Independence, in Fourth of July speeches, in extracts from Daniel Webster, in Mr. Lincoln's Gettysburg address.

He grows up and finds them—not here—just beyond, always beyond; in a country where all things are possible he has found exactly what ought not to be possible.

He keeps on longing for these principles with an aching, voice-less longing; with Chateaubriand's "Exile" he sighs:

"Their memory makes me sorry every day."

Is he mocking himself? The cold fear strikes him that perhaps there is no such country. The Greek—if he is lucky—will return to his island of the sea. He knows it is there. The Italian will go back to Italy sometime. At least the Jews *have* lived in Jerusalem. But the black American is something entirely new under the sun. Shall he ever realize the land where he would be?

"For thee, oh dear, dear country,
Mine eyes their vigil keep!"

The second lieutenant is doomed to know homesickness of both body and spirit. In France he will want the comforts of America; in America, he cries out for the rights of man which he knew in France.

A nostalgia of body and soul—there is nothing harder to bear.—JESSIE FAUSET, in *Crisis*, August, 1921.

It is true that the foregoing scenes and criticisms of Negro life present widely varying and somewhat con-

tradictory pictures. But those who know Negroes best
are the last to make easy generalizations about them.
The newspaper is too veracious to generalize.

Moreover, when we use the term "life" with reference
to any group, we must include the little things as well as
the big, all intimate passages between man and man that
throw their light and shade over human association.
"We speak," says John Dewey, "of the life of a savage
tribe, of the Athenian people, of the American nation.
'Life' covers customs, institutions, beliefs, victories and
defeats, recreations and occupations."[1] He goes on to
say that the process of communicating and sharing all
this is what makes society. If this be true, then the newspaper, regarded simply as an agency of communication,
is a unique social instrument. Its motto is, "Now it can
be told." Through it, individual experiences are shared
over wide areas, and the group comes to know itself.

The press supported by the Negro comes in this way
to be a means for making his life significant to himself.
The long years of slavery resulted in the impression that
the black man did not count in the real world. But now,
on the printed page, not only does a man's name appear
before his fellows, but the whole race seems to become
articulate to mankind.

Instead of merely reflecting "life" the newspaper, in
setting themes for discussion and suggesting the foci of
attention, helps powerfully to create that life. No part
of the Negro race in America is quite stagnant. It may
be that those who are on the frontiers of their world,
chiefly in the cities and the ranks of the educated, are
most sensitive to the new forces and new standards. But

[1] *Democracy and Education*, New York, 1916, pp. 1-5.

back in quiet rural areas, others are reading their news and arguments, and the whole mass is responding to the printed suggestion.   A young Negro is sent to Annapolis: through this press he becomes a symbol for all.   The Anti-Lynching Bill passes the House, and publicity engraves it in Magna Carta.   Even a street fight, if the racial issue enters in, stiffens the whole line of conflict and sounds the call to a holy resistance.   The advertising pages play their part in influencing the standard of living.   And so the press, ephemeral as it is, keeps moving on the main currents of interest, and helps to bring into being the life that its pages report.

BIBLIOGRAPHY

Alice Dana Adams, *The Neglected Period of Anti-Slavery in America (1808–1821)*, Radcliffe College Monographs No. 14, Boston, 1908.

Associated Negro Press, *Annual*, Chicago, 1920.

N. W. Ayer and Son's *American Newspaper Annual and Directory for 1920 and 1921*, Philadelphia, 1920, 1921.

John S. Bassett, *Anti-Slavery Leaders of North Carolina*, Baltimore, 1898.

Benjamin Brawley, *The Negro in Literature and Art*, New York, 1918.

———, *A Social History of the American Negro*, New York, 1921.

Centennial Encyclopedia of the A.M.E. Church, Philadelphia, 1916.

Chicago Commission on Race Relations, Unpublished Notes.

D. W. Culp, *Twentieth Century Literature, etc., Relating to the American Negro*, Naperville, Illinois, 1902.

Frederick Douglass, *Life and Times of Frederick Douglass*, Hartford, 1882.

W. E. Burghardt Du Bois, *Darkwater*, New York, 1920.

——— (ed.), Atlanta University Publications, Atlanta: No. 8, *The Negro Church, a Social Study*, 1903. No. 12, *Economic Cooperation Among Negroes*, 1907. No. 14, *Efforts for Social Betterment Among Negro Americans*, 1909.

Alice Dunbar-Nelson, *The Dunbar Speaker and Entertainer*, Naperville, Illinois, 1920.

William Lloyd Garrison, 1805–1879, the Story of His Life Told by His Children, New York, 1885.

George W. Gore, *Negro Journalism*, Journalism Press, Greencastle, Indiana.

Stephen Graham, *The Soul of John Brown*, New York, 1920.

W. N. Hartshorn, *An Era of Progress and Promise*, Boston, 1910.

L. M. Hershaw, "The Negro Press in America," *Charities*, XV (1905), No. 1.

Frederic Hudson, *Journalism in the United States*, New York, 1873.

Robert T. Kerlin, *The Voice of the Negro, 1919*, New York, 1920.
James Melvin Lee, *History of American Journalism*, Boston and New York, 1916.
Samuel J. May, *Some Recollections of Our Antislavery Conflict*, Boston, 1869.
Robert Russa Moton, *Finding a Way Out, an Autobiography*, Garden City, 1920.
National Association for the Advancement of Colored People, *Annual Reports*, New York, 1921, 1922.
———, *An American Lynching*, New York, 1921.
National Negro Press Association, *Proceedings, etc., 1917–1919*, Nashville.
J. L. Nichols and W. H. Crogman, *The New Progress of a Race*, Naperville, Illinois, 1920.
R. E. Park and H. A. Miller, *Old World Traits Transplanted*, New York, 1921.
G. H. Payne, *History of Journalism in the United States*, New York, 1920.
Irving G. Penn, *The Afro-American Press and Its Editors*, Springfield, Massachusetts, 1891.
Clement Richardson, *The National Cyclopedia of the Colored Race*, Montgomery, Alabama, 1919.
Carl Sandburg, *The Chicago Race Riots*, New York, 1919.
Emmett J. Scott, *Official History of the American Negro in the World War*, Washington (?), 1919.
———, *Negro Migration During the War*, Carnegie Endowment for International Peace, New York, 1920.
Herbert J. Seligman, *The Negro Faces America*, New York, 1920.
United States Bureau of the Census, *Bulletins*, Washington, 1920, 1921.
———, Department of Labor, *Negro Migration in 1916–17*, Washington, 1919.
———, *Investigation Activities of the Department of Justice*, 66th Congress, First Session, Sen. Doc. 153, Washington, 1919.
Booker T. Washington, *The Story of the Negro*, 2 vols., New York, 1909.
———, *Frederick Douglass*, Philadelphia, 1907.
———, *The Negro in Business*, Chicago, 1907.

George W. Williams, *History of the Negro Race in America*, 2 vols., New York, 1885.

J. B. Williams, *A History of English Journalism to the Foundation of the Gazette*, London, 1908.

Carter G. Woodson, *The Education of the Negro Prior to 1861*, New York, 1915.

Monroe N. Work, *Negro Year Book, 1918–1919*, Tuskegee Institute, 1919.

INDEX

(Numbers refer to pages)